D1254118

LEADERSHIP THROUGH SUPERVISION

In Industrial Education

LEADERSHIP THROUGH SUPERVISION

In Industrial Education

M. J. RULEY, Director
Industrial Arts and
Vocational-Technical
Education
Tulsa Public Schools
Tulsa, Oklahoma

McKNIGHT & McKNIGHT
Publishing Company
Bloomington, Illinois

COPYRIGHT 1971

by McKnight & McKnight Publishing Company

Lithographed in U.S.A.

Library of Congress
Card Catalog Number: 78-146483

SBN: 87345-450-2

iv

Preface

This book has been written as a guide for teachers, department chairmen, consultants, supervisors, and directors of industrial education to suggest techniques which will help improve instruction. It should also have definite value for the superintendent of schools and the principal who have responsibility for this area of education. They must develop skills which will attract, challenge, and develop students and teachers they lead.

The ideas contained in this book are the product of thirty-nine years of teaching and supervision in the area of industrial arts and vocational education. Actual classroom teaching involving an association with hundreds of elementary, secondary, and college students has sharpened the ability to devise learning situations and develop incentives to meet individual needs. The privilege of working closely with scores of teachers and leaders in the field has brought into focus the techniques and methods used by master teachers as well as the major personal and professional weaknesses which curtail success in the area of supervision.

Each student in my classes and each coworker has contributed in some measure to the content of this book. The final distillation of ideas, mistakes, solutions, methods, and techniques which have been a part of my experiences make up the content.

A study of the material covered in this book will reveal that the duties of a modern supervisor have been formulated by a philosophy of administration and supervision of industrial education which stresses democracy. In this concept of supervision, teachers share in planning, policymaking, and in evaluating results.

This manuscript took a number of years to develop with much of the material being used taken from Tulsa procedures and from courses in supervision taught by the writer in summer session on a number of different college campuses.

In the interest of industrial education and its place in the educational leadership of the public school curriculum, this book has been written.

M. J. Ruley

Acknowledgments

I am indebted to many people for their assistance in the development of this book. The many people who have helped to develop much of the material included and exerted educational leadership as they discussed problems of industrial education in inservice classes, group meetings, and through individual initiative.

I wish to acknowledge the help of Mrs. Gwen Davidson, secretary for the Tulsa Department of Industrial Arts and Vocational-Technical Education. Dr. Jess Hudson and Dr. Hiram Alexander have given stimulus for educational leadership in the Tulsa Schools where I have received most of my experience in the field of supervision and educational leadership. Also, the many teachers, fellow supervisors, and principals with whom I worked have helped in achieving any success that I may have had as a local director of industrial arts and vocational-technical education.

Many others with whom I have worked throughout the United States have helped to give direction. Professor Glenn Smith, Dr. Fred Strickler, Dr. Delbert Dyke, Dr. George Henry, Dr. William A. Bakamis, Dr. Kenneth Brown, and Dr. Ralph Gallington gave me an opportunity to teach graduate courses in supervision on their college campuses during summer sessions.

I am especially grateful to my wife and family for their encouragement and understanding.

M. J. Ruley

Table of Contents

Chapter 7   Staff Improvement   134

Chapter 8   Good School-Community Relations   154

Chapter 9   The Industrial Teacher As a Manager of Learning Experiences   164

Chapter 1

Industrial Education

in American Schools

The free public school was begun as an extension of the home, representing an attempt by parents to build a future for their children and a desire of the community to meet its needs as well as the needs of the nation. The public school has served effectively as an agency to amalgamate the variety of peoples making up the United States and has contributed to the prosperity of our country.

In determining the kinds of educational programs that will most nearly meet the needs of young people today, training for occupational competence — vocational education — is given considerable emphasis. Youth must have experiences which will enable them to assess their interests and talents, then secure and develop the special skills and information to enter upon and progress in an occupation. The goal of education is to develop a well-balanced individual who will be able to earn a livelihood.

Vocational Education

Vocational education means education for occupational competence. Since a functioning democratic society requires its citizens to be occupationally proficient, vocational preparation should be an integral part of the educational program for every boy and girl coming of age in the second half of the 20th century. There is no question that preparation for citizenship and vocation should claim the attention and efforts of those charged with the responsibility for planning an effective school program.

Courses in a secondary school curriculum may properly be designated as vocational when the following conditions or characteristics are found:

1. The aim of the course is to train individuals to meet an occupational standard of proficiency.

2. The teaching content is based upon an up-to-date analysis of the occupation as practiced by the most successful and efficient workers of it.

3. The students have made a tentative vocational choice based on their own interests and aptitudes as they meet the requirements of the occupation.

4. The instructional environment approximates, to the maximum possible degree, the present working conditions of the occupation.
5. The teacher has had appropriate training, experience, and is skilled in the occupation he is to teach.
6. The course is sufficiently complete to develop a degree of vocational competence.
7. The instruction includes skills, technical knowledge, insights, attitudes, safety habits, and related information essential to success in a chosen occupation.

Some form of vocational education has existed in the United States since the nation was founded. Apprenticeships and indentureships are educational methods which have been used for centuries and are still used today. Vocational education courses were introduced in the public and private schools as demands increased for trained manpower to serve agriculture, trades, industries, and other occupations.

The national programs of vocational education were established as a peacetime measure to assist and stimulate a growing economy. These cooperative endeavors between the Federal government and the states were launched only after intensive research and investigation. In 1914, Congress authorized the creation of a Commission on National Aid to Vocational Education. The report of the Commission led to the passage of the Smith-Hughes Act and supplementary acts which stimulated the development of comprehensive programs of vocational education. This cooperation in the allocation of federal monies helped state and local communities move forward in developing vocational programs.

Vocational education attempts to train young people in school and adults out of school for useful employment. Vocational programs develop abilities, talents, attitudes, and work habits which contribute to future successful employment and a full life. Employed workers are able to update themselves in their field and to improve the quality of their work through vocational programs. During World War II and the depression, vocational programs trained manpower for government and industry. Since the National Vocational Acts were passed in 1917, (8) vocational education programs have been added in many areas. Currently many State-Federal cooperative vocational programs exist. A problem that needs to be investigated is the organization of vocational programs in small communities where inadequate finances, staff, and facilities restrict the opportunities. (8)

In most states, a Division of Vocational Education under the State Board or Department for Vocational Education has the responsibility for the administration and implementation of vocational programs in conformity with a state plan for Vocational Education, the Federal Education Acts, state laws, federal and state rules and regulations, and policies pertaining to vocational education.

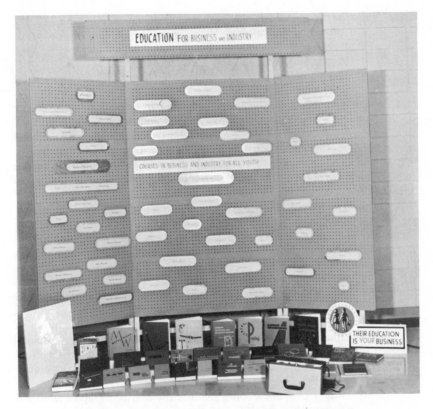

Fig. 1-1. From Business Machines and Clerical Practice to
Welding and Woodworking, the Vocational Program
Spans a Wide Range of Occupations
(Tulsa Schools)

The specific functions of a state board or department include:

1. Maintaining a qualified vocational education staff to administer,
    supervise, **and** evaluate vocational education programs as pro-
    vided in a **state** plan for vocational education.
2. Assuring that the standards, provisions, requirements, and pur-
    poses contained in the state plan are met.
3. Approving programs of vocational education including area
    vocational-technical schools.
4. Making contracts and cooperative agreements with local school
    districts and other public educational institutions and agencies
    for the training of qualified vocational education teachers.

5.   Preparing budgets.
6.   Approving and paying claims for vocational education expenditures.
7.   Maintaining fiscal and statistical records.
8.   Making required reports to the U. S. Office of Education and the State Legislature.

Vocational education includes programs in agriculture, distributive occupations, business, home economics, trades, industrial work, health services, and personal services. Persons may be served in high schools, community colleges, area vocational-technical schools, through adult education, and in work-study programs. Guidance and counseling is an important service to all trainees. In some states, the supervision of industrial arts is a responsibility of the division of vocational education.

There are over 40,000 separately identified job skills in the nation. Preparing a student for the correct one of these thousands of jobs presents a tremendous challenge to education. The galaxy approach is one response to this challenge. This organizational effort groups instructional areas into four broad classifications:

1.   *Materials and Processes:* this complex is that multitude of operations which produces and makes useful objects of materials. It includes the skills and knowledge in producing, shaping, forming, and assembling metals, woods, plastic, fabrics, and ceramics—to name some of the most familiar materials. Some typical occupations and courses are cabinetmaking, machine shop, pre-technical chemistry, welding, horticulture, and industrial cooperative education.

2.   *Visual Communications:* includes the drafting, graphic arts, and photographic industries. In the broadest sense it includes office practice, art, writing, and data processing. Courses and occupations include commercial art, drafting, offset printing, photography, printing, business machines, secretarial, technical drafting, design, and cooperative office education.

3.   *Energy and Propulsion:* consists of the development of energy and harnessing it for useful work. This includes internal combustion engines, external combustion engines, electrical power, solar energy, fuel cells, nuclear energy, etc., and the use of this energy in its many forms and applications such as electrical power and light systems, electronics, automobiles, aircraft, trains, and marine applications. Some jobs and courses are aeromechanics, autobody repair, auto mechanics, diesel mechanics, electronics, refrigeration, air conditioning, small engine repair, and technical electronics.

4.   *Personal Services:* comprises those jobs which involve a maximum of contact with human beings or servicing human beings. It includes such areas as commercial foods, health service, cosme-

tology, clothing, recreation, distribution, public safety, etc. Some courses are cosmetology, tailoring, upholstery, dental office practice, medical office practice, child care, food service, sewing, and distributive education.

The functions and purposes of typical operating divisions are described in the following paragraphs.

Trade and Industrial Education

The Division of Trade and Industrial Education provides for those who have entered, or are preparing to enter, a trade or industrial occupation. Such occupation may include any craft, skilled trade, or semiskilled occupation which directly functions in the designing, producing, processing, fabricating, assembling, testing, modifying, maintaining, servicing, or repairing of any product or commodity. Training may be given as appropriate to develop manipulative skills, technical knowledge, and information such as job attitudes, safety practices, and trade judgment. The functions of the division are the approval of trade and industrial education programs, setting administrative and certification standards for trade and industrial education teachers, making cooperative agreements with approved teacher training institutions, development of instructional standards, and sponsoring the Association of Vocational Industrial Clubs of America as a training program with leadership and participation activities.

Technical Vocational Education

The Division of Technical Vocational Education provides training for highly skilled technicians in recognized occupations requiring scientific knowledge in fields necessary for the national defense. Functions include the approval of technical-vocational education programs, establishing certification standards for technical-vocational education teachers, making cooperative agreements with approved teacher-training institutions, and development of instructional standards.

Area Vocational-Technical Education Schools

The Division of Area Vocational-Technical Education Schools provides for the designation of such schools serving population areas of at least 50,000 people. The training provided in such schools is based upon the number of students, their needs and desires, job requirements and opportunities, and community needs for trained personnel in business and industry. The func-

Fig. 1-2. Technical Electronics Is a Rapidly Growing
Occupational Area (Tulsa Schools)

tions of the division include recommendations of designated areas for schools, approval of facilities and equipment, approval of curriculum, establishing teacher qualifications, and general administration, supervision, and evaluation of area school programs.

Special Service Division for Adults and Work-Study

The Division of Special Services includes adult education and work-study programs. The work of training adults in vocational education subjects is coordinated with the work of other divisions in vocational education. Functions of this division include approval of vocational education programs, approval of qualifications and certification of instructors, establishing standards for instruction and operation, and general administration, supervision, and evaluation of vocational programs for adults. This division enters into agreements with local school districts for work-study programs which are designed to assist worthy students to stay in school to continue their training in vocational education subjects. Other functions include approval of schools for work-study, approval of cooperative arrangements between the school and other public agencies for work-study programs, and general administration, supervision, and evaluation of all work-study programs.

Vocational-Industrial Education

Industrial education is a broad term including industrial arts, vocational-industrial, and technical education. It has generally come to mean those phases of education which have to do with the materials, tools, processes, and technical knowledge involved in the production and utilization of industrial products and services.

Vocational-industrial education and industrial arts are closely related yet different types of education. There are clear-cut distinctions between industrial arts and vocational-industrial education in objectives, character of work, and students served. Industrial arts courses are general, basic in content, exploratory, and designed to familiarize students with various facets of our industrial technological civilization. Vocational-industrial education is designed to produce occupational competency in a specific trade or industrial job. Both types are essential parts of a good program of public education. Some school systems offer industrial arts and vocational-industrial education as parts of a unified program of industrial education; in other schools they are offered under separate administrative organizations; still other schools offer only one of the programs.

Technical education prepares for employment in occupations which require a mastery of more advanced mathematics and science. Persons in technical occupations generally have continued in school beyond grade twelve.

Efficient organization and administration of a program of industrial education necessitates a clear understanding of the differences and relationships between industrial arts and vocational-industrial education. They both involve a study of the tools, materials, processes, products, and the problems of occupational life in industry. In a *properly organized* program, the two supplement each other.

Industrial arts gives a broad, basic training to all who enroll without regard to vocation, socio-economic status, or where they might live. At the same time, a limited number of students find the education prepares them for employment in industry or for more specialized training in vocational classes. Thus, while industrial arts is essentially a program of general education, it also serves as preemployment training and as a self-selection device for vocation-industrial classes.

Philosophy of Vocational-Industrial Education

The philosophy of vocational-industrial education is consistent with the general philosophy of education. Professional vocational educators recognize that as the student grows, his habits largely determine his course of action. As he learns, his need for external controls should be lessened and his power to discipline himself for his own good and for the good of the environment in which he lives should be increased.

Fig. 1-3. Welding Instruction May Be a Part of Industrial Arts or a
Specific Occupational Objective (Tulsa Schools)

The wealth of a nation depends upon the degree to which it utilizes its human natural resources. The wealth of a state within the nation, likewise, depends upon the degree to which it has and is able to utilize its natural resources in the production of manufactured products. As an example, much of the natural wealth of the state of Oklahoma has gone to other sections of the country for processing. The transportation of raw products to and from those sections and the manufacturing of products outside of Oklahoma has not helped in its industrial growth. The best means of encouraging people to develop the natural resources within a state is to teach the skills and technical knowledge necessary for production of these resources. An increasing need now exists for upgrading workers in every community. Vocational-industrial education is devoted to the further training and increased efficiency of out-of-school youth and adults who are preparing for, or are already engaged in, trade and industrial jobs. Its goal is the competent industrial worker — competent economically, socially, emotionally, and physically.

Approximately 70% of the students who fail to complete high school drop out because of the limited educational opportunities and economic circumstances that require them to find employment in order to support themselves and their families. Many of these dropouts are handicapped because of their lack of training; therefore, they drift from one job to another.

Vocational trade and industrial education can serve in large measure to alleviate these conditions. It provides training for useful employment and contributes to the social and economic welfare of a state.

About half of the payroll jobs in the United States today are industrial in nature. The basis of economic progress has become largely dependent upon the capacity of industry, and production is largely dependent upon the supply of trained labor. It is thus doubly important that youth be well prepared for industrial jobs.

Technical Education

Since the beginning of the industrial expansion in the early part of the present century, the need for a "team" in industry has arisen. Technological developments today are products of teams. Scientists and engineers formulate ideas to create new products and services; engineers and industrial technicians help develop, test, and apply these ideas and creations; and technicians and craftsmen make the product and supervise the manufacturing and processing.

Technical education is designed to prepare individuals for the "middle level" occupations or the so-called technical positions of the occupational spectrum. There are two general groups of technicians: (1) the *engineering technician* who has a broad academic background and who works directly with the engineer, assisting him with design, testing, design modifications, etc., and (2) the *industrial technician* who has a more specialized background within his field and who completes the communication link between the engineer or engineering technician and the craftsman. Both types of technicians require intensive, specialized education based on a solid foundation of mathematics and science. A common knowledge of science and mathematics enables the technician and the engineer or scientist to communicate effectively. The industrial technicians's mathematics and science, however, are more specialized than that of the engineering technician. Technical education programs for both types of technicians are conducted at the post-high-school level, normally by a technical institute, a junior college, or an area school technical program. They require two years of study and usually lead to an associate degree.

Job Opportunities

One of the largest areas of employment for technicians is in research, development, and design work. Technicians in this type of activity generally work directly with engineers or scientists. In the laboratory, they conduct experiments or tests; set up, calibrate, and operate instruments; and make calculations. They may assist scientists and engineers in developing experimental equipment and models, make drawings, or assume responsibility for certain aspects of design work under the engineer's direction.

Industrial technicians sometimes work directly with engineers and scientists, but generally their work is closely related to production. They may aid in the various phases of production planning, such as working out specifications regarding needed materials and methods of manufacture. They often serve as production supervisors or inspectors, devise tests to insure quality control of products, or make time and motion studies designed to improve the efficiency of operations. Industrial technicians may also act as coordinators between departments such as research or engineering and production. In the installation, operation, and maintenance of complex machinery and equipment, industrial technicians often handle or supervise work which would otherwise have to be done by engineers. They sometimes are responsible for "troubleshooting" and repair work requiring considerable theoretical as well as practical knowledge.

Some of the various technologies in which engineers and industrial technicians are provided education and find employment are: Aerospace Technology, Architectural Technology, Building and Construction Technology, Chemical Technology, Civil Engineering Technology, Data-Processing Technology, Drafting and Design Technology, Electronic Technology, Electrical Technology, Instrumentation Technology, Mechanical Technology, and Nuclear Technology.

Educational Opportunities

Pretechnical education programs are conducted at the high school level for grades 11 through 12. The purpose of high school pretechnical education programs is to develop interest among capable and qualified high school students to enter post-high-school technical programs. Students should complete a regular high school curriculum with special emphasis on mathematics, science, and technical industrial courses. Most graduates of good high school pretechnical training programs should be capable of passing advanced-standing examinations and thus obtaining credit for some of the beginning post-secondary school technical courses.

Most post-secondary school technical programs require approximately 70 semester hours of credit for completion. The student should expect to spend about two hours in outside study for each hour he is in class.

The American Society of Engineering Education recently forecast a need in the United States for approximately 4,000,000 technicians by 1975. In 1969 approximately 40,000 technicians were graduated and entered technical jobs. The accumulated shortage by 1975 is forecast as being nearly 3,000,000. Leaders in vocational education must constantly strive to improve vocational education working with the local community and with state and federal officials. A continuing supply of trained manpower is vital to the economic and social progress of an industrial nation.

Industrial Arts Education

Industrial arts cannot be defined as something separate and apart from general education. The ultimate purpose of education is to transmit the social culture and to assist the individual in becoming an asset to himself and to society. Industrial arts, being of several areas, contributes to the realization of this objective through five channels:

1. Extension of the education of the individual.
2. Development of manipulative skills in the use of tools and materials.
3. Promotion of the conservation of human and material resources.
4. Providing experiences in common avocational avenues.
5. Aiding social and personal development.

Since half of all workers in the United States are employed in some phase of production industry, it seems imperative that the schools provide for an understanding of the role, functions, and methods of industry. Every person uses the products of industry in his day to day activities — from the alarm clock that awakens him to the late evening news report. It follows,

Fig. 1-4. Spot Welding in an Industrial Arts Class Provides
First-Hand Insights into a Common Industrial
Process and Job Category (Tulsa Schools)

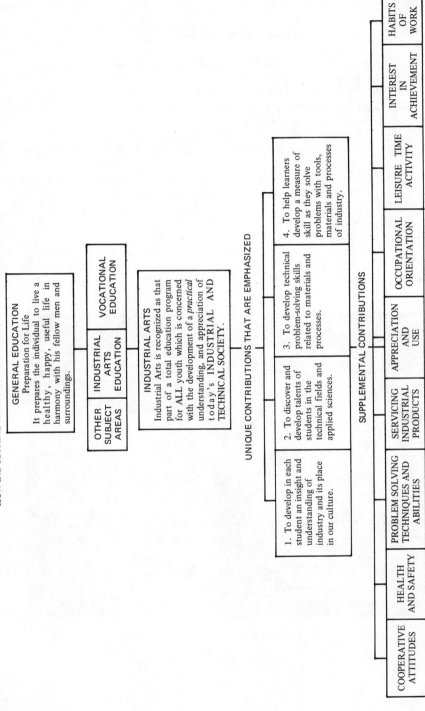

HOW INDUSTRIAL ARTS FUNCTIONS IN THE EDUCATION OF YOUTH

GENERAL EDUCATION
Preparation for Life
It prepares the individual to live a healthy, happy, useful life in harmony with his fellow men and surroundings.

OTHER SUBJECT AREAS	INDUSTRIAL ARTS EDUCATION	VOCATIONAL EDUCATION

INDUSTRIAL ARTS
Industrial Arts is recognized as that part of a total education program for ALL youth which is concerned with the development of a *practical* understanding, and appreciation of today's INDUSTRIAL AND TECHNICAL SOCIETY.

UNIQUE CONTRIBUTIONS THAT ARE EMPHASIZED

1. To develop in each student an insight and understanding of industry and its place in our culture.

2. To discover and develop talents of students in the technical fields and applied sciences.

3. To develop technical problem-solving skills related to materials and processes.

4. To help learners develop a measure of skill as they solve problems with tools, materials and processes of industry.

SUPPLEMENTAL CONTRIBUTIONS

COOPERATIVE ATTITUDES	HEALTH AND SAFETY	PROBLEM SOLVING TECHNIQUES AND ABILITIES	SERVICING INDUSTRIAL PRODUCTS	APPRECIATION AND USE	OCCUPATIONAL ORIENTATION	LEISURE TIME ACTIVITY	INTEREST IN ACHIEVEMENT	HABITS OF WORK

Fig. 1-4A. Contributions of Industrial Arts

therefore, that industrial arts must furnish guided experiences in the use of tools, materials and machines, and insights into those phases of industry that have become an important part of our social culture.

The purposes of industrial arts as listed in the *ACIAS Bulletin, Industrial Arts Education*, are as follows:

1. To develop in each student an insight and understanding of industry and its place in our society.
2. To discover and develop student talents in the industrial-technical field.
3. To develop problem-solving abilities related to the materials, processes, and products of industry.
4. To develop in each student skills in the safe use of tools and machines. (1)

Values of Industrial Arts Education

Industrial arts shares the responsibility with other curriculum areas of transmitting the social culture which is becoming increasingly technical. To define the role of industrial arts fully and accurately, however, requires that attention be directed to its unique functions in the school program. (See Table 1-1.)

Table 1-1
ANALYSIS OF VALUES OF INDUSTRIAL ARTS

Unique Contributions	Values				
	Cultural	Civic	Occupational	Professional	Avocational
1. To develop a degree of skill as students solve problems with tools, materials, and processes of industry.	x	x	x	x	x
2. To provide exploratory experiences in a variety of industrial activities.	x	x	x	x	x
3. To develop the skills and knowledge necessary to produce working drawings.	x	x	x	x	x
Secondary Objectives a. Prevocational experiences		x	x		x
b. Interest in industry	x		x	x	x
c. Self-discipline and initiative	x	x	x		
d. Appreciation and use of industrial products	x	x	x	x	x
e. Industrial intelligence		x	x	x	
f. Health and safety	x		x		x
g. Cooperative attitudes	x	x	x	x	x
h. Drawing and design	x		x	x	x
i. Shop skills and knowledge			x		x
j. Orderly performance	x	x	x	x	x

Cultural values pertain to the way of life of a people or the artistic and intellectual aspects of human activity and the traits learned and transmitted by man as a member of society. Simply stated, cultural values of education refer to the means whereby a culture recreates itself.

Industrial arts is an experience or activity curriculum which has as its main function the teaching of the relationships of man and technology. The emphasis on experience or activity is predicated on the belief that one cannot truly appreciate the cultural heritage without the quality of understanding that is produced from experience with it. In the relationship between man and the technology, the emphasis is on the complete fulfillment or self-realization of man. All members of society must learn to be aware of and to live effectively in today's technological society. Through industrial arts experiences, the learner utilizes and develops creative abilities through which he comes to know himself better.

Learning activities in industrial arts provide opportunities for many students to experience success who are not able to achieve satisfaction in other curriculum areas. Success experiences are essential for those who must leave school early and those who continue on to graduation; for the student with low scholastic ability and for the student on the honor roll; for the future factory worker and for the future professional person and for those of both high and low income status.

Changes can and do take place in the learner as a result of industrial arts experiences. These changes may take the form of an interest in the man-made world—its materials and products and how goods are produced and fabricated; the place of the tool, the machine, and man in these processes; the evaluation of one's attitude toward constructive work; the utilization of such work for health and recreation, as well as for its economic value; and the development of a favorable attitude toward creative thinking. Further, character improvement—knowing and making the most of one's self and the assuming of self-expression and control over one's environment—are evidences of this change.

Civic values pertain to the functioning, interpreting, and development of a civilized community involving the common public activities and interests of the body of citizens. All members of society must learn to be aware of and to live effectively in today's technological world. The industrial arts student develops new insights in important aspects of daily living. He utilizes and develops creative ability through self-expression.

Occupational values pertain to the principal business of one's life — a craft, a trade, or other means of earning one's living. Industrial arts provides technical skills and knowledge basic to many occupations and professions. With its tools, materials and machines, industrial arts enables the future scientist and engineer to solve technical problems; future craftsmen or technicians to develop skills and obtain technical information; and it enables all students to receive meaning from concrete experiences which aid in the understanding of abstract ideas.

Experiences in industrial arts help the learner to use tools and materials to solve technical problems and to synthesize concepts. Through direct experiences in conceiving, designing, planning, and arranging procedures, through producing and evaluating the results, the learner does develop new insights in important aspects of daily living. It also provides opportunities for learners to discover and develop their talents and abilities in the areas of technology and applied sciences. In achieving this, each learner acquires fundamental skills in the efficient and safe use of common tools and machines.

For instance, as a student is exposed to a series of different experiences in a broad and complete offering of industrial arts subjects, he will gain insights into a number of occupational clusters. From the activities in these clusters and with proper teaching and guidance services, the student should have a better understanding of the requirements, types of work, conditions, and future possibilities in many occupations.

As more and better guidance services are provided, along with expanded and new directions in industrial arts and pre-vocational courses, industrial education should and will take on new dimensions.

Professional values pertain to occupations requiring high levels of training and proficiency.

Avocational values pertain to activities pursued in addition to one's regular work, especially for relaxation and enjoyment.

An AIAA publication has stated that:

One of the most important aims is to assist boys in becoming more efficient in the work that must be done about the home. Another is to help satisfy the creative urge which most boys have. A third aim is to help boys in becoming acquainted with methods and living in modern industrial life. In localities where a comprehensive industrial arts program is found, it is possible for a boy to have experiences in woodwork, metalwork, electricity, drafting, graphic arts, industrial crafts, and power mechanics, so that guidance values may be attained. In such broad programs, a boy may be able to decide what occupation he will choose for his life's work, and in this way industrial arts may directly contribute to vocational education, while the latter area furnishes the specialization not found in the industrial arts program. (6)

All of the industrial arts programs have a number of characteristics in common. The two most important are (1) program breadth and (2) close representation of industrial practices.

Industrial Arts has taken great steps in innovative curriculum during the past decade. Programs in the galaxy approach and the organic curriculum represent a wide array of curriculum approaches for our profession. There are numerous common elements, for they all emphasize the introduction of new instruction which is more representative of current industry with an understanding of technical knowledge and the development of broad subject areas related to the current organization of an industry. A school may accept any or a continuation of the innovative curriculum patterns now being developed.

INDUSTRIAL ARTS

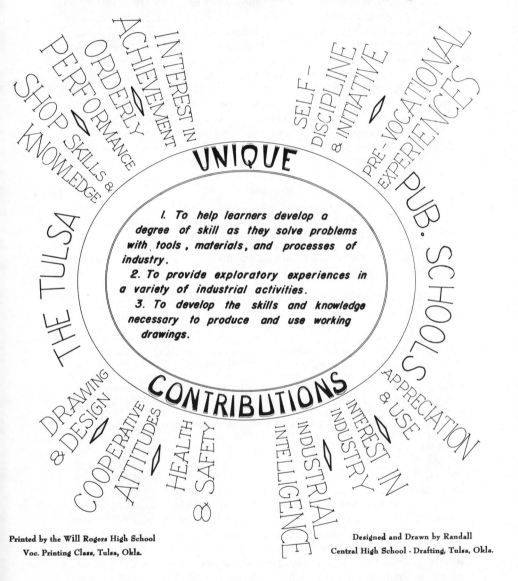

SHOP SKILLS & KNOWLEDGE
PERFORMANCE
ORDERLY
ACHIEVEMENT
INTEREST IN
SELF-DISCIPLINE & INITIATIVE
PRE-VOCATIONAL EXPERIENCES
PUB. SCHOOLS

THE TULSA

UNIQUE

I. To help learners develop a degree of skill as they solve problems with tools, materials, and processes of industry.

2. To provide exploratory experiences in a variety of industrial activities.

3. To develop the skills and knowledge necessary to produce and use working drawings.

CONTRIBUTIONS

DRAWING & DESIGN
COOPERATIVE ATTITUDES
HEALTH & SAFETY
INDUSTRIAL INTELLIGENCE
INTEREST IN INDUSTRY
APPRECIATION & USE

Printed by the Will Rogers High School
Voc. Printing Class, Tulsa, Okla.

Designed and Drawn by Randall
Central High School - Drafting, Tulsa, Okla.

Fig. 1-5. Communicating with Students, Parents, and Public
Requires a Variety of Devices (Tulsa Schools)

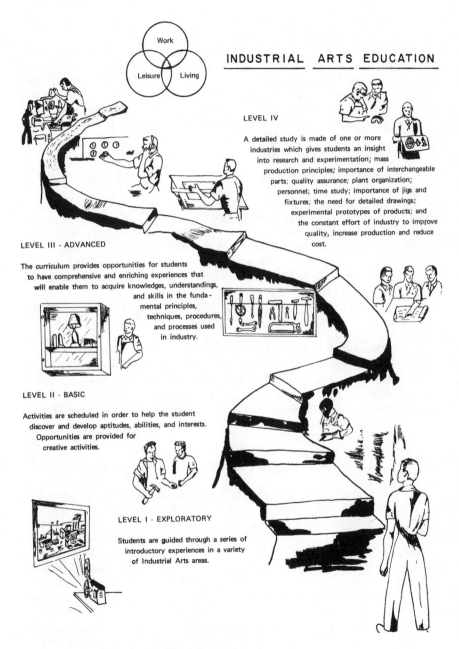

Work

Leisure   Living

INDUSTRIAL ARTS EDUCATION

LEVEL IV

A detailed study is made of one or more
industries which gives students an insight
into research and experimentation; mass
production principles; importance of interchangeable
parts; quality assurance; plant organization;
personnel; time study; importance of jigs and
fixtures; the need for detailed drawings;
experimental prototypes of products; and
the constant effort of industry to improve
quality, increase production and reduce
cost.

LEVEL III - ADVANCED

The curriculum provides opportunities for students
to have comprehensive and enriching experiences that
will enable them to acquire knowledges, understandings,
and skills in the funda-
mental principles,
techniques, procedures,
and processes used
in industry.

LEVEL II - BASIC

Activities are scheduled in order to help the student
discover and develop aptitudes, abilities, and interests.
Opportunities are provided for
creative activities.

LEVEL I - EXPLORATORY

Students are guided through a series of
introductory experiences in a variety
of Industrial Arts areas.

Fig. 1-5 continued.

In order to implement and update curricula, educational media offers a wide variety of materials. Textbooks, overhead projection transparencies, slides, teaching systems, project ideas, student manuals, closed loop films, programmed instruction, and other media have been developed to match the new curriculum patterns. These materials are invaluable to the industrial arts instructor in conducting his program. He schedules the activities a student is going to perform in the laboratory and he uses the audio visual materials to help convey the knowledge for the activity in the classroom.

Organization of Industrial Arts

Organization of subject areas may fall into the following categories or clusters:

1. *Visual Communications* — includes drafting, printing and lithography (graphic arts), and photography.
2. *Materials and Processes* — includes woods, metals and machines, plastics, textiles, adhesives and laminates.
3. *Energy Conversion and Power Transmission* — includes source of power, transmission through fluids, mechanics and electricity and uses, such as transportation and aerospace.
4. *Electronics and Instrumentation* — includes the study of electronic circuitry, instrumentation, and devices used in the home and industry.

Both the American Industry Project and the Industrial Arts Curriculum Project, which are research and development programs in the area of new curriculum patterns, point out that implementing a new program in industrial technology requires an organized process of change. Implementing this process will require three considerations: (1) innovative curriculum, (2) educational media, and (3) inservice education.

Vocational Education Supplements General Education

It is a mistaken idea that vocational and general education are in competition. These two aspects of a school curriculum complement each other. High schools, to render effective educational service to all youth, must prepare the boy who is going to be a mechanic as well as the boy who is going to college. Vocational courses cannot be a "dumping ground" for retarded or delinquent students. All vocational students should meet specific aptitude requirements for the training and employment they seek. Students should have a natural talent for and interest in the vocational program they seek to enter. (7)

A sure way to destroy a vocational-industrial education program is by arbitrarily assigning to it students who do not succeed in academic classes. Vocational-industrial education can be, and is, a part of the 11th and 12th

INDUSTRIAL EDUCATION
M. J. RULEY, Director—323 Education Service Center

Instructor	Room	1 M T W T F	2 M T W T	3 M T W F	4 M T T F	5 M T W T F	6 T W T F
G. E. Brewer	IE24	Soph. Drafting 1	Drafting 1 (IE24)	Drafting 1	Drafting 1	Drafting 1	Drafting 1 (IE11)
John Duncan	IE6	Soph. Machine Shop 1	Machine Shop 1 (IE6)	Woodwork 1	Machine Shop 1 (IE6)	Woodwork C	Woodwork 1 (IE11)
Wayman Penner, Dept. Chairman	IE10	See Voc. & Technical Ed.	See Voc. & Tech. Ed.	Woodwork 1	Woodwork 1	Woodwork 1 (IE10)	
Jim Ramsey	IE14	Jr. Photography 1	Photography 1	Photography 1	Photography 1 (IE14)	Photography 1	Photography 1
Richard L. Rice	IE3	See Vocational & Technical Ed.	See Voc. & Tech. Ed.	Machine Shop 1		Machine Shop 1 (IE3)	
Verlin Ringle	IE22	See Vocational & Technical Ed.	See Voc. & Tech. Ed.	Machine Shop 1 (IE3)	Printing 1	Printing 1	
Gene Stone	IE4	Jr. Power Mechanics	Power Mechanics	Power Mechanics	Power Mechanics	(IE4)	Power Mechanics
George Wright	IE23	See Vocational & Technical Ed.	See Voc. & Tech. Ed.	Engineering Drafting & Technical Drafting	Power Mechanics (IE23)	Architectural Draft. & Technical Drafting	

VOCATIONAL & TECHNICAL EDUCATION
M. J. RULEY, Director—323 Education Service Center
ALLIE DALE LAMBERT, Supervisor of Business Education—324 Education Service Center

Instructor	Room	1 M T W T F	2 M T W T	3 M T W F	4 M T T F	5 M T W T F	6 T W T F
Freda Bell	IE27	Sr. Home Room Grades Coordination	Coordination	Coordination	Voc. Office Ed. —Two Periods	Coordination	Related English Voc. Office Ed.
Lorene O'Hara	IE27	8:00-10:05 Sr. Voc. Office Ed. (Two Periods)	Related English Voc. Office Ed.	Coordination	Coordination	Coordination	Coordination
Louelllah Kirkpatrick	IE28	8:00-8:55 Jr.-Sr. Distrib. Ed. 8:55 Related English—D.E.	Office (IE26)	Coordination	Coordination	Coordination	Coordination
Elmer Mabry	IE26	8:00-8:45 Jr.-Sr. ICT Related 8:50 Office	Office	11:29-12:15 Daily ICT Relations	Coordination	Coordination	Coordination
Cora MacDonald	222	8:55 Related English Industrial Coop. Training	See English Dept.	See English Dept.			
Wayman Penner, Dept. Chairman	IE10	8:00-11:16 Jr.-Sr. Voc. Cabinet Making—Three Periods Thursday—8:00-10:01	See Industrial Ed.	See Industrial Ed.	See Industrial Ed.	See Industrial Ed.	See Industrial Ed.
Richard L. Rice	IE3	8:00-11:16 Jr.-Sr. Voc. Machine Shop—Three Periods Thursdays—8:00-10:01	See Industrial Ed.	See Industrial Ed.	See Industrial Ed.	See Industrial Ed.	See Industrial Ed.
Verlin Ringle	IE22	8:00-11:16 Jr.-Sr. Vocational Printing—Three Periods Thursdays—8:00-10:01	See Industrial Ed.	See Industrial Ed.	See Industrial Ed.	See Industrial Ed.	See Industrial Ed.
Roy Trimm	IE5	8:00-11:16 Sr. Vocational Auto Mechanics—Three Periods Thursdays—8:00-10:01			Vocational Auto Mechanics—Three Periods M-T-W 1:09-3:40 Th-F 11:58-3:40		
George Wright	IE23	8:00-11:16 Sr. Vocational Drafting—Three Periods Thursdays—8:00-10:01	See Industrial Ed.	See Industrial Ed.	See Industrial Ed.	See Industrial Ed.	See Industrial Ed.

VOCATIONAL-TECHNICAL CENTER OFFERINGS
JOE W. LEMLEY, Principal

Aeromechanics
Auto Body Repair
Auto Mechanics
Business Education (Bookkeeping and Office Procedures)
Business Education (Stenography)
Business Machines
Chemical Technology—Post Graduates
Commercial Art
Cosmetology

Data Processing—Post Graduates (Computer Programming)
Dental Office Assistant
Diesel Mechanics
Food Services
Horticulture
Machine Shop
Medical Office Assistant
Offset Printing

Refrigeration and Air Conditioning
Sewing Services
Small Engines Repair
Technical Drafting and Design
Technical Electronics
Vocational Drafting
Vocational Electronics (Radio-TV Service)
Welding

Fig. 1-6. Comprehensive Program of Industrial Education
As Offered in One High School

grade high school program. There is a definite trend, however, to making these programs an integral part of the post-high-school program of the 13th and 14th years.

Industrial arts is related to vocational-industrial education and is considered essential as an avenue of guidance as well as a foundation upon which these programs can be built. It serves life needs and vocational-industrial education in the same manner as arithmetic serves life needs and algebra and calculus. Far from being synonymous, industrial arts and vocational-industrial education are distinct phases of education for the technological age in which we live. If the programs are of good quality, it is difficult to tell where good industrial arts ends and good vocational-industrial education begins.

Table 1-2 summarizes the differences between industrial arts and vocational-industrial education. In a well-organized system the two do not compete, but supplement each other. (5)

Industrial Arts in the Elementary School

Industrial arts in the elementary school most often consists of construction activities which grow out of the classroom situation. Interests and insights can be quickly and surely stimulated by first-hand experiences within the ability of the children. (4)

Handwork with tools and materials in the elementary schools has been widely carried on in this country for more than half a century. However, the organization of the program and its purposes have changed almost entirely in recent years.

Industrial arts in the elementary schools is sometimes taught by special teachers in rooms equipped for this work. However, many systems include this area in self-contained classrooms and use the experience to complement the overall curriculum of the school. The equipment is limited to portable benches, hand tools, and some special tools. In the lower grades, the activity consists of building projects within the interest and performance range of the pupils and with a minimum number of tools. In the upper grades the activity is continued and handwork introduced to meet individual needs and interests. A reasonable degree of skill is expected in the use of hand tools. The whole program is one of gradual development of the child's knowledge and skill. In the first year only a few tools are used. In each succeeding year new tools and new skills are introduced until at the end of the 6th grade the child has learned to use a number of tools in many different manipulative operations. Kindergartens are generally equipped to carry on construction activities.

Many desirable habits and attitudes will result from an intelligently planned and administered program of elementary industrial arts. Such a program furnishes opportunities for necessary psychological and social adjust-

Table 1-2
DIFFERENCES IN INDUSTRIAL ARTS AND
VOCATIONAL-INDUSTRIAL EDUCATION

Characteristic	Industrial Arts	Vocational-Industrial Education
Aims and Objectives	General education involving exploratory and developmental experiences; consumer knowledge and appreciations; skill in care and use of common tools; understanding of and interest in industrial life; development of desirable habits and character traits.	Specialized training for useful employment, involving job skills and procedures; technical and related information; employer-employee relationships; occupational health and safety.
Groups Served	All comers; elementary; junior and senior high school pupils; usually offered as part of activity program in lower grades, required in junior high school, and elective in senior high school; classes somewhat homogenous.	Selected groups; must be at least 14 years of age in day classes, 16 in evening classes; students must be either employed in trade or industrial pursuit or have made definite selection of same before they can legally enroll; need for and ability to profit by instruction further selective criteria; older groups, heterogenous in character.
Time of Enrollment, Time Allotment and Length of Course	Enrollment conforms to regular school program; classes meet from 1 hour per week up to 10, usually 5 single periods; courses run for a semester or year, for shorter periods when scheduled for exploratory purposes; school is bound only by state regulations.	Part-time and day classes conform closely to regular school schedule; evening classes started when need arises; day classes must offer at least 30 hours of instruction per week for school year of 9 months; at least 15 hours per week must be spent in shop.
When and Where Classes Meet	Classes ordinarily meet during day time only, in regular school or in special shop building on school grounds; increasing number of schools offering industrial arts along with recreational activities in summer program.	Trade preparatory classes meet generally during the day and in public school; part-time classes meet during day or evening at any place under public supervision and control; evening trade extension classes meet any time after working hours at any place under public supervision and control.
Content and Nature of Work	Activities represented in program and course content much the same from school to school; general shop, drawing, metalwork, woodwork, electricity are most commonly offered.	Subjects taught and the content thereof vary with the industries of the community and the needs of the workers; instruction based on an analysis of what the individual workers need to know and be able to do.
Methods of Teaching	Shop work centered around projects of individual type; much group instruction given; individual instruction used to some extent; readings, visual aids and excursion trips used; achievement tests similar to those in other fields used.	Shop work organized around group projects; production procedures followed as closely as possible; instruction largely individual, supplemented by group methods; readings reduced to a minimum skills emphasized; few tests other than practical performance used.
Type of Teacher	College graduate with broad technical and professional training; practical experience highly desirable but not required; a lover of boys and boy activities; must meet minimum requirements as set up by State Department.	Competent tradesman; acceptable to group; 3 years or more of journeyman experience; leadership qualities and ability to teach; minimum of professional training; must be approved by State Supervisor:

ments and for the development of desired manipulative skills. It also enables the teacher to observe and evaluate the interests and abilities thus indicated, and may aid in the solution of problems encountered in other areas of learning and relationships in the school program. Many new avenues of learning will be opened by the observation of important and sustained interests.

The ability to use materials well and to create with one's hands gives the child a feeling of satisfaction of work done. Personal satisfaction often leads to the improvement of the general work habits and standards of the individual. A good school program provides for many experiences that contribute to the feeling of security and belonging that is so essential to the spiritual and emotional growth of the child. A sense of belonging to the group and joy in accomplishment is derived from contributions made in the field of practical arts that otherwise might never be experienced.

Industrial arts at this level should not be considered as an isolated subject, but rather one that contributes to the enrichment of the many areas of experience necessary to the growth and development of the child. It helps in the clarification of concepts encountered in many branches of learning. Social studies, play experiences, seasonal interests, a creative urge, or the challenge of environment provide many opportunities for use of manipulative skills and practices. The course of study for the elementary school should be planned to develop thinking, self-expression, planning, solving problems in construction, hand skill, safety in the use of tools, thrift and economy in the use of materials, accurate and precise work, and appreciation of a job well done.

The work carried on in the industrial arts area can enrich the social studies and implement the other academic subjects by providing facilities for committee work. Activities and projects such as the following are motivational and give students an opportunity to create:

1. Hand puppets — stage, scenery, lights, etc.
2. Dramatization revolving around large construction.
3. Small construction for diorama table layout.
4. Small construction for manipulation, lumbering, etc., forest station.
5. Rhythm instruments for South American study.
6. Electrical experiments and projects — circuits, magnets, compass, etc.
7. Series of displays showing principles of simple machines — lever, inclined plane, pulleys, screws.
8. Weather station — working models of weather instruments.
9. Cages, traps, mounts, racks, bins, shelves. (Play up science displays.) This may be for rock collections, etc.
10. Containers for growing things — glass to show growth, flats, planters, window boxes, etc.

In industrial arts the children should have the *purpose* of the construction work clearly in mind.

Social studies understandings are often furthered through the medium of dramatic play. In order to make the dramatic play life-like a wide variety of objects will be needed. Whether the objects constructed will be large or small will depend upon the plans set out by the class. The construction work should help the child clarify his ideas. The construction work should cause the child to question and to do further reading.

When it is impossible to use authentic materials the child should seek substitutes. At all times he should be aware of the fact that he is using such substitute material.

Industrial Arts Education in the Junior High School

Industrial arts courses, as such, are ordinarily first offered in the early secondary school years. Prior to this time, industrial arts work was integrated with the regular classroom program and was not generally an entity in itself. Regularly scheduled industrial arts classes normally begin in the 7th grade.

A course in comprehensive general shop or the equivalent is recommended for all junior high school students. The basic course is all-inclusive and is designed to provide for exploration and to meet the other objectives previously cited. In this course, students have an opportunity to sample various phases of work in drafting, electricity, metalwork, graphic arts, industrial crafts, woodwork and power mechanics. In doing so, they became aware to some extent of their interests, abilities, and aptitudes in working with a variety of tools and materials.

Industrial arts is generally offered in grades 7 and 8. For many students, this is the only formal industrial arts educational experience they will have. Therefore, it is desirable to provide an opportunity for them during these two years to experience all six or seven of the industrial areas represented in a comprehensive industrial arts education program.

In a school which contains two or more general shops, the equivalent of a comprehensive general course can be offered by rotating classes through these shops. This is basically the same as a comprehensive course, except that the instruction takes place in two or more shops instead of one.

Industrial arts at the 9th grade level serves two purposes. It acts as a culminating experience for some students and also sets the stage for future work in this curriculum area. The elective course in this grade, while being the first course in any high school sequence, is still part of the total comprehensive general shop program in junior high schools. For this reason, it is desirable to organize it in such a manner that it is not a complete repetition of the 7th and 8th grade work, nor to the other extreme, completely limited to one area of instruction. Opportunity should be provided to take advantage of the interests of the individual. Facilities for work in the six or seven industrial arts areas should be provided so that students may avail themselves of opportunities to explore and experiment with any material or materials they desire. While the broad exploratory concepts of junior high school industrial arts should be maintained in the 9th grade, it seems desirable to allow some concentration of work according to individual student desires.

In schools where industrial arts is required in the 9th grade, some modification of the suggested organization for the 7th and 8th years can be made so that two sections of work are offered at each grade level. The teacher is admonished, however, that a considerable amount of organization, planning, and direct guidance is necessary to avoid a potentially chaotic situation. In grades 7, 8, and 9, boys should have the opportunity to receive instruction in multiple-activity shops. The instructional program should be designed to encompass a variety of beginning experiences with the common tools, materials, processes, and problems of industry.

Organization, or a lack of it, will make or break a program of industrial education. A lack of organization of student responsibilities in care and management of equipment, tools, and supplies will result in the teacher doing the checking, supply handling, and clean up after each class leaves. With an organization chart that is effective and working, students will learn to work with one another through the democratic process. With students handling the various assignments in the shop, the teacher has time to do an effective teaching job, and give individual attention to those in need of it.

Organization of all types is one of the most important factors in maintaining a good teaching-learning situation in industrial education classes.

The program for the junior high school should include at least 9 weeks in each of the exploratory areas for at least 1½ years, allowing for experience in each of six areas. Further instruction (½ year in the 8th grade, and 1 year in the 9th) should be scheduled in basic areas or in others not listed. The elective program should be scheduled for one semester in a single phase of industrial arts as previously experienced in basic exploratory areas. Such programs should be carried on if one teacher or a multiple-teacher program exists.

Exploration through investigation and experimentation is a characteristic of many early secondary school students. Their interest in the things around them becomes more pronounced because of natural curiosity. Their attention is captivated by the ever-increasing changes in the world about them and the products of industry that cause these changes. The opportunity to use tools and materials in the industrial arts shop can help to satisfy these interests and desires. Here they are encouraged to develop an appreciation for workmanship and industrial process. They acquire knowledge, insights, and appreciation as well as develop skill in the use of industrial materials as they research, study, plan, and build.

A program such as just described allows the student to experiment with and explore the application of these processes as they are used in industry and to sample the different activities so that they can determine at least partially their likes and dislikes, their interests, and their aptitudes. In addition, they can develop an interest in adult activities of various kinds and enjoy trying out ideas that are new to them.

Work of this nature can include assigned study, visits to industrial plants, class discussions, and other similar activities that help to develop an intelligent understanding of the industrial age in which we live.

Arranging for men from industry to talk with classes on new techniques, materials and processes; along with working in a class situation that is organized similar to modern industry, will help students to see how industry functions. Films from industry will also give helpful information.

Keeping a notebook on how American industry operates, as well as making a study of occupational clusters related to the various areas experienced through activities of the various industrial education courses, is a must.

Industrial Arts Education in the Senior High

Two types of industrial arts courses are generally offered in the senior high school grades. These are general-unit and unit courses. A general-unit course is one in which instruction is based on several kinds of work in one major industrial section. Such a course is broad in scope and has an appeal to many students. General woodwork is an example of a general-unit course. A well-rounded course might include hand and machine work, carpentry, concrete form construction, furniture-making, model work, patternmaking and wood finishing. General-unit courses offered in schools throughout the country include woodworking, electricity/electronics, metals and machines, power mechanics, graphic arts, drafting, and industrial crafts.

A unit course is one in which instruction is based on one specific kind of shopwork in an industrial section. This type of course is narrower in scope than general-unit industrial arts courses. It usually appeals to fewer students because of its intensive nature.

Courses in grades 10, 11, and 12 should be offered in especially designed and equipped shops, laboratories, or drafting rooms. When possible, courses should be limited to a single phase of industry which will meet the needs of students with varying abilities, aptitudes, desires, and interests. Each course should be designed to extend for at least one regular school year (36 weeks—a minimum of five periods per week). In some areas, a double period should be allowed. It is here that some of the course offerings need to be upgraded to meet the needs of students and present technology.

Many practical applications of science, mathematics, art, language arts, and other subjects may be given meaning and thereby enhance the instruction in industrial arts as well as in the other subjects. Technological changes are of intense interest to many young men in high school. Curiosity, as well as the desire to experiment and create, may be developed to a high degree.

Industrial arts can provide challenging experiences for students and give them an opportunity to increase their ability to think and to solve problems. It appeals to youth whose capacities and interests have developed to almost a mature level. If an industrial arts course is general in nature but provides for a degree of specialization and for further exploration in industrial fields of the student's own choosing, the total school objectives are furthered. Also, the student gains information that will assist him in making a wise occupational choice or in determining his needs for further training.

The type of work and the operations and processes experienced by students in senior high school classes generally involve a greater degree of difficulty than those in lower grades and brings forth the highest possible standards of workmanship consistent with the maturity of the students. Much of the craftsmanship displayed meets adult standards. Student interest, of course, remains the primary consideration, for an opportunity to investigate, plan, construct, and evaluate must be provided.

There should be a limited amount of group project activity (production) each year for the school community. Such activity, however, must not be extensive enough to exploit the student's time at the sacrifice of instruction. In comparison with junior high school industrial arts, more occupational information should be offered at this level. This guidance instruction should be a part of the daily instruction of advanced students.

Industrial arts and trade training classes should be coordinated in the advanced grades. There should be a differentiation with cooperation. Community activity, geographical location, and the needs of the citizenry should have some influence on the choice of courses to be taught in the advanced grades. This, however, should not be permitted to the extent of eliminating any of the basic fields of industry from the instructional schedule. In the senior high school, some instruction should be given in the subjects of industrial organization and management, labor relations, and labor legislation.

Basic courses for students who plan to become engineers, technicians, or industrial education teachers should be developed. Courses such as descriptive geometry, pre-engineering drawing, basic electronics, industrial materials, and industrial processes are of value. Most engineering schools do not require engineering drafting courses or engineering shopwork because of time needed for theory courses. Most colleges will recommend that students take such courses while in high school. Such a statement should be in all student handbooks.

Vocational-industrial classes provide preliminary instruction in a definite industrial occupation for high school students who have chosen their field of work. This program provides for shopwork and related subjects to complete the student's high school course. Typical courses offered in the senior high school are: machine shop, cabinetmaking and millwork, drafting, printing and lithography, auto mechanics, carpentry, diesel mechanics, auto-body repair, refrigeration and air-conditioning, aeromechanics, welding and many others.

The cooperative part-time industrial training program is designed to provide an opportunity for high school students to obtain both instruction and experience in industrial occupations. Bridging the gap between school and employment is the major purpose of this program. Students attend school for one-half day and work one-half day in an occupation of a trade or industrial nature. Such part-time employment offers actual experience to the student and at the same time provides for related and technical information to be studied in school.

The industrial coop student completes all his required subjects such as English, history, etc., and graduates from high school along with the rest of his class. In addition, he has had an opportunity to study occupationally related materials. On the job, the student spends a minimum of 20 hours per week learning a trade or occupation and gaining experience which will enable him to continue working full time after high school graduation. The student receives school credit and is paid for time spent on the job. This salary has, in a number of instances, made it possible for the student to complete his high school education. Training can be given in practically any industrial occupation which requires a training period of at least 2,000 clock hours. The occupation must be suited to the apprenticeship type of training and there must be sufficient related and technical information available for study. Some of the more common coop occupations are: auto mechanics, baking, beauty culture, business-machine repair, cabinetmaking, carpentry, cleaning and pressing, drafting, dental technician, welding, laboratory technician, machine shop, nurse's aid, patternmaking, photography, plating, printing, radio and TV repair, sheet metalwork, watch repair, and plumbing.

Industrial Arts for Adults

Adult education of an industrial arts nature will increase as more time is available for supplementary instruction, hobbies, interest, and leisure time activities. Adult courses should offer basic training if the adult student has no basic skill or knowledge. Flexibility should be the keynote for all adult classes.

The American Council of Industrial Arts Supervisors has this to say about adult education: "Industrial arts helps them (adults) to develop worthwhile avocational interests; in organizing home workshops, in making useful household articles and in discovering personal interests and aptitudes. For the physically handicapped, industrial arts experiences provide practical and effective motivation as well as mental and manual therapy essential to the rehabilitation of the individual. Industrial arts activities have many recreational values which are fundamental to programs in the armed forces, hobby shops, out-of-school activities, youth work, and for adults before and after retirement." (2)

Industrial Education in Special Education

Courses for the handicapped should be available in all special education programs. Classes in industrial arts are accepted in programs for the physically handicapped. Much still needs to be done in this area, for industrial arts is too often set up as a special program and is not always considered a part of general education. Some of the classes include courses for the gifted student as well as the slow learner. Gifted students who excel in manipulative skills as well as other types of learning are in a position to make ingenious application of the skills and information acquired. Through participation in industrial arts, the slow learner also experiences the morale-building stimulus that comes with successful accomplishment.

Industrial Education at the College Level

The four-year or two-year industrial arts program serves three basic functions: (1) provides general education course work, (2) offers specific courses for industrial technology majors (junior colleges include only those major courses appropriate for the first two years of college work.), and (3) prepares teachers for industrial arts instruction. A U.S. Office of Education conference found that: "In preparation of teachers in institutions offering teacher education, basic understandings of the philosophy and objectives of all education first must be developed. Following these basic education requirements, the future industrial arts teacher develops an appreciation and understanding of the objectives of the program by participating in industrial arts classes ... Throughout the entire teacher preparation program, the professional responsibilities that are basic to education are encouraged." (3)

References

1.   American Council of Industrial Arts Supervisors, *Industrial Arts Education*, Washington, D. C.: American Industrial Arts Association, 1961.
2.   *Bulletin to the Members of the American Council of Industrial Arts Supervisors.* Washington, D. C.: American Industrial Arts Association, October 12, 1959.

3. *Industrial Arts Education*, Washington, D. C.: U.S. Office of Education Conference, 1960.
4. *Industrial Arts Education – Organization and Administration.* Albany, New York: The University of New York, The State Department of Education, 1960.
5. *Industrial Arts Handbook, Bulletin 7B.* Jefferson City, Mo.: State Department of Education.
6. *The Industrial Arts Teacher,* January-February, 1959.
7. *Vocational Education for American Youth.* Washington, D. C.: American Vocation Association.
8. *Vocational Education in the Next Decade,* Washington, D. C.: U.S. Department of Health, Education, and Welfare, January, 1961.

Chapter 2

The Role of Leadership in Education

Whatever the scope or level of his authority may be, the primary function of an educational leader is to further the educational development of all those for whose welfare he is responsible. Thus, the superintendent, the principal, or the supervisor of an area of instruction is the administrative head of a specific program. The ultimate responsibility for the success of an educational program rests with these various administrators. Their authority may be delegated, but responsibility may only be shared, for the community will find them accountable for all actions.

Good administrators subject all school practices to periodic evaluation and they examine proposals for further programs in the light of present research. Alert leadership stimulates research by individual teachers and by groups, and encourages experimental centers. The weakest aspect of educational research is the slow rate of proof. A way of speeding up this process must be found.

A good leader supplies initiative, experience, and personality to the school community and is cognizant of individual needs and ideas. He must be able to work well with others, whether participating in a small planning session or functioning as the head of a larger group. He must be aware of his responsibility to improve the community of which he is a part, and able to assist groups in arriving at effective conclusions and courses of action. He must be a catalyst in the developmental process.

A major concern of any administrator is the use that can be made of youth organizations to further the growth of young people. These organizations can be character building, socially orienting, educational, of benefit to the community, or a combination of these characteristics. Educational leadership must be able to correlate the community and educational activities of youth to the benefit of the individual, the group, and the community.

Changes in Working Relationships

The school administrator cannot function effectively if he feels he must have all the ideas, make all the plans, and put these ideas and plans to work. Rather, he is an activator of groups of capable, hard-working parents, civic leaders, teachers, and other professional educators.

The true role of the administrator involves identifying, clarifying, and meeting new and broader opportunities for service. He must delegate, yet share the responsibility for outcomes. Because the development of the school policy is in the hands of the community it serves, an educational leader must work vigorously, skillfully, and honestly with lay and professional people alike.

The classroom teacher is a professional person, with a unique opportunity to observe the impact of school policies, curriculum, organization, and regulations on the student body. Administrative philosophy and action must involve teachers in the improvement of the school's services to students and the community.

The teacher observes students (and other teachers) in many situations and can be a valuable counselor to them and to the school organization—through his awareness of potential trouble. The teacher sees the over- or under-achievers, the students with indications of emotional insecurity, and hears the undercurrents of question about policies and curriculum. Further, his professional preparation for teaching has encouraged him to improve the educational process, and to seek avenues of participating in the process of change.

Teachers are increasingly better prepared and educated today for these undertakings. First, they have had a better basic college training; more specialized course work and practical work experience; greater participation in real teaching internships; and they are influenced and assisted by professional organizations and certification requirements.

Second, they have broadened concepts of individual worth, rights, and privileges; increased opportunity for travel; a tendency to take more graduate work; and an opportunity to pursue individual hobbies and interests.

Third, they have a broader outlook on life because of present-day trends in psychology and related sciences; the lifting of many fetishes, taboos, and superstitions; and the gradual maturation of civilization.

Responsibility for leadership is not an exclusive province of administrative and supervisory persons group but rests in every individual who deals with learners.

Changes in School Philosophy

A school philosophy emerges from group action and should be the product of the critical thinking of many persons under optimum conditions of communication. The Tulsa Public School system relates that:

From the concepts of democracy as a way of life—concerned with the needs, interest, and welfare of man — and the democratic process, which places the burden on the individual working with others as a means of achieving this welfare, the purposes of education emerge. (6) Such a philosophy, to be effective, should become the personal conviction of all those concerned with the instruction and motivation of youth.

The acceptance of these concerns obligates any school system to provide experience for the development of certain interests, knowledge, insights, skills, and activities which are basic to educational achievement.

The Administrator

Industrial education, along with other areas of the school program, must have the approval and active support of the superintendent. He must recognize the need for a comprehensive program, be imbued with the overall philosophy, and able to convince the Board of Education of the need and desirability of this phase of the educational program. An effective supervisor of the industrial education program must work with the superintendent to keep him abreast of needs, trends, and changes in this educational area.

It is important for the administrator to understand that the industrial education curriculum is a continuing development, through the selection of skills and information adaptable to the school shop and drafting rooms from the vast reservoir of modern mechanical and scientific knowledge; that industrial education is an integral part of the school curriculum; and that industrial instruction applies learning from other subject areas as well as teaching its own unique content.

The Supervisor

The role of the industrial education supervisor is one of leadership for this area of the curriculum with a joint responsibility for the overall educational program. The duties and responsibilities of such an assignment are similar to these of other department supervisors with variations necessary to carry on a program of industrial arts and/or vocational-industrial education.

He is also a "middleman" in educational administration. Midway between central administration and faculty and the school and the community, a supervisor never sees all the effects of his accomplishments in the lives of individual students; his aim is to contribute to the improvement of instruction in industrial education.

The supervision of a staff of professionally trained persons might well be described as the effective coordination of efforts. A supervisor must assume initially that inadequacies are oversights rather than incompetence. As professional to professional, the supervisor must function to coordinate the efforts of the total staff, to assist with problems of equipment and material,

Fig. 2-1. Supervisory Positions and Administrative Assignments
Exist Only to Improve Instruction

and to bring news of new methods used in industry and in other schools. In general, a professional teacher is aware of his role and responsibilities in school and in society.

Characteristics of Teaching As a Profession

A good teacher meets students with vigor and instills a desire for growth. Democratic principles of leadership and the participation of all students in problem-solving activities are both strong factors in American education. Therefore, a teacher should motivate others in learning activities or leadership.

The community expects a teacher to be well read and conversant with contemporary developments, both in his field and generally. Outstanding teachers possess a desire for additional training and education and growth in the profession. Continued success in teaching means advanced study for degrees and certification through attending college, summer sessions, or extension courses, plus participation in inservice training programs.

Effective leadership of professional teachers cannot be achieved if the supervisor does not treat them as professionals and exhibit at all times his own professional values and beliefs.

Leadership Organization

A variety of organizations are to be found in school systems. This wide variety of administrative organizations is a result of the rapid growth of school systems. Superintendents and principals have been so burdened with administrative problems that they could direct little attention to supervisory matters. This rapid growth has led to the establishment of agencies or offices as a means of coping with various instructional problems.

Most analyses show a definite similarity in the types of school organization. The types of organization for school supervision have fallen under three main groupings: (1) dualistic, (2) line and staff, and (3) coordinate.

The dualistic organization has two lines of authority on which the principals and supervisors occupy similar positions. In an organization of this type teachers are responsible to both the principal and supervisor.

The "line" in supervisory organization represents a flow of authority extending from the superintendent of the school system through his assistants and the principals to the individual classroom teachers.

In the coordinate type of supervisory organization, the departmental activities of supervisors and the administrative activities of the principals operate as coordinate functions. Both the supervisor and principal are on the same line of authority; both share authority and responsibility; and both are directly responsible to the superintendent.

The *line function* is the responsibility for and the authority over other employees while the *staff function* is to provide information or assistance. In the line-and-staff structure, the superintendent, his assistants, and the principals form the line organization – the channel of delegated authority. Supervisors, whatever their title, have a dual function. They must assist the superintendent and the principal and yet function effectively with teachers to improve instruction and curriculum.

The supervisor has been given many varied titles including Director, Educational Consultant (or Advisor), Technical Consultant (or Advisor), Counselor, Instructional Consultant (or Coordinator), and Resource Person. One of these names may eventually replace the term supervisor with its connotations of inspection, rating, imposed improvement programs, and the superiority-inferiority relationship between the groups of coworkers.

A Typical Administrative Structure

Assistant Superintendent of Instruction

The Assistant Superintendent of Instruction, under the direction of the of the superintendent of schools, is responsible for the general administration and supervision of instruction. The assistant superintendent is responsible for curriculum planning and development. He must provide for a study of educational purposes and organization, the coordination of the various areas of instruction, improved teaching methods and procedures, provision of the best available teaching materials, and carry on a continuous evaluation program.

One important activitiy of this office is initiating and supervising in-service programs. Such programs involve the cooperative efforts of teachers, principals, supervisors, and administrators and often serve a dual purpose. Besides bringing about the improvement of teaching methods and procedures through study and research, inservice classes frequently become the birthplace of new and vital curriculum materials.

Supervisors

Supervisors of various areas work with the assistant superintendent of instruction as staff persons; that is, unless specifically authorized, they serve in an advisory capacity. As specialists in their respective fields, they bring information and help to both teachers and administrators.

Principals

The principal is the administrator and supervisor of the school or schools to which he is assigned. To the people of the community he is the representative of the superintendent of schools. He is also directly responsible to the assistant superintendent or the director of elementary or secondary schools for the general organization and efficient administration of his school.

A principal must know and administer the general policies and procedures of the Board of Education as they apply to his school. For example, he must be familiar with various services that may be needed by the pupils. He must know when special services are needed, by whom they are needed, and how to obtain these services. The principal should not only know the school policies and services but he must also be able to explain, interpret, and intelligently discuss these with teachers, parents, and students. He is responsible for the validity, adequacy, and safe keeping of all records required by state and federal law or by the Board of Education and the superintendent of schools.

As chief supervisor of the building or school to which he is assigned, he works with teachers toward the identification and solution of problems that are concerned with instruction and learning. As an administrator, the principal must provide reasonable safeguards for the health and general welfare of the students so that there is a physical environment conducive to worthy school life.

The principal is responsible for the general quality of instruction and guidance maintained by teachers, counselors, or guidance officers in his assigned school. He must take the initiative in promoting an educational program that is consistent with the expressed and implied policies and plans of the Board of Education and superintendent of schools.

The supervisor should know that the principal is the final authority in the building for which he is responsible. Supervisors function in an advisory capacity to school principals on any matters pertaining to the subject area. They interpret policies to principals, and assist them in making desirable adaptations of these policies to their own schools. In most cases, the supervisor actually supervises the work personally. Under no conditions should a supervisor make suggestions to teachers about such fundamental matters as changes in the time schedule without first clearing the way for these changes with the school principal. The supervisor may, however, make suggestions directly to a teacher regarding a method of teaching a specific skill. The effective supervisor should always keep the principal informed of his activities in the school.

A good supervisor will try to work with the principal in ways that will avoid any differences. If serious differences do arise, and no agreement can be reached, either the principal or the supervisor should request a conference. An effective supervisory program requires a clear understanding on any point, to avoid confusion.

Occasionally the principal may instruct a teacher to pursue a given course of action, and the supervisor, without the knowledge of the principal, makes contradictory suggestions. In this unfortunate situation, the teacher does not know how to proceed. The teacher should be informed that, whatever plan of organization the school system employs, his immediate superior is the principal. Proper relationships between the supervisor and the principal will minimize many of the problems concerning final authority.

A Supervisor's Relationship with the Principal

When visiting a school a supervisor should first report to the principal's office to let it be known that he is in the building. A follow-up conference with the principal should be held when needed.

The supervisor serves as a consultant to a principal in the placement of teachers, curriculum changes, and physical facilities in the building. He should support the policies and programs of the principal and keep the principal informed on new trends in the subject area. Among his many activities are: arranging for inter-school visitation as a part of the school inservice program; consulting with principals on school and other exhibits and fairs; serving in an advisory capacity on any matters pertaining to a particular field; coordinating matters that affect both principal, teacher, and supervisor; helping to establish lines of communication; helping to develop a continuous program of evaluation of the curriculum; keeping the principal informed on objectives of courses; explaining purposes of curriculum, scope and sequence; and arranging for meetings with school counselors to explain the program of instruction, providing counseling information, and assisting in the selection and scheduling of students. The guidance counselors in the school system are generally persons with training and experience in academic fields—the supervisor must help them learn more about industry, and the contributions that industrial education has to make.

Supervisor's Relationships with Teachers

A supervisor has two major responsibilities to the individual teacher. First, he must orient new teachers to the total functioning program of the school and to the purposes of supervision. Second, he must work with the teacher to improve areas of classroom instruction, and the special skills of classroom visitation are important in this endeavor.

The supervisor orients new teachers to responsibilities in instruction, school environment, local school policies, and the local community. (6) The orientation process includes the many informal contacts between teachers and supervisor, and is continuous, for every contact should demonstrate how the supervisor intends to coordinate the program of instruction and to provide service to individual teachers.

Working with the teacher to improve instruction can take many forms:

1. Observing instruction through visitation.
2. Holding conferences to discuss strengths and weaknesses.
3. Giving recognition for improved instruction.
4. Assisting in evaluating day-to-day instruction.
5. Assisting in developing teaching plans and outlines.
6. Assisting in selecting, developing, and using needed instructional materials.
7. Assisting in selecting and using needed equipment.
8. Providing opportunities for exchanging ideas and materials with other teachers.
9. Making it possible for teachers to have professional experiences and contacts.
10. Recommending and developing inservice studies and activities. (6)

The supervisor also provides leadership for curriculum change and improvement by coordinating the development of course content and resource units, teaching guides, and other curriculum materials.

Classroom Visitations

A certain etiquette must be observed by the supervisor in visiting classrooms. Good manners should govern him at all times. Specifically, he should:

1. Be on time.
2. Cause as little disturbance as possible.

3.   Nod and take a seat.
4.   Remain silent unless invited to participate. (2)
5.   Set a friendly situation in any conversation.
6.   Take only mental notes.
7.   Encourage the teacher as he leaves.

Brief but frequent visits are preferred to fewer, longer observations. The success of a visit will depend on the supervisor's approach, what is accomplished, and what use is made of the data. (2)

Supervisors may use a variety of types of visiting procedures. Each has its own advantages and disadvantages.

1.   Announced Visit — eliminates surprise, but may give the teacher the idea that the supervisor has come to show him how to teach.
2.   Unannounced Visit — is all right when the supervisor is considered a coworker— there to help but not to judge.
3.   Visitation on Call — permits the supervisor to be present when commendable work is being done, but teachers tend to prepare elaborate demonstrations.
4.   Brief Visits — can be made for different purposes such as equipment or supply needs, repair request, open house, etc.
5.   Period Visits — made for different purposes, such as to discuss safety program, inservice course, graduate work, etc. (2)

Teachers and supervisors must work together to improve instruction. To that end, the objectives of the classroom visit include the following:

1.   To build a good working relationship with the teacher.
2.   To assist with problems confronting the teacher.
  a.   Grouping for effective instruction.
  b.   Adjusting instructional materials to ability groups.
  c.   Planning activities suitable to age levels.
3.   To determine adequacy of equipment, supplies, and instructional materials.
4.   To promote a desirable working environment.
5.   To help with organization of materials.
6.   To bring about understanding and effective use of teacher's guides and textbooks. (6)

The classroom visit is especially effective when an early conference follows the visit.

Acceptance of social position and certain standards of conduct are part of the profession's responsibilities. Teachers should maintain high personal standards because their actions influence the actions of their students, perhaps more than their words. Teachers must possess sound judgment and be understanding, tolerant, fair, just, and have the ability to work with many differing personalities. The ability to get along with people, a pleasing personality, social maturity, clean-cut personal appearance, and acceptable social conduct are some of the personal prerequisites of the teacher.

Characteristics of the Supervisor

The supervisor's first responsibility in implementing a philosophy of education, based on respect for the individual, is to practice such a philosophy in his relationships with coworkers.

In order to form a good relationship with others, the supervisor should possess certain characteristics of behavior and action:

1. Be well informed in his area of professional responsibility.
2. Be open-minded.
3. Be emotionally mature.
4. Be enthusiastic and resourceful.
5. Be skillful in promoting good school-community relations.
6. Be loyal.
7. Be effective in oral and written communication.
8. Have good physical health and energy required for assuming his responsibilities.
9. Have good personal relationships.
10. Recognize supervision as educational leadership.
11. Know his job and do it.
12. Know his administration and work cooperatively in this relationship.
13. Make his department an integral part of the school.
14. Keep his administrators informed as to what he plans to do and what he has done.
15. Know and follow school administrative policies.
16. Give credit where credit is due.
17. Be an active citizen in the community.
18. Be an effective public relations contact for the entire school.

The purpose of supervision is to help school personnel to provide a better program of education. Changes may be needed in philosophy, content, emphasis, techniques, classroom organization and management, and/or working procedures.

Outline of Leadership Qualities

   I.   Personal Characteristics
       A.   Faith in the democratic system of education.
       B.   Superior intellectual capacity.
       C.   A high degree of social sensitivity.
       D.   Resourcefulness, drive, inventiveness.
       E.   High moral character.
       F.   Sound judgment.

      G.   Common sense.

      H.   Evidence of possessed skills.

          1.   Faith in the efficacy of group action.

          2.   Respect for the worth of every individual.

          3.   A willingness to obtain genuine participation in policy-making.

          4.   Ability to stimulate group thinking.

          5.   Fosters possible potentialities of individuals.

          6.   Understands and appreciates group techniques.

II.   Basic Convictions

      A.   The welfare of the group is assured by the welfare of individuals. There is no conflict between the two.

      B.   Decisions reached through cooperation are more valid than individual decisions. There is loyalty to the idea and more conscious effort to maintain it.

      C.   Every idea is judged on its own merit. One of the dynamics is that an idea when once thrown out is no longer a personal idea but a group idea.

      D.   Growth comes from within the group.

      E.   Democratic methods are efficient. Although they move slowly in the beginning, this seeming delay is compensated for by the enlightenment of the groups. The tempo then increases and goes far beyond the accomplishments of an authoritarian method.

      F.   Every person merits respect.

      G.   The total group must develop and understand the social responsibilities of education and what can be done.

      H.   The democratic concept of educational leadership must be defined and developed.

      I.   The democratic form of organization must be established. There must be permissive "trickling down" and "bubbling up" of ideas.

      J.   There must be participation of all people who are to receive benefits and/or be handicapped.

      K.   All people involved must define the role of the teacher. If the group is to gain the concept of good leadership, the group must share and live the experience. All people have rich experience, and each has something to contribute.

III. Outward Expressions

      A.   The pronouns used; *We* and *Our* as opposed to *I* and *My*.

      B.   Senses where the group enjoys working together, from the custodian on up to the principal.

      C.   Informs all personnel; an informed personnel leads to better planning and execution of plans.

      D.   Accomplishments indicate participation by many people; "We did" approach.

The degree to which a supervisor possesses the above leadership qualities determines, to a great extent, the degree to which he will be accepted by teachers and principals. He should be able to listen and participate rather than dominate and directly control and to assist rather than to master. He should never be overly dominant, forceful, or timetable conscious. The supervisor has many opportunities to strengthen the morale of the teachers and principals with whom he works. His manner can do much to maximize his contribution to the educational effort.

Duties of an Industrial Education Supervisor and Staff

The person responsible for supervision must be a leader skilled in human relations, group procedures, personnel administration, and evaluation. Outside the school, he must consider the values of working memberships in public service organizations, church groups, and fraternal lodges.

William Melchoir in *Instructional Supervision* enumerates the duties of a supervisor as: "The supervisor plans cooperatively; . . . he is coordinator of activities; he can carry forward the curriculum program; he is expert in methods and techniques; he is there to supplement the teachers. He can justify his position only to the extent that he can offer leadership as a teacher of teachers . . . . He is not there to show the teachers 'how to teach,' but he is there to encourage creative teaching. Supervisors are teachers of teachers and therefore concerned with adult education. It is essentially an educative process in which the supervisor should apply the same philosophy of education in working with the teachers as he would want the teachers to use in working with students. The old authoritarian idea is essentially static. We have moved over into the area of the growth conception of supervision. This is even more important than just getting a particular program of action." (4)

I. General Duties
    A. Provide assistance to administrators and director in the interpretation and initiation of industrial arts and vocational-technical programs.
    B. Assist in coordination of industrial arts and vocational-technical programs on the elementary, junior high and senior high school levels.
    C. Make appropriate professional and community contacts.
    D. Attend staff meetings.
    E. Attend and participate in school, community, and professional meetings and conferences.
    F. Receive visitors.
    G. Conduct tours of schools.
    H. Review books, publications, periodicals, and visual aids.
    I. Work with advisory committees.

J.   Work with state employment service.

K.   Correlate industrial arts and vocational-technical activities with teachers, department chairmen and directors of other areas, in order to promote an integrated, coordinated educational program.

L.   Assist in the recruitment of industrial arts and vocational-technical teachers.

M.   Conduct orientation program for new teachers.

N.   Assist teachers in writing articles for local and national professional publications.

O.   Help conduct follow-up job surveys.

P.   Help keep records on all equipment.

II.   Professional Improvement

A.   Conduct individual teacher conferences.

B.   Hold departmental meetings.

C.   Interchange ideas and information between teachers.

D.   Help evaluate the services of industrial arts and vocational-technical education departments and individual teachers.

E.   Visit as many teachers as possible during each year.

F.   Arrange for displays and exhibits.

G.   Promote participation in local and national awards programs.

H.   Encourage teachers to write articles for professional publications.

I.   Introduce experimental procedures in selected schools.

J.   Visit each instructor as needed and at least each quarter.

K.   Submit written or oral report to individuals requesting visit.

L.   Make written or oral report to teacher, principal and director, concerning conclusions reached in visit.

M.   Report in writing or orally to principal the conclusions reached by the visit:

1.   Evidence of good student-teacher relationship.

2.   Appearance of teacher.

3.   Size of class.

4.   Teaching procedures used.

5.   General appearance of shop.

6.   Ventilation and lighting.

7.   Condition of shop tools and equipment.

8.   Safety devices and safety rules employed.

9.   Mannerisms of teacher.

10.   Instructor's use of English.

11.   Instructional aids used.

12.   Extent to which desired outcomes are met.

13.   First aid equipment and supplies.

14.   Instructor's lesson plan.

15. Records of student progress.
16. Records of inventory, purchase, and requests.

III. Instructional Program
A. Hold individual and group conferences for consideration of instructional problems.
B. Help compile tentative outlines and courses of study.
C. Assist in the development and publication of instructor guides (including course of instruction outlines) for all areas.
D. Implement (help in implementing) the courses of instruction.
E. Assist teachers to adapt instructional material.
F. Help keep instructional material up-to-date (revision and supplemental material).
G. Assist in establishing a safety program.
H. Assist in textbook studies preparatory for adoption.
I. Encourage instructors to use new industrial products and procedures.
J. Assist teacher committees (subject area groups and department chairmen) in developing instructional material.
K. Assist in developing teaching aids.
L. Assist teachers in planning field trips.
M. Distribute material concerning occupational information.

IV. Equipment and Supplies
A. Assist in setting up standards for equipment and supplies.
B. Advise concerning the purchasing of equipment and supplies.
C. Assist in preparing specifications.
D. Recommend changes, repairs, and replacements.
E. Meet with and participate in equipment and supplies standardization committees.
F. Assist in installation of equipment.
G. Assist in inventories.
H. Help prepare standard lists for equipment and supplies.
I. Help supervise procurement, storage, and distribution.
J. Help with department budget.
K. Help with requisitions and process for all teachers.
L. Help handle supplies and charge out equipment, resale, board, etc.

V. Housing
A. Assist in planning of construction and remodeling shops with building and planning.
B. Help plan shop layouts.
C. Assist in preparing preliminary plans and estimates for constructing, remodeling.
D. Make recommendations on lighting, heating, and ventilation.

VI.   Specific Vocational Education
  A.   Assist in the organization, coordination, promotion, and devel-
        opment of a comprehensive program of vocational education for
        in-school and out-of-school youth and adults.
  B.   Help provide proper supervision needed for vocational schools or
        classes organized and conducted under the provisions of the state
        plan.
  C.   Establish advisory committees for vocational education programs.
  D.   Cooperate with outside agencies aiding in the further develop-
        ment of vocational education.
  E.   Cooperate with teacher training staffs in the development of the
        pre-service and inservice teacher education programs.
  F.   Assist teachers in the improvement of methods and content of
        instruction through individual or group conferences.
  G.   Help promote youth programs.
  H.   Help supervise, evaluate, and recommend for approval or dis-
        approval the vocational instruction carried on in the schools, or
        the vocational program, operating under the state plan.
  I.   Promote by discussion, conferences, and the use of printed mate-
        rials, the establishment of vocational courses wherever needed,
        and explain to school authorities the operation of federal and
        state laws for vocational education.
  J.   Assist in the preparation and promotion of courses of study in
        the schools operating under the state plan.
  K.   Assist in the conduct of surveys, studies, and investigations af-
        fecting the vocational education programs.
  L.   Assist in developing sound relationships with interested public
        groups by interpreting the vocational education program in their
        respective fields.
  M.   Assist in providing adequate records and reports to be submitted
        to federal and state boards on work accomplished in the voca-
        tional education program.
  N.   Perform any other duties assigned.

Certification of Vocational Supervisors

        The certification of supervisors as outlined in the Oklahoma State Plan
for Vocational Education is typical of the supervisor's educational requirements.
        A local supervisor of trade and industrial education shall be a graduate
of an accredited 4-year college or university, preferably with a major or
minor in trade and industrial education. He shall have completed or
shall be required to pursue 20 semester hours of professional trade and

industrial education courses as approved by the state supervisor and by the approved teacher trainer in the authorized teacher training institution.

Professional training shall include:

History and Philosophy of Vocational Education
Supervision of Vocational Education
Trade and Job Analysis
Industrial Planning
Instructional Procedure and Techniques
Conference Leadership
Organization and Management of School Shop

Two semester hours from:

School-Industry Relations
Evaluation of Instruction
Job Training Procedures
Procedures in Diversified Occupations
Survey Techniques in Industrial-Vocational Education
Organization and Administration of Adult Vocational
Education Programs (5)

Local supervisors shall have had at least three years of successful experience as a teacher of approved trade and industrial classes which meet the standards of the state plan.

Department Chairmen

A department chairman's job differs from other industrial education staff members only in that he assumes certain delegated responsibilities, such as coordinator between the administration and individual staff members. A department chairman takes part in the supervision of instruction, course content, classroom procedure, and teaching methods. He may also be responsible for the accounting of budget money and reporting to the administration all situations that affect the department in general. Aiding in the selection of teachers is another way that the department chairman can help with the overall school administration.

Classroom Teacher

The most important duty of the individual teacher is to maintain a program that will result in effective teaching. This can be done by following the basic course of instruction, keeping the program of instruction up-to-date, constantly reevaluating teaching methods and course content, and systematically checking and reporting student programs.

Other duties of individual staff members include effective teaching, record keeping, cost accounting, shop maintenance, aiding fellow staff members, and such extracurricular responsibilities that are inherent in any teaching job. Work in industry to insure keeping up to date may be a most important extra responsibility.

Usually the teacher adopts a recordkeeping system that will fulfill his own particular needs. There is a particular prestige attached to keeping accurate records of purchases, maintenance, distribution of supplies, receipts and expenditures of funds, and evaluation of students.

Industrial education teachers are often the most versatile teachers on the school staff. For this reason they can be valuable in other areas of instruction and thus must be willing to give their time, energy, and talents to improve the effectiveness of teaching throughout the system.

The homeroom program affords the teacher of industrial education an opportunity to pass along information regarding occupational opportunities and to give students a general understanding of their industrial culture through a group guidance program.

Summary

A statement by Chester Mathews will serve as an appropriate conclusion to this section:

Supervision is a two-way street. The supervisor not only may give information, guidance, a feeling of security, and deep satisfaction to those with whom he comes in contact, but he may receive these same kinds of gifts if the process is operating adequately. Inadequacy in giving and receiving help, at times, stems from inadequate leadership. It is highly important that improvements be constantly sought which will keep it on the highest possible level. (3)

References

1.   Adams, Harold P. and Frank G. Dickey, *Basic Principles of Supervision.* New York: American Book Company, 1953.
2.   Harman, Calvin and W. E. Rodenstengal, *Public School Administration.* New York: Ronald Press, 1954.
3.   Mathews, Chester O., "Self-Improvement of Supervisors," *Educational Leadership*, May, 1959.
4.   Melchoir, William T., *Instructional Supervision.* Boston: D. C. Heath Company, 1950.
5.   *Policies and Procedures* Oklahoma City, Okla.: Oklahoma State Department of Vocational and Technical Education.
6.   *The Role of the Supervisor in Educational Leadership*, Tulsa, Okla.: Tulsa Public Schools, April, 1960.

Chapter 3

General Principles of Supervision

Educational supervision has been defined in the *Dictionary of Education* as efforts by school officials to provide leadership for the improvement of instruction. The stimulation of professional growth and development of teachers; selection and revision of educational objectives, materials of instruction, and methods of teaching; and evaluation of instruction are the agents of improvement. (3) Industry, business, the military and government have found supervision a necessity and a wise investment. The public schools should not be an exception.

In large school systems, someone must assume the responsibility for coordinating programs, upgrading teachers, and developing a unified spirit among the staff members. This can best be accomplished by the designation of one staff member as department chairman or supervisor. In smaller systems with perhaps two schools, the department chairman might also teach several classes a day. However, with more than ten teachers, it is best that the supervisor spend full time in the organization, coordination, and operation of the program.

Administration

While the general administrative responsibility in any school system is vested in the superintendent or the supervising principal, certain phases of administrative work can best be carried out by a person with a special background of training and experience. In industrial education, this work can be done by the person who is designated supervisor.

System-wide administrative routines for records, reports, requisitions, and inventories are extremely helpful in large school systems. They contribute much to a well-organized program by reducing duplication of effort; simplifying ordering, replacing and maintaining equipment; and making it easier to establish budgets as well as allocate funds. These routines serve teachers by streamlining their paperwork, freeing them to plan instruction and teach. Assisting in the planning of new facilities should also be considered a part of the administrative responsibilities of a supervisor.

While the scheduling of students and teachers is usually a function of the principal of the individual school, the industrial education supervisor should have a relationship with the general school administrator that will allow him to make suggestions concerning these kinds of organizational decisions. It should be within the province of the industrial education specialist to review teacher assignments and work loads as well as the schedule of courses offered to assure that personnel and shop facilities are used to their best advantage.

The industrial education specialist assigned to a central office makes a definite contribution to the school system when he assists in planning a new department. His experience and understanding of the program will help affirm that all necessary work is provided and that supplies and equipment are available.

Supervision should be philosophical, always seeking after new truths; cooperative, providing ample participation of the teaching personnel; creative, allowing freedom and opportunity to try new ideas and techniques; and effective, showing definite growth and progress. (4)

Good administrative practices require that funds for industrial education in a large school system be allocated on the basis of student class load and material necessary to operate the shop. This would require that a budget be established and made known to the industrial education staff prior to the time at which orders would be submitted for the materials and supplies needed in the programs. Additional money might be set aside for the purchase of new equipment, repair and maintenance of existing equipment, and for special requisitions of individual teachers. These must be compiled by the administrator so that materials of a similar nature used in several schools can be combined into one purchase. A perpetual inventory of equipment and supplies is desirable. Individual teachers often find that a school record system assists them in reordering materials and supplies.

In summary, then, the supervisor is an educational official who discovers, marshalls, assists, and creates—but above all releases the energies of teachers for improving instruction.

The Purposes of Supervision

The main purposes of supervision are: (1) to help teachers see more clearly the real goals of education and the special role of the school in achieving these goals, (2) to help teachers identify the problems and needs of students, and to help them provide for these needs, (3) to build strong group morale and to create an effective team working with intelligent appreciative cooperation to achieve the same general goals, and (4) to evaluate the results of each teacher's efforts in terms of pupil growth toward approved goals.

Supervision aims at the growth of not only pupils and teachers but also the supervisory staff itself. Supervision is concerned with everything that directly concerns the development of every member of the faculty and student body toward physical and social competence. It is also concerned with, but not directly responsible for the factors indirectly related to their growth.

The purpose of supervision is to help school personnel to change in such a way that they will provide a better program of education. Change may be needed in philosophy, in content or emphasis, in procedure and techniques, in classroom organization and management, or in methods of working.

The basic structure of the present program of industrial education is sound. Depending upon the need in a given situation, it may need to be upgraded, given depth, and/or breadth. The effectiveness of a program cannot be evaluated by reviewing teachers' guides or course outlines. Such matters as guidance, correlation with other subjects, and relationships with industrial processes and materials need a first-hand, on-the-spot review. The teacher's methods, teaching aids, and classroom management are also important factors in achieving announced goals.

Supervision of Instruction

Supervision is *attitudinal* because it is based in part on the teacher's habitual modes of regarding anything, (any set of behavior or conduct) as indicating opinion toward life and the school in particular. Attitude toward the school as a social institution involves: (a) the purpose of education in a democracy, (b) the students, parents, and other citizens served by education, (c) the total curriculum or the total learning environment, (d) the effect of the teaching practices, and (e) the influence of the school in the local community, state, or nation.

A supervisor is cooperative. Cooperation at its best is based upon a clear understanding of the purpose of the school and its administrative divisions. This means that every person involved knows the reasons, the goals, the mutually desired results. Each person has at least some comprehension of the other person's ideas and responsibilities. Each knows the needs of others—physical and mental—and their emotional assets and habits. Each knows the part he plays and the part that every other person plays in the total program. If the supervisor stifles the teacher's initiative, desire and ability to exercise judgment, innate skill and acquired knowledge, he cannot expect to have wholehearted cooperation. As is generally understood by teachers, administration deals with externals—with people and with problems.

The tendency has been for supervision to be increasingly objective and experimental in its methods, increasingly participatory and cooperative, active among more individuals, and increasingly derived from the given situation rather than imposed upon it. (1) It has thus changed because of the widespread knowledge of philosophy and psychology of education. In the supervisor's position, less emphasis is placed on inspection, rating, direction, and imposition and the leader is expected to give democratic leadership, inspiration, coordination, and service.

The personal conviction of a teacher with regard to the ideal of the worth and dignity of the individual child in his classroom may be strong or weak as he views himself in his relationships with administrators and supervisors. The teacher, too, must sense the basic concepts of democracy; that is, he is accepted as an individual, his own dignity will not be violated, and his efforts will be recognized and accepted for what they are worth. The supervisor's responsibility then becomes to implement a philosophy of education based on respect for the individual. A philosophy of education that exists only as a written statement is of little value. It must be a personal belief with a sense of conviction and commitment so strong that it will guide one in all he does for children.

The Supervisor and Change

All individuals have certain basic needs, interests, and desires. Until those needs are met or the desires are satisfied, a tension or state of unrest exists within the individual. This tension is a prerequisite for change; conversely, it may act to oppose change. Tensions may be induced by forces in the environment or forces from within as he sees his needs or interests in a new light. Tensions induced by an external force often cause the individual to take an undesired action; and as soon as the external forces are eased, the individual may revert to his original behavior. In contrast, constructive tensions come from within the individual and tend to be created by a new interest, a shift in interest, or awareness of new needs. What was satisfactory to the individual at one time is no longer satisfactory because he has new values and new sets of goals. These tensions exist until the goal is achieved.

The role of the supervisor, then, is to help the individual set new goals for himself through sensitivity to new insights and values. How does the effective supervisor act in relation to the change:

1. The good supervisor does not bring about change through the *directives* approach which implies a threat or an external force. A directive will not cause a person to gain new insights and values which result in self-imposed action toward new goals. The goal most likely set by the individual protects his position or status by complying to the minimum extent.

2. The supervisor should be skilled in helping others recognize their own needs and solve their own problems. This is the beginning of change that is not externally forced.

    a. The supervisor is sympathetic, recognizing that it is normal for people to have problems and to make mistakes.

b.   He has faith in people—that they can usually identify and solve their own problems with proper motivation and the right kind of help.

c.   He understands that his role in helping another solve his problems is one of cooperation. He does not supply answers, but through motivation and guidance he helps the teacher analyze his problems and formulate possible solutions.

d.   He has patience, recognizing that solving one's own problems may be slow. He realizes that to rush the process will involve the use of directives and create pressure.

e.   He understands the steps in problem solving and knows how to apply them.

3.   The supervisor, as he works with people, should be able and willing to set the stage for action—a situation in which the atmosphere is permissive, for growth is an internal process and supervisors can only help supply the conditions that will nurture the growth. The kind of environment most conducive to growth is one in which:

a.   The teacher recognizes the supervisor as a sympathetic, understanding coworker.

b.   The teacher feels free to reveal a problem or admit a mistake and to ask for help.

c.   The teacher feels free to express an opinion contrary to the one held by the supervisor.

d.   The teacher senses his own worth and recognizes a peer relationship.

4.   The supervisor should encourage experimentation and creative effort.

a.   He should remain openminded and recognize that there may be other and better ways of doing things.

b.   He should, however, help the teacher to assume an objective, research attitude toward the proposed effort. All creative effort is not equally good, and some efforts may not be good at all. He should help the teacher to look critically at the proposal and to evaluate the effort.

5.   The supervisor should help provide resources for the professional growth of the teacher and for his teaching, such as books, pamphlets, films, recordings, and community contacts.

6.   The supervisor should strive constantly to broaden the base of leadership, recognizing that he is not necessarily the best leader in all situations or even a good leader in some situations. He should study and know the resources he has among the people

with whom he works—their strengths and potentialities—and use those resources.

7.   The supervisor should provide for the more formal aspects of professional growth by setting up such inservice education activities as professional meetings, conferences, and workshops.

8.   The supervisor, as an accepted member of the group, should feel free to bring his own problems and concerns to the group for action. If his relationships within the group have been properly established, he may be confident that his proposals will meet with a sympathetic, cooperative attitude.

The good supervisor recognizes that supervision is synonymous with educational leadership. He works within the group to bring about changes that will improve instruction and provide better learning situations for students.

Contrasts in Supervision

Supervision methods may be classified as autocratic or absolute, inspectional, scientific, and creative. All school authorities agree that the purpose of the supervisor is improved teaching. All imply that there is some agent or agency necessary to give direction to this purpose; all promote some methodology for attacking the problem of improving instruction. (2)

The authoritarian approach to supervising creates essentially a one-man show. While successful industrial enterprises have been operated in this way, it leads to the stifling of creative initiative and ability and makes it impossible to adjust a situation to individual pupil needs. On the other hand, a too-inspirational approach to the role of the supervisor, in the belief that the purpose is to inspire, lift, and reinvigorate teachers also has problems. Two dangers exist in this method. First, there is an assumption that a qualitative difference exists between teachers and supervisors; and secondly, the teachers are deceptive in that they look interested but go home thankful they do not have to be "inspired" every day.

A more traditional approach has been a method of inspection which practices visitation and conferences, focussed on fault-finding in teaching methods and equipment maintenance. The modern method is a study and analysis of teachers and material, focused on pupils and environment, organized, planned, and devised by many persons.

The Need for Supervision

Criticisms of the supervisory function in education have been that it costs too much for the aid rendered; it is undemocratic because it destroys the individuality of the individual teacher; it lacks basic principles that are objective, valid, and reliable; it is unorganized; the staff is inadequately trained; and it lacks sufficient criteria for self-evaluation. (1)

However, supervision is an accepted principle of administration in all difficult and complex undertakings. Education is particularly complex and intricate; furthermore, it is carried on with minimum public exposure (except to students) in relatively small classrooms, so there is a need for a coordinating force. The academic and professional training of teachers in the United States, despite excellent progress, is still far from a uniformly high quality. Even where large numbers of highly trained and professionally minded individuals work together, there is still a need for leadership and coordination of efforts, as in research laboratories in industry and government. Education is developing so rapidly that heavily scheduled teachers cannot possibly keep abreast of current developments in educational methodology and industrial technology. Supervision is necessary to bring new departures constantly into the school situation. The great extension of educational effort and opportunity, particularly on the secondary level, necessitates supervision. The teaching load, particularly in high school, is so diverse and so unrelated to a teacher's previous preparation that supervisory assistance is necessary.

A local supervisor of industrial education should be appointed in each school system where industrial education offerings are sufficiently extensive to justify such an appointment. Wherever possible, this should be a full-time official, even if provision needs to be made for a combined position. Adequate staffs should be appointed to assist with clerical, mechanical and maintenance functions. Such staff members should be properly trained and as wisely selected as the chief supervisory officer.

Clearer definitions should be made by the local supervisors of their duties and services. Differentiation is necessary between state and local supervision. Definitions should be based on comprehensive studies concerning the substance and procedure of the local supervision of industrial education. It is recommended that local supervisors contribute to the professional literature on a much greater scale. For the purposes of communication and professionalization, it is recommended that state and national associations of industrial education supervisors be organized. More research should be conducted concerning local supervision of industrial arts education.

At a conference to decide what kind of supervision they would welcome, one hundred eighty-nine representative elementary teachers decided that desirable characteristics were: planned, constructive supervision democratically applied; friendly, helpful supervision; expert individual help in bulletins; improved observation; and helpful, sympathetic, professional leadership. (5)

Manpower for Supervision

There seems to be no set formula for the number of teachers a supervisor of a department should be able to adequately supervise. In the past ten years, many department heads have had their staffs doubled with no added personnel to help orient the increase of new teachers and other added responsibilities of the position.

Visits to schools are cut in proportion to the number of schools and teachers in the department. In many cases, a supervisor finds himself making only those calls where help is needed. Visits to teachers on a semiorganized basis are almost a thing of the past. A chairman of a department may have a period free to look after department business or he may be required to teach a full schedule. The systems used are many and varied. Some suggest that a person be assigned full time to the supervision of a department where there are a number of teachers in the field. Certification of supervisors is generally requested when more than one-half time is spent in supervision of the industrial education program.

The following study was made by a graduate student:

Problem: Based on a national survey of industrial arts supervisors at the public school level, what is (1) the present teacher load of industrial arts supervisors, and (2) the maximum number of teachers that industrial arts supervisors think they can supervise adequately under present circumstances?

Limitations: The study was an attempt to portray only a factual presentation of the data as collected by a one-page questionnaire. No attempt was made to interpret either the collected data or the comments made by the participants in the study, nor was any attempt made to provide suggestions or recommendations in the solution of supervisory problems pertaining to teacher load.

Sources of Data: Name and addresses of persons with membership in the American Council of Industrial Supervisors were obtained, and after a detailed study of the list, 98 persons were chosen to represent full-time supervisors in industrial arts. Supervisors returned 86 questionnaires (87.8%) and of this number, 36 were unsuitable for the study.

Conclusion: Based on the purposes of the study and the data collected, the following conclusions were made:

1. The mean number of teachers a supervisor presently works with is 69, but the number ranges from 21 to 108.

2. The mean number of teachers a supervisor thinks he is capable of effectively working with is 57, but this ranged from 29 to 85.

3. The comments made by supervisors when asked how many teachers could be adequately supervised under present circumstances were varied. In general, however, they commented that more teachers could be adequately supervised if their duties were concerned only with the improvement of instruction. The

comments made suggested other areas of industrial arts supervision where research could be carried out. (6)

References

1. Barr, A. S., William H. Barton, and Leo J. Brueckner, *Supervision, A Social Process.* New York: Appleton-Century-Crofts, Inc., 1955.
2. Bartley, John A., *Supervision as Human Relations.* Boston: D. C. Heath & Company, 1953.
3. Goode, Carter V. *Dictionary of Education.* New York: McGraw-Hill Book Company, 1945.
4. *Industrial Arts Education – Organization and Administration.* Albany, New York: University of New York, State Department of Education, 1960.
5. Kyte, G. C., "This is the Kind of Supervision that Teachers Welcome and Appreciate," *Nation's Schools,* 48, July, 1961.
6. Veri, Clive C., "Survey of Supervisors." College Park: University of Maryland, 1962 (course paper).

Chapter 4

Planning a Program
of Industrial Education

Curriculum is defined as "all the experiences of the child both within and without the school over which the school exerts influence." (9) The two bases for planning curriculum lie in the purposes and objectives of education in accord with democratic principles and in the growth and development of the child. (9)

Curriculum planners must consider the functions of education in a democracy, the first basis of curriculum selection, for the democratic process places the responsibility for the general welfare upon each individual. The people of the states, therefore, provide for competent, educated children through a process of interaction of ideas concerned with principles of successful living. (9)

Curriculum planning is also influenced by the known educational and environmental experiences of the individual child. The insight a child gains from a learning situation will depend upon his background, ability, and personality. The teacher should try to understand each child and help him plan experiences suited to his capacities for growth and development. (9)

The Industrial Education Department

An industrial education department refers to the total industrial education organization in a single school or a school system. It includes all the industrial education teachers, shop and laboratory facilities, vocational trade and industrial arts equipment in the school.

Multiple factors are involved in planning an industrial education department. The nature of the school, school enrollment, sizes of classes, time allotments, number of shops, types of shops, and scheduling of classes must be considered. (6)

Nature of the School

The special characteristics of a school play an important part in the organization of an industrial arts program. If the junior high school offers a comprehensive general shop program, facilities should be geared to it. If a senior high school places emphasis on a general unit, facilities should be prepared. Facilities for the two individual programs (industrial arts and vocational-industrial) often must be separate. (6)

School Population

The size of the school and the size of the industrial arts enrollment are other major factors of consideration in planning the industrial arts program. A projection of enrollment in industrial arts courses in schools of different sizes may be made from statistical information. (6)

As an example, 56% of the boys enrolled in Tulsa's 7, 8, and 9th grades are enrolled in industrial arts classes, with industrial arts being required of all boys in the 7th grade and elective in the 8th and 9th grades. In grades 10 through 12, 60% of the boys are enrolled in industrial arts courses. In a large comprehensive high school of grades 10 through 12 where vocational classes are scheduled, 15% of all students may be expected to enroll. (6) With the new vocational legislation, the percentage of enrollment can be expected to increase for in-school and out-of-school youth, and for adults.

Determining Facilities Required

The number of shops and facilities needed can be ascertained only when information includes anticipated enrollments by represented grade level, the number of periods each day the facility will be used, the number of students per class, time allotted for each, and the basis for which enrollments in the classes are predicted. (6) In some cases, the determination of number of shops needed will end with a fraction. In these cases, the shops may need to be used for more than a normal school-day schedule or another shop may need to be added.

In cases where exact enrollments are not available, such as in proposed new building programs, the experience in other schools and the policy under which industrial education courses will be scheduled, either required or elective, should help to determine facilities for this area of the curriculum.

Teacher Help in Planning the Curriculum

If teachers are to participate effectively and meaningfully in planning the curriculum, certain criteria must be present. According to John A. Dewar, these conditions are:

1. Time must be provided for teachers to work effectively on curriculum improvement and revision.
2. Teachers must receive encouragement from the administration to carry on curriculum work.
3. Teachers must receive guidance from the administration in the progress of their curriculum planning.

4. Work which the teachers do on curriculum must be recognized and considered by the administration.
5. Effective and creative curriculum revision appropriate to the particular school district should be adopted and carried out by the administration.
6. Teachers should feel free and be encouraged to conduct research either in their own classes or on a district-wide basis.

Curriculum Construction

Barr, Barton, and Brueckner have devised some criteria for evaluating staff participation in developing curriculum:
1. Does the curriculum work grow out of an expressed need, or is it superimposed?
2. What workshop activities have been used and how successfully are they implemented?
3. What efforts are being made to bring out and utilize teacher suggestions?
4. What machinery is used to select texts, readings, and equipment?
5. What efforts are being made to develop leadership in the group?
6. How are committees selected?
7. How are the results of committee work used? (1)

Determining Curriculum

Purposes — Industrial Arts or Vocational?

Selected readers of a major publication in industrial education were asked whether the emphasis of a comprehensive high school shop should be industrial arts or vocational. (7) In response, 75% voted for a major emphasis on industrial arts in the curriculum of the comprehensive senior high school. A teacher educator, voting for industrial arts, justified his choice by stating that "Industrial arts teaches more youngsters, it gives a background for numerous areas of work or further formal education, and has many other attributes for general education people." The same educator believes this emphasis should vary with the size of the school — as the school becomes larger, "a good general industrial arts program should precede a more specific type of program in industrial arts with a good trade or vocational program added as justified." (3)

The Industrial Arts Curriculum

Industrial arts is an area in the school curriculum that can demonstrate opportunities for high-level creativity, problem solving, and a study of the vast technology of the industrial culture. The industrial arts laboratory stands unique as one of the few facilities in which all education can be brought together and synthesized. Functional industrial arts curriculum design and teaching will exploit this uniqueness and extent its benefits to all ages and levels of learning. It has the subject matter and activities to challenge the more able student. Attention should be given to the establishment of industrial arts classes that will attract students interested in science and engineering and offer opportunity to put into practice the principles of many areas. Minimum programs for the more able, average, and less able need to be established. These programs should be geared to the needs of youth, characteristics of youth, and present-day technology.

Industrial arts in the elementary grades should include constructive activities which are part of the common learning of elementary children. Such activity should be correlated with the basic units for elementary education so that the result is an integrated program of education. Usually the activities can take place in the classroom under the direction of the elementary teacher.

In grades 7, 8, and 9, boys (and girls) should receive instruction in industrial arts, designed to encompass a variety of beginning experiences with the common tools, materials, processes, and problems of industry. The areas of instruction should include basic exploratory experiences in drawing and planning, woodworking, metalworking, electricity, graphic arts, power mechanics, and industrial crafts. The program should include at least 9 weeks in each exploratory area thus continuing 1½ years. Further instruction (½ year in the 8th grade, and 1 year in the 9th) should be elective in these basic areas or in new areas.

Girls should have more opportunity to take industrial arts. A required semester of industrial arts for girls and home economics for boys at the 8th grade level gives girls a better knowledge of industry and the types of jobs women can do and some experience with the skills necessary. Experiences in home economics provide boys a better understanding of homemaking and the roles of man and wife in modern society.

Grades 10, 11, and 12 should be maintained in shops, laboratories, or drafting rooms especially designed and equipped. Whenever possible, courses should be limited to a single phase of industry and be designed to meet the needs of students with varying abilities, aptitudes, desires, and interests. Each course should be designed to extend for at least one regular school year (36 weeks with five periods per week). In some areas, a double period should be used.

After a one-year course, the more able students should be ready to do intensive research and planning; utilize new materials, processes, modern machines, and tools; and engage in problem-solving activities that will give them an opportunity to do advanced work of an industrial nature. Thus, the work in a second year-long course could very easily be considered occupational in nature, whether a course be called special, vocational, or general. If such courses provide a basis for entry into and success in a future or immediate occupation, they have occupational characteristics. A curriculum might well provide specific training for the college-bound student who intends to enter any type of technologically oriented field. Programs for the below-average student have been and will continue to be a problem. Some courses might be classed as special education, and in this area industrial arts will have to assume a heavier responsibility. Experiences in disassembly of industrial equipment have seemed to work well with severely retarded students who have trouble in regular industrial arts classes. Such a program may sound like busy work, but there is a relation to industry, materials, processes, and simple tools.

In the junior college, experimental laboratories, shops, and drafting rooms offer practical work in industrial arts related to industry and find many enrollees. Here again, such courses can and will become specific and give meaning to one's future employment even though not considered as terminal and vocational courses.

General Industrial Arts Program

There should be well-equipped industrial education shops in every school where grades 9 through 12 are enrolled. Since a large number of high school graduates who do not go to college will be engaged in industrial jobs, a major in industrial arts for those interested in this work is effective preparation for later job success. A boy graduating from high school should have the opportunity to take 4 to 6 hours of work in industrial arts subjects. Drafting should be required of students who major in fields such as woodwork, metalwork, and plastics, as well as being offered as a major subject. (4)

Pattern of Courses

This section contains general descriptions of courses for five levels of industrial education identified as Level I, *Exploratory*; Level II, *Basic*; Level III, *Intermediate*; Level IV, *Advanced*; and Level V, *Vocational*. Levels I and II may be provided in grades 7, 8, and 9. Factors that may limit the scope and pattern of courses of a particular industrial education program are (1) the size of the school, (2) the physical facilities available, (3) the amount of time devoted to each course. (4)

Level I, Exploratory — Areas: Drawing and planning, electricity, printing, industrial crafts, metals, and woodwork. An introduction to an industrial area is provided through a variety of experiences and activities. The correct and safe use of a variety of tools and machines is emphasized. Certain machines and operations are introduced by the instructor through the use of demonstrations. Students share responsibilities for the organization and management of the shop. They are oriented in the relationship of shop activities to the other subjects in the school curriculum. Attention is given to the selection, use, and manufacture of materials of industry and its products as related to the home and community through student activities, discussions, and instructor demonstrations. Technical, general, and occupational information is provided. Interest in the instructional area is developed through projects having "boy appeal." Pupils make a number of useful articles involving a broad selection of tools, materials, and processes. Experiences in planning, designing, and drawing are an integral part of the instructional program.

Level II, Basic — Areas: Drawing, electricity, printing, industrial crafts, metals, and woodwork. Emphasis is placed on the development of tool and machine skills in all major subareas of an instructional area of industrial arts and the use of materials and processes. Instruction is concerned with developing safe work habits in the shop and on the relationship of these safe practices to everyday living in school and community. Students participate actively in the operation and management of the shop. Attention is given to the development of skill, accuracy, craftsmanship, and judgment. Technical abilities and interests are discovered and occupational information is provided. Shop activities are correlated with class discussions, demonstrations, and study and

Fig. 4-1. Industrial Crafts in Junior High School (Tulsa Schools)

these provide for the practical application of mathematics, science, and language arts. Students have opportunity to select, design, plan, and make appropriate articles.

Level III, Intermediate — Areas: Power mechanics, drafting, electricity, radio, electronics, printing and lithography, machines and metals, tailoring, photography, and woodwork. Students acquire extensive knowledge and skills through the use of tools and machines and related information in all major facets of an instructional area of industrial arts. Accuracy and neatness are stressed. Each subarea is specifically identified and students are encouraged to select certain subareas for emphasis. Special attention is given to the development of safety habits, good working relationships, and economical use of time and materials. Opportunities to participate in activities involving production methods and processes are provided. Emphasis is placed on the practical application of mathematics, science, and language arts. Occupational guidance is an integral part of the instruction offered. Students plan and design their projects, compute costs involved, and assist in the selection of material.

Level IV, Advanced — Areas: Automotive and power mechanics, drafting, electricity, radio, electronics, printing and lithography, machine shop, welding, tailoring, photography, and woodwork. Students are encouraged to concentrate in a selected subarea. Emphasis is placed on the project-problem approach in acquiring skill through the use of tools and machines and applying mathematics, science, and language arts. Instruction in using complex machines and equipment is provided. The latest industrial techniques and materials are introduced. Students are encouraged to design articles and to experiment with tools, materials, and processes of industry. Detailed information concerning the requirements of and opportunities in occupations related to the particular subareas is provided. Both individual and group projects are encouraged. Methods of obtaining accuracy in quantity production are studied and used. (3)

Level V, Vocational — Vocational education in the schools is that part of public education which is devoted to the purpose of providing training opportunities for high school age youth in preparation for entrance into useful employment in the various trades, industry, and distributive occupations. It is not merely preparation for specific skills in job competency, but also the knowledge and information needed by workers to enter and make progress in employment on a useful and productive basis. The goal of vocational education is the competent worker; economically, socially, emotionally, physically, and in a civic sense.

Dr. Lindley Stiles, Dean of the School of Education at the University of Wisconsin, says:

If the high school is to be the foundational unit, it will have to improve the learning skills of individuals, through increased understanding of the educational process and increased effectiveness of educational techniques to keep the human scrap heap as small as possible despite the fact that half of our people are below average. More and more the total life experience is based upon a solid foundation in the basic skills. Educators who seek dumping grounds and perform social promotions rather than provide serious remedial service to those who can profit are indulging in academic snobbery, reducing our manpower, and debilitating the nation. Basic skills in mathematics, science, communications, and humanities are needed indeed whether the student goes to college or to trade or technical schools. The educator who refers the academically unprepared to a vocational track may be passing a life sentence on the individual and hamstringing a program vital to our national survival. Until we in post-high-school vocational-technical education can enroll students with the basic skills and understandings, we are in a make-do situation. (4)

Tables 4-1 and 4-2 show a pattern of courses in grades 7-12.

Selection of Subject Matter

The supervisor and the instructional staff will need to consider carefully the overall industrial education curriculum, and the selection of subject matter to be included at each level. In addition to general objectives, the age range of students, their background and abilities, the grade level, length of class periods, duration of course, facilities of the school, and personality of the teacher must be taken into consideration. (4) Outlines of the various courses should be prepared for the general guidance of all those who will be working — counselors, other teachers, administration, parents, and perhaps most important, the students.

Fig. 4-2. Available Facilities and Equipment Must Be
Considered in the Design of Curriculum

Table 4-1
SCOPE AND SEQUENCE OF THE INDUSTRIAL ARTS
EDUCATION CURRICULUM

Seventh and Eighth Grade Industrial Arts

7	(Exploratory)	Drawing and Planning, Electricity Metals and Woodwork

8	(Basic)	Industrial Crafts, Metals, Printing and Woodwork

Drafting

9	Drawing and Planning

10	Drafting 1

11	Technical Drafting 1	Arch. Drafting	Drafting 1	Pre-Engineering Drafting

12	Technical Drafting 2	Technical Drafting 1	Arch. Drafting	Drafting 1	Pre-Engnr. Drafting

Electricity and Electronics

9	Basic Electricity

10	Electronics 1

11	Electronics 2	Electronics 1

12	Electronics 1	Electronics 2

Industrial Crafts

9	Industrial Crafts (Basic)

Metal Technology

9	Metals

10	Machine Shop 1	Welding 1

11	Machine Shop 2	Welding 2	Machine Shop 1	Welding 1

12	Machine Shop 1	Welding 1	Machine Shop 2	Welding 2

Photography

10	Photography 1

11	Photography I	Photography II

12	Photography I	Photography II

Power Mechanics

10	Power Mechanics 1

11	Power Mechanics 2	Power Mechanics 1

12	Power Mechanics 1	Power Mechanics 2

Table 4-1 (cont.)

Printing and Lithography

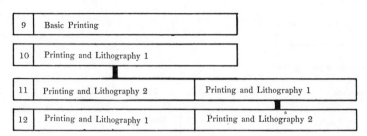

9	Basic Printing	
10	Printing and Lithography 1	
11	Printing and Lithography 2	Printing and Lithography 1
12	Printing and Lithography 1	Printing and Lithography 2

Stagecraft

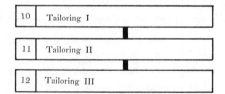

10	Stagecraft 1	
11	Stagecraft 2	Stagecraft 1
12	Stagecraft 3	Stagecraft 2

Tailoring

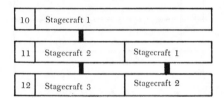

10	Tailoring I
11	Tailoring II
12	Tailoring III

NOTE: Refer to Vocational-Technical curriculum for occupational oriented courses in industrial and technical areas.

Wood Technology

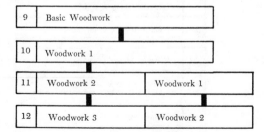

9	Basic Woodwork	
10	Woodwork 1	
11	Woodwork 2	Woodwork 1
12	Woodwork 3	Woodwork 2

Table 4-2
SCOPE AND SEQUENCE OF THE VOCATIONAL-TECHNICAL
EDUCATION CURRICULUM

Agricultural Education

11	Horticulture 1
12	Horticulture 2

Business Education

12	Cooperative Office Education

12	Business Machines-Data Processing (Card Punch Operation)

12	Business Education (Stenographic) Business Education (Bookkeeping and Office Procedures)

Distributive Education

10	Cooperative Distributive Education 1
11	Cooperative Distributive Education 2
12	Cooperative Distributive Education 3

Health Occupations

12	Dental Office Assistant
12	Medical Office Assistant

Home Economics Education
(Gainful Employment)

11	Sewing Services 1
12	Sewing Services 2

12	Child Care Services 1

11	Food Services 1
12	Food Services 2

Technical Education

11	Drafting and Design 1
12	Drafting and Design 2

11	Electronics 1
12	Electronics 2

12	Pre-Technical Chemistry

Trade and Industrial Education

11	Aeromechanics 1
12	Aeromechanics 2

11	Auto Body Repair 1
12	Auto Body Repair 2

11	Automotive Mechanics 1
12	Automotive Mechanics 2

11	Cabinet Making & Millwork 1
12	Cabinet Making & Millwork 2

11	Commercial Art 1
12	Commercial Art 2

11	Cosmetology 1
12	Cosmetology 2

Table 4-2 (cont.)

11	Diesel Mechanics 1
12	Diesel Mechanics 2

11	Drafting 1
12	Drafting 2

11	Electronics (Radio-TV) 1
12	Electronics (Radio-TV) 2

11	Industrial Cooperative Training 1
12	Industrial Cooperative Training 2

11	Machine Shop 1
12	Machine Shop 2

11	Material Fabrication 1
12	Material Fabrication 2

11	Office Machine Repair 1
12	Office Machine Repair 2

11	Offset Printing 1
12	Offset Printing 2

11	Photography 1
12	Photography 2

11	Printing and Lithography 1
12	Printing and Lithography 2

11	Refrigeration and Air Conditioning 1
12	Refrigeration and Air Conditioning 2

11	Small and Basic Engine Repair 1
12	Small and Basic Engine Repair 2

11	Tailoring 1
12	Tailoring 2

11	Upholstery 1
12	Upholstery 2

11	Welding 1
12	Welding 2

Post Secondary
Technical Education

13	Computer Programming
14	Computer Programming

13	Chemical Technology
14	Chemical Technology

Analysis Technique

The analysis of the course outline is made according to what should be taught, how it is to be taught, and to whom it should be taught. In an analysis, every operation should be listed. The operation and information units should be listed separately, disregarding teaching or learning sequences. The course planner then selects those units from his list that contribute to the realization of course objectives required under normal local conditions. When selecting course content, it is wise to consider the following criteria in the light of course objectives because it tends to make a course of study more objective:

1. In what way will the unit contribute to the attainment of course objectives?
2. Is the unit adapted to the age level?
3. Can the unit be made interesting?
4. Can the unit be adapted to the facilities? (4)

What to Teach

Careful planning makes teaching valuable to the student and provides for evaluation of progress. A logical outline keeps the class and the teacher moving toward the same goals at the same time. Each instructor should adapt the course of study for his subject area since all teachers and classes are different.

New York City has set forth the following rules for making a good lesson:

1. **Course Outlines**
    Plan a course outline or instructor's guide including the titles for units, topics or activities that are to be studied during an entire course and arrange them in instructional order. Course outlines are available for teachers in most of the areas covered in industrial and vocational education. The course outlines or instructor guides should be compiled by the combined efforts of the teachers in a subject area.

2. **Types of Teaching Plans**
    a. *A Unit Teaching Plan* is a detailed, written plan prepared and used for any one topic or unit taken from the course outline. A unit may require from a few minutes to two or more weeks to teach. It should include related safety instruction and background information for the four phases of the lesson.
    (1) Preparation – of the material takes the form of advance knowledge, prerequisite material to the new area.
    (2) Presentation – introduces the student to the new material and ties in with previous knowledge.
    (3) Application – is extensive practice in a new area.

(4)   Evaluation – of the unit plan makes provision for examination or tests to determine student mastery of the new area.

b.   *A Project Teaching Plan* is a series of notes compiled to aid the teacher as he presents the instruction for a typical project in the shop. The shop teacher will, in most cases, need to make these himself. A project teaching plan will include these features:

(1)   Introducing the job.

(2)   Titles of operations and informational topics involved in the project.

(3)   Useful teaching aids.

(4)   Lists of needed tools, equipment, and supplies.

(5)   Drawings and sketches.

(6)   Operational procedure with checking levels indicated.

(7)   A job test or evaluation.

(8)   Instructional sheets:

(a)   Job sheet

(b)   Operation sheet

(c)   Information sheet

(d)   Assignment sheet

(9)   Safety topics to be stressed throughout.

(10)   Provision for the student to draw and design his own project.

c.   *A Daily Lesson Plan* is the teacher's notes for a specific class period. Many shop teachers find it difficult to arrange time to prepare daily lesson plans, but they are very useful in the event a substitute teacher is needed. A lesson plan is used by a teacher as a craftsman uses and works from a print. As a road map, so to speak, it gives direction and meaning in the presentation of technical and related information. The lesson plan serves the teacher as notes do a speaker and serves as a reminder to cover all key points and steps in the lesson.

3.   **Writing and Caring for Instruction Plans**

a.   The type of plan most useful in the given shop situation should be used.

b.   It is advantageous to use the same general format for each plan.

c.   Some unit plans will not be used a second time because they were not effective. Sometimes such plans can be rewritten and made to work effectively.

d.   The teacher should have a definite time for writing instructional plans.

e.   Storing the lesson plans:

(1)   Manila folders can be used, with plans stored in a steel file cabinet.

        (2)   Instructional plans can be mounted on cards and filed.

   f.   For valuable help in making instructional plans refer to such books as:

        (1)   G. Harold Silvius and Estell H. Curry, *Teaching Successfully* (Bloomington, Ill.: McKnight and McKnight Publishing Company, second edition, 1967).

        (2)   John F. Friese, *Course Making In Industrial Education* (Peoria, Ill.: Chas. A. Bennett Co., Inc., 1946).

        (3)   Emanuel E. Ericson, *Teaching the Industrial Arts*, (Peoria, Ill.: Charles A. Bennett Company, 1946 and 1956).

        (4)   G. Harold Silvius and Ralph C. Bohn, *Organizing Course Materials*, (Bloomington, Ill.: McKnight & McKnight Publishing Company, 1961).

4.   **Related Study in Junior High School**

      Approximately 20% to 25% of the time spent in industrial arts and vocational industrial classes is used in demonstrations and a study of related and technical information.

      A demonstration may be given to the entire class, to a small group of students in the class, or to an individual. Usually today's teachers make an effort to identify basic instruction that may be taught to the entire class. Where an operation can be successfully taught to an entire class at one time, it reduces the need for small groups or individual demonstrations on this basic instruction. By reducing need for individual instruction on fundamentals, the teacher increases his time for important phases of highly individualized instruction. Many of the same techniques used to make demonstrations for an entire class effective can also be used with small groups or individuals.

      Carefully planned demonstrations are an effective way to conserve teacher effort and improve instruction, reducing the time and teacher effort for "patch up" instruction. If class demonstrations are poorly done or omitted, the teacher will find his time being spent helping students, one step after another. The teacher also discovers that he does not have adequate time to carry out many other responsibilities that need to be met in a class situation.

      By giving class demonstrations the teacher knows that all students are given instruction on basic operations. Where demonstrations are given only to individuals or small groups, several students in a class may never receive basic instruction from the teacher. It is then necessary for these students to observe operations as they are performed by other students or just do them the best way they can. This practice results in poor work habits on the part of many students.

      Industrial education instruction lends itself to demonstrations. The activities that make up the programs in this area can be observed visually.

5.   **Practical Work in Shop Classes**

Planning for practical work on the part of the instructor and the student is something that must be done if objectives are to be accomplished. Who else has a better opportunity to teach students those things which we say all individuals need and should have? Certainly, the project is not the only means through which we may teach boys and girls the basic skills and the fundamentals necessary to make a worthwhile contribution to the total education of the individual. The course work should be planned with the following considerations in mind: Why are we doing the things we do, when should we present our various units, what should be included for the particular area and grade level, and how should it be done? If these questions can be answered and a program planned within the framework of the area being taught with proper planning and guidance on the part of the teacher and with pupil participation, the objectives will be more nearly achieved.

Projects activities and experiences selected will depend on many factors. They should take into account the interests and experiences of the pupil and should be appealing and have utility. The activity must incorporate operations to be taught. Each project should introduce

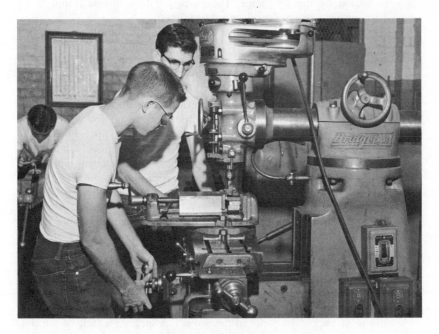

Fig. 4-3. Projects Should Introduce New
Instructional Material

new instructional material. The project must be within the student's ability to make. A project must be well designed. The project must permit completion within a reasonable time limit. The project must be reasonable in cost. The sequence of activities selected and planned by the pupil, under the guidance of the instructor, should be progressively difficult in design and processes. Development of skill comes through repetition of the processes involved in the sequence of projects throughout the term and not through formal drill exercises. The quality of workmanship for each project will depend upon individual ability. However, a reasonable standard of achievement should be expected in connection with the construction of projects.

Basic Projects are those that are undertaken at the beginning of a course in order to develop some measure of skill with fundamental tools and processes, so that the student may proceed readily to individual and group projects for the values inherent in them. As a general rule, each member of the group works upon a basic project at the same time. The number of basic projects to be constructed will vary with student ability.

Individual Projects may be of the pupil's own choice or suggested by the instructor. They incorporate elements found in the basic projects or involve advanced processes.

Group Projects are those that require the combined activity of two or more pupils. They are valuable in that they foster such traits as leadership, cooperation, respect for the activity of others, and citizenship. Group projects may be carried out for the benefit of the school or other departments of the school.

Line Production can be a significant educational experience for both the teacher and pupils. The important reason for a production project is to let the students see by actual participation how the assembly line in industry produces items more quickly and more economically. It emphasizes the principle of interchangeable parts which is basic to all modern production. A production project can also serve to broaden the value of industrial arts and fill the gap between industrial arts and industry.

An experience in line production makes industry more readily understood and makes pupils aware that industry has many problems to solve. A production shop means that junior high students are provided a method of learning while doing. All students must learn and know their jobs, work efficiently and safely in order for a production shop to be a success.

Setting the stage for the production shop experience is probably the most important phase of the project. A special meeting of the class needs to be called to get their thoughts and reactions for setting aside a few weeks for production shop. Discussion should involve the type of project, materials to be used, practicality of project, and interest and enthusiasm of the students.

The ground work is laid for the organization of line production, if student activities are patterned on procedures used by management in industry. In producing the hamburger press, a study was made on the number of work stations needed to produce it. The number of different work stations needed for the setup was ascertained; then under the direction of the instructor, the workers were selected for each job according to the capabilities of the student.

Upon completion of the final drawings, there are jigs to be designed and perfected.

A production flow chart, similar to practice in industry shows the progressive steps. Each station records the number of parts the workers produce each day. This keeps all stations up to date. To complete the production steps, a crew "steelwools" and waxes the production unit and keeps a tabulation of the total number of finished units.

A careful record of all material used could be compiled and the total cost figured and divided by the total number of units produced.

The greatest personal satisfaction in organizing a production shop is the development of the awareness of economic concepts in a tangible way. It is gratifying to see how well boys work with each other in the various work stations, even though they are busy doing the same job over and over. Whatever else that may be gained from production shop, the students will understand better the important part industry contributes to our American way. The complexity of modern life makes it essential for each student to be able to work side by side and to get along with his fellow man.

Making preparation for line production will require careful planning, skillful presentation to the class, and accurate apportioning of time. Students can be introduced to mass production by various types of presentation. Show 8mm film or slides of previous line production jobs. This will help the students to get an overall picture of the full operation of a production shop.

Give an assignment for the students to do some research on planning and design. This is an organized way of thinking to solve a special problem. When these plans are presented and discussed by the group, the students will have a closer feeling, as they become a part of the project they have selected. This method is very successful with older secondary students, but because of the lack of knowledge and experience in the lower age groups, it is necessary to modify this approach. The instructor should present a project or two that he knows would be within the abilities of his students. After group discussion about possible projects, a vote could be taken to determine the line production project.

After a choice has been made, the next step should involve the best way to make the product. A model is made at this time in order to gain the knowledge necessary to make the item to be line produced. This part of the planning will save a lot of time and help to set up arrangements for the production line. Students will gain much experience by re-designing and changing the model. They will learn that appearance, simplicity, and utility are the best ingredients for a successful production job. The model need not be a completely finished and final product.

Once a satisfactory model has been made, the class can analyze and break down the item into various operations. Each student should receive a set of plans, so he may list all the essential operations, tools, and machines. He must make decisions on the easiest or best way to perform a certain operation or step. The instructor should go over these plans with the students in order to arrange the operations in the proper order. A class discussion on the processes will bring out some very valuable aids. At this point it is very essential to combine a number of operations into *one* single operation at each work station, if possible. The amount of equipment and the number of students in each class will affect this portion of line production.

Production costs are figured on material, time and wages. This brings into the discussion types of materials, methods of working, wage and plant costs necessary to produce the item, methods of financing, credit, interest on money, labor laws, working conditions and many other points involved in industry and business.

it should be a part of the learning experiences of all students at all levels of grade and ability. It provides students an opportunity to learn about the theoretical and practical aspects of industry and technology — two basic and dominant elements of our society.

Industrial arts should provide a meaningful sequence of content from the seventh through the twelfth grades to acquaint students with:

Industrial Manufacturing Processes — a study of the methods, machines, and materials as typified by means of mass production industries. Industrial arts is an organization of subject matter which provides opportunities for experiences concerned with developing insights into the broad aspects of industry; such as construction, transportation, communication, manufacturing, and research and development with the resulting personal and technological effects.

Man's Technological Achievements — a study of the history, developments, and contributions of man's mastery over nature's raw materials, and his inventiveness in the creation and utilization of a broad spectrum of tools and machines to improve his way of living.

Industrial Organization and Occupations — a study of the ways in which contemporary industry organizes men, materials, and machines into a common endeavor in such industries as communications and transportation — and in such functions as engineering, manufacturing, and research and development. It also involves the study of the occupations related to the areas of management and labor within these and other industries.

Social and Economic Problems — a study of the social and economic problems and benefits resulting from the influence of industrialism on American culture.

These programs are implemented in a classroom, shop, and laboratory combination that provides students with an opportunity to study the materials, machines, processes, products, and related problems of the previously mentioned areas through such activities as planning, organizing, creating, constructing, experimenting, testing and evaluating.

Leisure Time Projects should be encouraged and students helped in constructing projects at home in their spare time. These projects should involve training in project analysis with regard to design, proportion, cost and type of material, processes and tools involved, and proper methods of procedure and finish.

Planning the Physical Facilities

Four distinct kinds of industrial arts shops are in common use today: the comprehensive general shop, the general unit shop, the general shop, and the unit shop. (8) Each has a place in industrial arts education.

Comprehensive General Shop

The comprehensive general shop is the basic type of industrial arts shop recommended for all schools having only one shop. It possesses equipment for instruction in four to as many as six or more areas of industrial arts in one room under the direction of a single teacher. Each of the major industrial sections can be subdivided into activities representative of the several types of work found in the industry. For example, a printing section may include facilities for instruction in letterpress and offset printing, binding, silk-screen printing, blockprinting, papermaking, photography, and stenciling. Similar subdivisions may be identified in other major sections.

The comprehensive general shop fits well into a school with only one teacher in the industrial arts department. This type of shop permits the addition of a part-time teacher as enrollment demands. It is an economical plan for providing a wide range of activities and, as a minimum, the opportunity for experience in drawing, general woodwork, general metals and electricity. Experience in other industrial areas can be included. (6)

Fig. 4-4. Area Devoted to Junior High School
Letterpress Printing (Tulsa Schools)

General Shop

General shops are usually found in a two- or three-shop industrial arts departments. A general shop contains equipment for instruction in two or more major sections of industrial work. In a department with two general shops, each may contain equipment for instruction in three major sections of work while a department having three shops would have each equipped for two major sections of work. When the multishop department is regarded, due consideration should be given to the many factors of equipment needs, selection of suitable and compatible sections of work, scheduling considerations, and teacher abilities. (6)

General Unit Shop

The general unit shop contains equipment for instruction in several phases of one area of industrial arts. An example would be a general metal shop with work centers for art metal, foundry, forging, heat treatment, machine shop, ornamental iron, sheet metal, and welding. General unit shops are practical only in large junior or senior high schools where enrollment justified four or more shops. For scheduling purposes in some schools, more than one instructor may be assigned to this shop during the week. (6)

Unit Shop

The unit shop contains equipment for instruction in only one phase of an industrial area. Typical unit shops would be furnituremaking, machine shop, letterpress printing, automobile mechanics, and radio. Unit shops, the most specialized of industrial education shops, are usually found in a large senior high school because enrollment must require more than six general unit shops.

The unit shop provides work experiences in a single phase of the field of industry; for example, the machine shop would offer a depth experience beyond the general metals area and cabinetmaking would be a similar narrowing from general woodworking. (6)

Planning a Shop

Shops should be on the ground floor for easy admission of supplies, machinery, and movement of large projects. Size of industrial education facilities varies with the type of shop; the safest rule to follow is size based upon area required for each pupil. Many states set a minimum which varies from 75 to 200 square feet per student. A good average is 125 to 150 square

Fig. 4-5. General Metal Area

feet for each pupil. This does not include storage space, etc. It will vary as to the type of shop.

The following are space allotments recommended for open shop areas in vocational trade and industrial shops (20 students).

"HEAVY" SHOPS
(auto, machine, cabinet, electric, sheet metal,
body and fender, welding, graphic arts)

Space	Square Feet per Student	Square Feet Total Open Shop Area
Minimum	100	2000
Adequate	150	3000
Desirable	200	4000

"LIGHT" SHOPS
(drafting, electronics, industrial crafts, etc.)

Space	Square Feet Per Student	Square Feet Total Open Shop Area
Minimum	50	1000
Adequate	75	1500
Desirable	100	2000

The shop should be rectangular in shape (a ratio of 2 to 1 length to width is suggested) and well-lighted with 50-70 foot-candles of maintained illumination at bench height. Duplex 120-volt outlets should be remotely controlled by a safety cutoff switch. Maple flooring, with concrete for some working areas, is recommended for most shops. Ceilings should be treated for sound insulation. Other items that need to be considered are a sink with a large trap, a gas supply, ventilation to remove fumes and dust, a source of compressed air, display cases, and adequate storage. (6)

All working areas should be visible for supervision and the teaching area should be provided with a chalkboard and with facilities for showing educational films and using all types of instructional media. A tool panel should be placed for easy access by students. The passage aisles should be four feet wide and no less than three feet should be provided between machines where no passage is involved. A storage room and auxiliary room, serving as a classroom and office, should be planned to meet the needs of every shop. (5)

The following general descriptions are typical of material provided to the Board of Education and General Superintendent during early planning phases of new facilities.

Preliminary Outline of Requirements — Senior High School

After study and meetings with those concerned with industrial arts and vocational subjects at East Central, after studying the enrollment of the department at this school and city wide, also study of the existing shops and others available through school shop planning manuals, we arrived at an average requirement for the types of installation being recommended. Because of all the factors listed and many others, the following proposal is made for offering courses in Industrial Arts and Vocational Education for the proposed new high school: (Listed in order)

1. *Drafting* — 32 students each room, with an overall area of 2100 sq. ft., including reproduction room and storage. Room 50' x 42'.
2. *Power and Auto Mechanics* — 28 students, 4000 sq. ft., including planning area, storeroom, welding booths, etc. Planned for industrial arts and/or vocational auto mechanics. 50' x 80' — need balcony space for storage.
3. *Woodwork* — 28 students, 3,400 sq. ft., including lumber room, storage room, class and planning area, finish booth. Does not include balcony which is needed. 50' x 68' available for flexible use.
4. *Electricity and Electronics* — 28 students, 2800 sq. ft., including assembly and planning area, storerooms, test booths, area 40' x 70', plus balcony if possible.
5. *Metals Shop* (machine, welding, etc.) — 28 students, 3,250 sq. ft., to include class and planning area, supply rooms, welding booths, lockers. 50' x 65' with balcony for storage.
6. *Industrial Cooperative Training* — 36 students, 1,250 ft., to include office and conference space. This room would be available for other classes one-half day when one such program is in operation or full time until such time as the Industrial Cooperative Training Program is scheduled. 25' x 50' including storage.

Display, toilets and office this area — see plan — 200 sq. ft.

Preliminary Outline of Requirements — Junior High School

1. *Exploratory Woodwork and Drawing and Planning*, 32 students maximum, 2500 sq. ft., 42' x 50' overall. This shop to be flexible so subjects listed may be offered. Total shop area to be approximately 2,516 sq. ft., not including balcony, but including finish area, supply room, planning and assembly area. Working

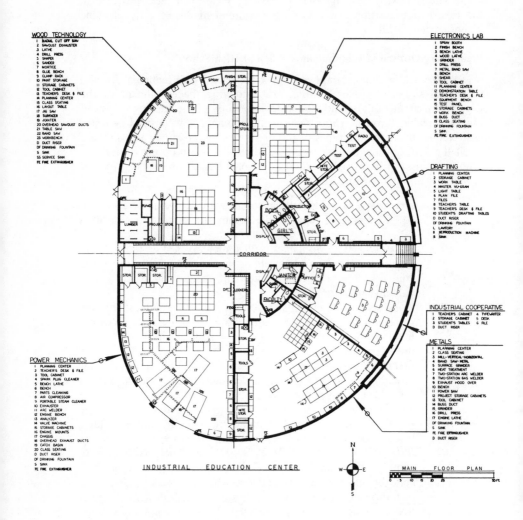

Fig. 4-6 General Plan of Facilities at East Central
High School, Tulsa Schools

Fig. 4-6A. Model of the East Central High School, Tulsa

space approximately 1,800 sq. ft. Shop to be in dimension of 34′ x 74′ or ratio for 3 shops together with supply and lumber storage rooms, finish room, and planning-assembly area at the end.

2. *Industrial Crafts and Printing*, 32 students maximum, 1,920 sq. ft., 32′-36′ x 50′ overall. This shop to be flexible so subjects listed may be offered. Total shop area to be approximately 1,920 sq. ft., not including balcony, but including finish area, supply room, dark room, and planning area. Working space approximately 1,560 sq. ft. Shop to be in dimensions of 30′ x 64′ with supply room, finish area, and dark room at end of room, or 32′ x 50′ with supply room, balcony, finish area and dark room on the sides, worked in with metal shop space.

3. *Exploratory Metalwork and Exploratory Electricity*, 32 students maximum, 2500 sq. ft., 42′ x 60′ overall. This shop to be flexible so subjects listed may be offered. Total shop area to be approximately 2,500 sq. ft. not including balcony, but including finish area, supply room, and planning-assembly area. Working space approximately 1,800 sq. ft., shop to be in dimensions of

34' x 74' with supply room, steel storage, finish room and planning-assembly area at end.

Arrangement of a Good Tool Rack

1. Mountings should be made of metal or hardwood.
2. For junior high students, the tools most commonly used should be near the bottom.
3. Chisels, scribers, etc. should be protected so that students will not receive an injury when removing them. Cutting edges and sawteeth should be covered.
4. Tools should be mounted so that their removal is possible with normal arm movement. Tools should not have to be lifted their full length to be removed from the rack.
5. Holders should be tilted to the front 20° for some tools such as try squares. Bottom-type holders should be avoided.
6. Tools of similar function should be grouped together.
7. All tools should be properly marked.
8. Tool silhouettes may be placed on tool panels to show location of tools.
9. Precision tools and equipment should be in special containers and locked up in a drawer of a cupboard.

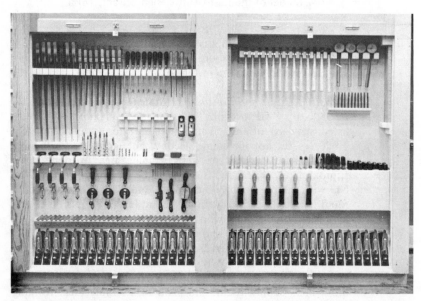

Fig. 4-7. Well Planned Provision for Tool Storage Is Important

10. Tool storage facilities should be placed most conveniently for students.

11. As much space as possible should be conserved.

Color

Since some behavior is affected by color, careful consideration should be given color combinations in the shop. Yellow suggests warmth; blue is cool and calming; red is associated with danger and excitement; green suggests freshness; violet means luxury; and orange is cheerful. A safety color code suggested for application in the school shop from specific recommendations of the ASA:

Red (fire protection) for emergency stop buttons and fire alarm boxes.

Yellow (hazardous areas) for safety zones around machines and for accentuating obstructions.

Green in combination with *white* (first aid) for the first aid cabinet and fire blanket container.

Black and white and combinations of them in stripes and squares (housekeeping and traffic marks) for location of aisles, directional signals, and areas to be kept clear.

Orange (alert for parts of machines) for inside of gear and switch boxes, inside pulley covers, safety alerting buttons, and a line of path for circular sawblades.

Blue (caution against moving machines) for electrical switch plates, handles of levers, and controls that start or stop the equipment.

Grounds Adjacent to Shop

1. Provide a surfaced motor-vehicle parking area of adequate capacity for staff, students, and visitors.

2. Provide an appropriate back exit for delivery of supplies and equipment and for easy emergency exit.

3. Provide for surfaced driveways and concrete walks.

Plant Adaptability

1. A curriculum can only be carried out effectively if the school building is planned to meet the needs of the diversified activities and associated services prevalent in a vocational-technical school shop.

2. It is suggested that the building be in harmony with the activities it houses and portray a modern simplicity in design, reflecting in its various components the most recent advancements of proven merit.

3. The school shop, furthermore, should be planned and so located on the site to facilitate expansion of the center.

General Building Recommendations

1. Orientation of the building should be such that classrooms and laboratory-type rooms have a western and/or eastern exposure. All shops having southern, eastern, or western exposure should have windows equipped with heat-retarding and glare-reducing devices.

2. Each shop should include space for lockers, washing facilities, tool racks, equipment, aisles, classroom, storage, and special rooms.

To be sure that shops built in the next decade adequately serve the needs of the school, the following principles should be considered:

1. Members of the profession should work closely with school architects in order that the latter be well acquainted with the needs of the industrial education areas of education.

2. Administrators and architects should be convinced that shops and laboratories must be completely equipped with tools, machines, benches, and cabinets.

3. Consultant service should be available at the state level so that small and medium-sized towns can obtain expert advice as to the kinds of shops that best suit their communities.

4. Planning of industrial education facilities should not take place without involving the industrial education teacher and/or groups of teachers. When supervisors are available, they should direct the planning with the assistance of teacher committees.

5. The location of necessary utilities such as gas, air, and electricity determines the specific location of benches, machines, and other items in the shop.

6. The advice of commercial concerns in selecting benches and equipment should be sought, but the job of school shop planning should not be completely turned over to any single company. Equipment of high quality should be used.

Selection of Students in Vocational Subjects

Enrollment in vocational-industrial classes should be limited to those persons who have signified their desire to prepare for employment in the occupation for which training is offered. Acceptance of students in the course should be based on the physical, mental, and educational qualifications required for training and work in the occupation. These qualities will be partially revealed by the job analysis.

A schedule of requirements for enrollment in the course should be adopted. This schedule should be prepared in cooperation with the advisory committee, potential employers, and appropriate consultants. Actual recruitment of students by the school may be accomplished through referrals by members of the advisory committee, employers, unions, public employment agencies, and public information on the course and its objectives through local newspapers.

Criteria Used

1. Vocational Objective — The first consideration is the vocational objective of the applicant. Adequate vocational guidance and counseling must always consider the utility of the education.

2. Educational Plan — The educational plan of the applicant must be considered very carefully. The plan must be analyzed realistically in terms of the present school schedule and achievement, the student's economic status, and what plan the applicant has actually indicated on his permanent record.

3. Interests — Particular attention is given to areas of interest indicated by each applicant. Example: A student who has a "ham" radio operator's license is generally a good candidate for an electronics program.

4. Grades and Test Scores — All available information as recorded on the permanent record of each applicant is carefully observed and considered in terms of native ability and achievement. The greatest agreement and greatest variance between native ability, test scores, and achievement should be determined from a close examination of the student's record. Adequate vocational guidance and counseling will always consider these three items on the student's record as indicators of success in particular areas of vocational interest.

5. Attendance — Student's attendance is closely observed since a majority of students enrolled in specialized subjects will ultimately be punching an employer's time clock. Punctuality and attendance are among the first characteristics to be examined by potential employers.

6. Counselor's Recommendation — (a) The high school counselor's recommendation and written comments on the application are highly significant in terms of selecting the right applicant to be prepared for the right occupation; (b) the composite check marks, recorded from teacher's personal rating forms to the permanent record, prove to be excellent indicators of success or failure in each of the attributes or characteristics listed on the rating form; (c) when available, classroom teacher's personal recommendations made through daily observations of the applicant under classroom conditions prove to be most helpful in the success or failure of each applicant.

7. Personal Appearance — All students enrolled in any educational

course should be encouraged to be neat and orderly in manner, attire, and habit. Good grooming is generally considered to be dependent upon neat hair cuts, appropriate attire, and personal cleanliness.

8.   Activities — All student activities, both in school and out of school, are good indicators of potential leadership, character, maturity, and willingness to accept responsibility by serving his community. These and a host of other similar attributes are important in diagnosing the student's overall potential in an occupation.

9.   Miscellaneous — Miscellaneous items to be considered in the selection of an applicant for a particular occupation are: Parents' occupation and educational level, economic level, parents living or deceased, student has a guardian or step-parents, etc.

10.   Personal Opinion — The personal opinion of the counselor doing the interviewing is considered in the light of the above criteria.

The supervisor, administrator, superintendent, department chairman, or teacher can attract industrial education students by the following practices:

1.   Explaining benefits of the program to the students or faculty.
2.   Making home visits to inform parents.
3.   Insisting upon better training agencies and more careful placement of students.
4.   Obtaining better pay for students in co-op training.
5.   Using advisory committees in selecting students and in recruitment.
6.   Working with counselors to develop an understanding of the program and its standards as well as its opportunities.
7.   Working with companies who employ students in the summer.
8.   Using school bulletin boards to display items of interest and occupations available.
9.   Encouraging industrial arts clubs to set up school-wide projects in which other students can participate.
10.   Informing school administrators about the program.
11.   Helping prospective students to become aware of opportunities in various occupations. Organize an industrial education promotion, such as a double-page newspaper spread with pictures of students.
12.   Using want ads in the school paper.
13.   Proving that vocational students can go to college and keep records on those students who do go.
14.   Sponsoring a career day.
15.   Assisting in scheduling students.
16.   Having hall displays.

17. Maintaining follow-up records.
18. Setting up and maintaining standards.
19. Providing scholarships for advanced study.
20. Setting up downtown window displays, distributing auto decals, etc.

The need for close working relationship between industrial education teachers, administrators, counselors and teachers of other subjects can not be over-emphasized if a successful guidance program is to be carried on. To provide this team work, a planned program which involves these people should be worked out.

The following examples present some ideas that may be employed:

I. Meetings
   A. To become acquainted.
   B. To discuss guidance problems.
   C. To plan guidance programs.
   D. To outline responsibilities.
   E. To correlate guidance information with other subjects.
II. Programs (carried out jointly between counselor, industrial education teachers and others).
   A. Career fairs.
   B. Field trips.
   C. TV career programs.
   D. Career assemblies.
   E. Film presentations.

Guidance of Learners

Recent trends in education and the world of work require that increased and renewed emphasis be placed upon guidance in the industrial arts and vocational education programs. Growing up today is hard! Preparation for, and successful entry into, the labor market is a complex task.

Education and special skills represent the only means of entry into many job openings. Unless our schools start early to help youth understand the opportunities and demands of the labor market — to understand these opportunities and demands in relationship with their interests and qualifications — and to plan accordingly, graduates of the schools will have a difficult time in finding jobs.

As teachers of occupational education, we need to realize that we are in a position to exercise a lasting influence on helping students to make vocational choices. This decision is important in that it often determines the entire course of a student's life. Sound, effective guidance will lead the individual to decide wisely what should be his occupational objective, and therefore what should be his school program.

One of the most important objectives of industrial and prevocational courses involves exploration of industry. Information about the world of work should be a natural outcome of study and experiences found in practical arts courses using some of the tools and machines of industry.

Teachers in these areas should have a broad overview of the variety of job classifications found in the cluster of occupations that are related to the subject in which he or she teaches. If the teacher does not have knowledge of these specific job requirements, then work experience or research and study is a necessity.

From experience and knowledge, the student will become better acquainted with many industrial operations. They include: the nature of the work, the future in the occupation, and advantages or disadvantages in the occupations.

When a student shows interest in an occupation, encouragement should be given to the student to seek additional information about the occupation. This may be accomplished through interviews with workers, materials in the school and shop libraries, career conferences, visitation to vocational classes, or a visit to business and industry.

In addition to work experience, practical arts teachers can further reinforce their teaching by familiarizing themselves with all offerings in vocational, technical, and practical arts programs.

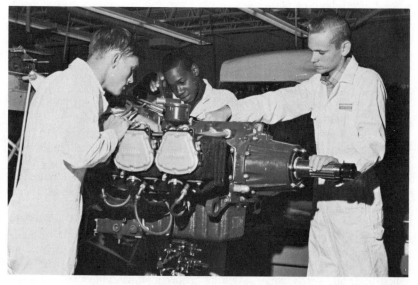

Fig. 4-8. Exploration Is a Vital Part of Occupational Guidance

Certain basic general rules concerning vocational guidance are applicable at all levels of education. The objectives of education, including planning and preparing for a career, should be directed toward the recognition that this is a world of change. Experiences, skills and learnings students will need in the work world of the future should be based on the expectation of change.

As the practical arts teacher begins to plan for vocational guidance, it is well to think of some basic facts:

1. Most students will eventually need and want to earn a living.
2. The economy and welfare of the nation depend upon the education of individuals, the productivity of individuals, and the employability of individuals.
3. Practical arts teachers must be realistic and should be geared to meet the needs of all youth for the best possible and most fitting education as preparation to enter the world of work.

Vocational Guidance, through all grades, should be devoted largely to development of self-concept, exploration, and gaining knowledge and understanding of the areas of work characteristics of the environment of each student.

Certainly the need to work should be stressed. The values of work to the individual are important concepts to be developed. The sense of satisfaction, fulfillment, and happiness which comes from the involvement with an occupation of one's choice, should be stressed. The knowledge that one is a constructive and contributing member of society, and is earning the right to live well and independently, is important to each individual's mental health and personal growth.

In order to implement the suggestions made, each teacher should develop a file of material for an instructional unit in vocational guidance, which should be a part of every subject area and each grade level.

The guidance of high school students cannot be performed adequately by counselors alone. Even in the most ideal situation, the counselor works with 200 to 300 students. With this counseling load he is able to see the majority of students only once or twice during a semester. To most students he can be hardly more than a skillful stranger. He is not likely to be a person the student has learned to trust, or one who has much real knowledge of the student's mental and emotional processes. In a very real sense, if guidance is to function in the secondary school, the classroom teachers will provide the major portion of it. The major function of the guidance specialist will be to serve as an essential resource to teachers and provide continuing help for students with serious disturbances or difficulties.

The world of work today is changing so rapidly that personal adaptation and development require a greater degree of self awareness. Industrial arts can play a very important part in providing pupils with information and problem solving experiences which can assist in obtaining constructive utilization of our most vital resource — manpower.

In former times, when occupational and professional life was less highly specialized, parents assumed a responsibility for informing their children about careers. Most parents today, however, find themselves severely limited in knowledge of the breadth and variety of opportunities possible for their children. This has led to a growing demand for the school to assume a greater responsibility in assisting young people in their career development.

Industrial educators have become dramatically aware of the role their curriculum offerings should play in assessing abilities and their obligations in an era when full utilization of all talents is essential to the nation's future well being.

There are vast numbers of youth enrolled in the nation's high schools who have special needs. The fact that there is a 25% dropout nationally, emphasizes the magnitude of the need to develop special vocational programs to better serve these youth. Youth with special needs are those who are unable to succeed in regular academic or vocational programs. They are often socio-academically handicapped but with a mental ability above the special education level. These are the youngsters who often see no relevance or "payoff" in terms of present, traditionally developed educational programs. They value education and desire it but their reasons for wanting education differ from those stressed by most schools in that they want vocational job-preparation-oriented education that will help them to get along in the modern world by providing them with an opportunity to learn and earn.

Industrial education programs designed specifically to motivate and provide youth with special needs with the necessary job preparation to enter the world of work are very much needed.

Topics for Class Discussion

What kind of jobs might the unskilled secondary school graduate be able to find in our community? (After response from students, you might exhibit a classified help wanted section from the Sunday edition of your newspaper. Have marked in one color those openings available to the unskilled and in another color those demanding special skills for which a youngster could be trained at a vocational or technical school or in special postsecondary school training. Read a representative sampling of each, including salaries where given.)

You hear a lot about automation these days. What is it? Can you think of any examples of how automation might affect your preparation for the future? (Machines taking over routine tasks once done by people . . . sorting, posting figures, addressing envelopes, simple manufacturing tasks. But people . . . trained people . . . are needed to design, build, program, and operate these machines.)

If a secondary school education is not enough, should everyone go to college? Why? (Not everyone has the interest in or ability for the academic life. While we need a certain number of professors, doctors, lawyers, etc., we need a great many more skilled workers and technicians to make the wheels turn.)

What alternatives are there? (Service, special training available there; apprenticeships; vocational and technical training.)

What is vocational and technical education? How is it different from college? (Shorter time—anywhere from a few weeks to two years, depending on course chosen; lower cost—compare tuition to that of state university; less emphasis on academic courses, more on learning to do as well as think, actual job training, practical application of theory.)

What kinds of jobs can it prepare you for?

What jobs do you know about that looked particularly interesting to you? What fields would you like to know about?

What types of education and training are available locally? (You may wish to secure catalogs from area schools and read a list of the various specializations offered.)

What do parents think about vocational and technical education?

Do you think a discussion and films on vocations might be valuable for parents to see? (Discussion on this point may lead to a decision for parents to view and discuss films on vocational and technical education.)

Suggested Class Projects

Take a field trip as a group to your high school or area vocational and technical center, and observe various kinds of training in action. Ask a guidance counselor to talk to the group about the various courses of training offered, and answer questions from the group. Or, if a trip is impractical, invite a vocational school representative to speak at your school.

Visit one of your community's large industrial plants to see the different kinds of skilled workers involved in the design, manufacture, and distribution of a product. Be sure to see office as well as production facilities.

Invite representatives of the major vocational categories in your community—for example: agriculture, health, distributive, service, manufacturing—to speak to the group about updating of job requirements in their fields over the past 10 years and in the next 10 years. Complete the series with a speaker from your State Employment Service. Ask him for an overall view of current and future demands in your local job market.

Placement

One of the most comprehensive and revealing studies of vocational education ever made was conducted by the Ford Foundation under the direction of Dr. Max U. Eninger. The study surveyed the post-high-school occupational and educational experiences of 10,000 vocational and 3000 academic graduates selected from 100 high schools. Half of the schools were vocational and half were comprehensive. The graduates were from the classes of 1953, 1958, and 1962.

Here in capsule form are some findings:

1.   Vocational graduates get their first full-time jobs after graduation much sooner than do academic graduates. (On the average, a month earlier.)

2.   Vocational graduates enjoy substantially greater employment security.

3.   Vocational graduates had greater accumulated earnings over the 11-year period of the survey. About 50% of the vocational graduates entered into the trade for which they were trained, and 15% entered into occupations related.

4.   The percentage of vocational graduates who enter the trades for which they are trained rises and falls with the general level of the U.S. economy. In the recession of 1958, only 28% of the graduates entered the trade for which they were trained.

A comparison of vocational and academic graduates without college training reveals no difference in conversational interests, leisure-time activities, and affiliation with community organizations. The findings contradict the contention that the vocational graduates are more poorly educated than academic graduates from the standpoint of education of the whole person.

A serious misconception is evident in the nation concerning vocational-industrial education in the senior high. The average citizen assumes that a young person taking industrial education courses begins with full job competencies after graduation. In reality, the schools cannot provide full competency but rather *job-entry competency.* This is the concept that makes sense in terms of what schools are equipped to do, of what industry and business expect, of what labor through the organized trade unions can accept, and of what young people should achieve. The service the schools should be providing students is job-entry competency — commensurate with the capabilities, interests, and motivation of the student.

The school administration, the public, and those responsible for the program must realize that schools can provide only job-entry competency. This will lead to more effective programs and full utilization of the opportunities available under education.

Placement of students in jobs should be considered as equally important to placement of students in colleges. The following questions should be asked of any school placement program:

1.   Is placement organized as a functioning part of the vocational program?

2.   Does the vocational instructor assume definite responsibility for placing students from his classes?

3.   Is the school's placement program closely coordinated with other placement programs in the community?

4.　Is there close cooperation between instructors of pre-apprentice-ship vocational training classes and local joint apprenticeship committees?
5.　Are students carefully screened for jobs that meet their interests, abilities, and aptitudes on the basis of training and work experience records?
6.　Is a permanent record kept of the number of different students who have been enrolled in vocational classes and the actual number of placements in the trade?
7.　Are students prepared for placement through orientation and training in the attitudes in addition to the skills of the trade?

Follow-Up

Along with a good instructional program and placement system in the school, follow-up programs should be conducted for proper guidance of future learners. Such questions as the following should be asked:

1.　To what extent does the school district maintain a well organized and functioning program for follow-up?
2.　What are the specific objectives of the school district's program of follow-up? What tangible evidence is available to show the extent to which these objectives are being realized?
3.　Are the records adequate?
　　a.　Are facilities for keeping records adequate in space, form, and files?
　　b.　Is there an effective system of records?
　　c.　Are they kept up-to-date?
4.　Do follow-up records show percentages of students placed in each occupation for which trained? Have they continued in the occupation?
5.　What percentages of former vocational students contacted through the follow-up program are enrolled in extension classes for their trade?

Curriculum Coordination

The problem of coordination has become acute since the junior and senior high schools have been separated in different buildings. An overall school organization should have a cohesive curriculum. A program generally requires "facilities for a comprehensive-exploratory program in the 7th and 8th grades as well as provision for offering the opportunity to continue this exploration in the 9th grade." The senior high school should have facilities that provide for specialization and the curriculum should be continuous so that senior high courses will not repeat junior high work. (6)

The post-secondary programs—junior colleges, community colleges, and area schools—should carry on the course of study of the high school with effective terminal courses for those who will end their schooling in the junior college. Junior colleges, community colleges, technical institutes and area schools offer technical, skilled, and specialty training.

One organizational trend is the middle school concept. Just what is a middle school, and what grades does it encompass? The answer is not firm nor clearcut and shows all kinds of variations. It covers, in most cases, grades 6, 7 and 8; but it can be 5, 6, 7, 8 or 7, 8, 9 or 7, 8; and just about any other combination of these grade levels. It is the school between elementary and high school.

We know that its concept has gained momentum, and some individuals even claim it may become the major educational development in our times. Just how fast is its growth is hard to judge, because research is virtually non-existent. Its rate of growth, however, seems to be phenomenal.

Two steps must be taken when industrial arts considers its role in the middle school. A set of working principles must be compiled, and the realities of the local situation must be adjudicated with the working principles.

Here are some generalizations of practice that should be the basis of the working principles.

1. The study of industry and its impact upon the lives of individuals should be an important part of the work in each grade of the middle school.

2. The organization of the middle school should exploit the use of the specialized industrial arts staff and facility in developing a curriculum that is characterized by unity and articulation.

3. Like all other subjects in the middle school, industrial arts should adapt itself to the transition from the self-contained classroom in the early grades to the more segregated offerings in the upper grades.

4. Industrial arts in the middle school must be characterized by exploratory experiences in a wide variety of media.

5. The middle school and all of the disciplines within it should emphasize individualized instruction.

6. The middle school, and industrial arts within it, should place primary emphasis on factors that lead to the continued quest for knowledge.

7. A continuing inservice program should assist teachers in understanding the middle school student and the methods which are most appropriate to the unique characteristics of this age.

In an editorial for *Educational Leadership* (ASCD Journal), 1965, Gordon Vars said, "Yes, junior high schools are changing. Yet the basic question remains the same. 'What shall be the nature of education for young adolescents in today's society?' Neither changing the institution's name nor moving its grade level brackets up or down a notch will necessarily affect the character of the education it provides. Instead, educators at all levels must seize the opportunity represented by the present state of flux to try once again to make of the intermediate unit a truly unique institution for the age group it embraces."

There may well need to be a shift in emphasis from the single exploratory approach of the junior high school to courses operating at three levels; for the *above average* student, for the *average* and for the *below average* student.

For the *above average* student the idea of an experimental laboratory, whether in the field of engineering or the field of art is suggested. From this group will come the creative people, the scientists, the research engineers, the industrial designers and inventors, etc.; thus the desire to experiment with three-dimensional materials must be fostered.

Students interested in mathematics and science should have an opportunity to solve technical problems involving tools, materials, and machines. Devices to demonstrate physical phenomena such as acceleration apparatus, static electricity demonstration unit, prony brakes, are typical examples of such activities. Such experiences develop a greater mechanical resourcefulness. It is generally recognized that discovery, research and planning can be conducted only to the degree that mechanical and manipulative work accompany theoretical developments. Under such conditions the ability to do is a vital addition to the ability to think.

There needs to be considerable emphasis on related information at a high level; machines should be seen as applications of scientific laws and principles; there needs to be analysis of design as well as development of the ability to judge quality of design both from the esthetic and the engineering viewpoint. To permit maximum efficiency it is recommended that related information lectures, films, etc., be given in a room away from the shops so that the equipment might be available for other classes.

Such activity does not exclude providing the opportunity for the above average boy to make, for example, a fine piece of furniture but does not restrict him to this type of activity.

For the *average* student the opportunity should be provided to work individually but with more emphasis on the development of skills. A high standard of workmanship can be demanded; it is of vital importance for the student to appreciate, to strive for and to achieve to the full extent of his ability, excellence in craftsmanship. There may be less emphasis on related information than in courses for the above average but should be more than in junior high school. Application of scientific principles in machines must be discussed as well as analysis of design; attention also needs to be given to development of taste and judgment in design. The major part of the related information, however, deals with materials, machines and processes involved in the work.

Opportunity should be provided for specialization or broad coverage according to the student's choice and the policy of the school. While those specializing are not preparing to be tradesmen or technicians, they are receiving training that will be of direct value in jobs closely related to those of the tradesmen and technicians.

For the *below average* student the industrial arts courses should provide an opportunity to learn more about care and maintenance of equipment. Shop safety must be given constant attention, but not because it is more important for the below average pupils than with the average or above average but because they do not see as readily the dangers of unsafe practices. The idea that machines and tools can always be dangerous must be emphasized constantly so that they will habitually seek to learn the safe way to operate a machine before attempting to use it.

As further advances in our industrial society will surely result in greater amounts of leisure time, the hobby interest of industrial arts assumes increasing importance. Whether or not the leisure of the 30- or 35-hour working week is used for debasement or enrichment will depend on the system of values developed largely in the schools.

Philadelphia's public schools are giving slow learners easier achievement tests than their classmates in an effort to get a more accurate measure of their achievement. Students are given tests designed for the previous grade so the tests will be more in line with their reading ability. However, an easier test does not mean a higher score, school officials say, because the student must get more items correct to obtain the same score. But school officials believe "out-of-level testing" will reduce a student's frustrations with tests and eliminate random guessing which produces inaccurate scores. This practice was suggested years ago by test manufacturers but was never tried on a large scale because of the difficulties involved, a school spokesman said. The Philadelphia experiment involves 15,000 to 20,000 children—about 15% of those in grades 4-8. In another first, the Philadelphia schools asked for test samples so students and teachers can familiarize themselves with the test format. Officials hope this will eliminate low scores caused by mechanical reasons and misunderstandings.

The educational view of "gifted children" is in the midst of a revolution. The National Association for Gifted Children, meeting in Chicago, agreed that giftedness can no longer be restricted to academic talent measured by IQ test. Leaders in the field agreed that giftedness now includes many kinds of talents such as the social ability to be a leader, artistic ability, humor, and many other kinds of creativity. Their aim: to uncover special talents at an early age and nurture them in study units which are a part of traditional courses.

It is time that the schools embrace the mission of career preparation. The manner in which they do so has implications beyond the disadvantaged student, though his need is the most urgent. The larger implications are of two kinds:

1. The integration of career consciousness throughout the schools will actually enlarge, not reduce, the number of options and alternatives for individual pupils—both in terms of occupation and higher education.

2. The work world is a valid component of academic content for all children—a powerful instrument for advancing relevance in the teaching of all subjects, academic as well as "vocational," and, in a fundamental sense, consonant with liberal education.

Relationship of Industrial Arts to Vocational-Industrial Education

Industrial arts is related to vocational-industrial education and is often considered essential as a foundation upon which these programs can be built. It serves vocational-industrial education in the same manner as arithmetic serves algebra and calculus. Far from being synonymous, industrial arts and vocational-industrial education are distinct phases of education for the technological age in which we live. The latter, however, is education for advantageous employment in a specific occupation.

In many communities programs of vocational-industrial education are not offered to students. For students in these communities, industrial arts is the nearest approach to the type of program they desire; not a satisfactory answer to their needs but at least a partial solution for their interest in schoolwork of an industrial nature and in many instances partial preparation for entrance into an occupation.

Industrial arts education cannot be substituted for trade and technical programs because of limited equipment and time as well as the necessity for a qualified trade teacher.

Terminology

Six terms defined as they apply to industrial arts and vocational-technical education:

Occupational education: Education designed to contribute to occupational choice, competence, and advancement. It includes occupational guidance, much that is provided by the practical arts and the other forms of general education, vocational education, technical education, and education for the professions.

Vocational education: Specialized education for a particular non-professional or non-technical occupation or a cluster of these occupations.

Technical education: Specialized education for occupations ordinarily requiring two years of preparation beyond the high school, which emphasizes the science, mathematics, and laboratory procedures related to the occupations for which the students are preparing.

Professional education: Specialized education for occupations requiring four or more years of college preparation.

Area Schools: Junior and community colleges, vocational schools, technical institutes, and branches of universities which serve areas usually larger than school districts.

Practical arts: Education in industrial arts, agriculture, business, distribution, home economics, and industry which is not designed to prepare for a particular occupation or a particular cluster of occupations.

Student Clubs

Various groups of individuals find value in participating in club programs. The following lists include some of the values expressed by students, educators, and business leaders.

Students

1. Participate in a group concerned with their chosen occupational field.
2. Associate with recognized leaders in community activities.
3. Secure prestige and recognition by participating in a variety of challenging projects.
4. Pursue excellence in peer-approved activities.
5. Live in a social atmosphere in which they have a feeling of acceptance.

Educators

1. Present techniques for developing motivation through self-determined student goals.
2. Develop, through practice, understandings of democratic principles which are essential elements to citizenship.
3. Present club activities which offer an opportunity to develop an understanding and appreciation of the free competitive system.
4. Develop a relationship of club activities to the classroom program as a means of motivating student achievement in the total school program.
5. Present activities of the club program which will be useful in

communicating essential aspects of distributive education to various community groups.

Business Leaders

1. Encourage students to explore industrial occupations.
2. Make a contribution to school activities.
3. Plan an approach for creating individual and group activities.
4. Present opportunity for students to practice elements of leadership.
5. Plan programs which help to explain the free enterprise system. (2)

The U.S. Department of Health, Education, and Welfare views a club program as:

. . . an activity which complements, supplements, and strengthens the instructional program. Combined with classroom instruction, the club program gives greater scope and depth to the total instruction program. Success in any occupation is dependent upon attitudes that lend themselves to development within an educationally-centered club program. The club program provides an avenue for the enrichment of the instructional program through activities planned by students under the teacher coordinator's guidance. (27)

References

1. Barr, A.S., William H. Barton, and Leo J. Brueckner, *Supervision, A Social Process.* New York: Appleton-Century-Crofts, Inc., 1955.
2. *Educational Values in Club Programs.* Washington, D. C.: U.S. Department of Health, Education, and Welfare.
3. *Guide for Industrial Arts Education in California.* Sacramento, Calif.: State Department of Education, 1958.
4. *A Guide to Improvement of Industrial Arts in Oklahoma Schools.* Oklahoma City, Okla.: State Department of Education, 1965.
5. *Guide for Planning and Equipping Industrial Arts Shops in California Schools.* Sacramento, Calif.: State Department of Education, 1956.
6. *Industrial Arts Education – Organization and Administration.* Albany, New York: State Department of Education, 1960.
7. "Opinion," IA/VE Editorial, October, 1960.
8. *Organization and Administration for Industrial Arts Education.* Columbus, Ohio: State Board of Education, 1959.
9. *The Role of the Supervisor in Educational Leadership.* Tulsa, Okla.: Tulsa Public Schools, 1960.

Chapter 5

Basic Consideration
in Planning Instruction

Nature of Learning

Learning is generally defined as any desirable change in the behavior of an organism. A teacher selects learning experiences based upon certain facts and assumptions about the ways in which learning takes place. These include:

1. Best learning results when there is some means of application of what is learned.
2. Learning takes place more readily when a purpose or desire is present.
3. Learning is simplified if it is built on something already known.
4. Learning, to be effective, must proceed in a logical order.
5. Learning is a problem-solving process and must be challenging.
6. More effective learning takes place when impressions come through more than one of the senses.
7. The first impressions are usually the most lasting; therefore, it is important not to convey wrong impressions that must be corrected.
8. Learning is more likely to take place if students have a reasonable chance to achieve success.
9. The more often learning is used, the longer it will be retained.
10. Learning requires motivation and interest.

Imperative Needs of Youth

The NASSP Bulletin has listed the ten imperative needs of junior high school youth. These have real meaning as a program of instruction is planned and implemented.

Imperative Need Number I

All junior high school youth need to explore their own aptitudes and to have experiences basic to occupational proficiency. They need to:

1. Explore various occupational fields and from exploration to choose fields to pursue further.
2. Analyze their own personal interests and abilities.
3. Have experiences which will give insight into the world at work, home, and elsewhere.
4. Have information regarding the activities and requirements of various vocational fields.
5. Learn about and practice safety in connection with occupations.
6. Grow in their ability to be accurate and to experience satisfaction in the completion of a job well done.
7. Learn to work effectively with others and to gain satisfaction from contributing to the welfare of the group.
8. Acquire certain skills which are basic to occupational success.

Imperative Need Number II

All youth need to develop and maintain abundant physical and mental health:

1. To comprehend the significance of health.
2. To covet health of body and mind.
3. To practice the various habits which result in a lifelong pattern of sound health.
4. To grow in physical coordination through cooperative and competitive play.
5. To succeed frequently and to have notice taken of their progress.
6. To achieve emotional stability sufficient to withstand the pressures of the environment.
7. Guidance in understanding and resolving their personal problems.
8. To understand the relationship between physical and mental health, with particular reference to changes taking place during adolescence.

Imperative Need Number III

All youth need to be participating citizens of their school and community with increasing orientation to adult citizenship:

1. To feel that they are *bona fide* members of the *body politic* of the school.
2. To feel that they are partners with the faculty in the management of the school and the promotion of its welfare.
3. That competence and personal worth grant status regardless of race or socio-economic background.
4. To realize that their role as citizens and their conduct are in-

timately related and that school citizenship provides privileges
and responsibilities, including a willingness to serve.

5.   To realize that their school community is organized along lines
     comparable with the civic organization of the adult community.
6.   To experience fully the function of representation in govern-
     ment and in other group activities.
7.   To understand and appreciate the processes and struggles by
     which America developed and continues to develop.
8.   To discover ways in which they can apply their school govern-
     ment experiences to classes, extracurricular activities, and stu-
     dent organizations.
9.   To look forward to a vital role in their senior high schools and in
     later adult citizenship.
10. A growing awareness of contemporary problems and the value in
     respecting honest differences of opinion.

Imperative Need Number IV

All youth need experiences and insights appropriate to their age and
development which are functions of successful home and family life.

(Some way is needed to give experiences and insights to those with no
home or family life.)

1.   To grow in appreciation, respect, loyalty, and a sense of respon-
     sibility toward their own home.
2.   To help in interpreting and resolving problems which they may
     experience in their own homes.
3.   To enrich home life through wholesome leisure-time activities.
4.   To understand the art of making the home attractive and to
     learn skills which can be used.
5.   To associate with members of the opposite sex in a variety of
     wholesome activities.
6.   To practice respect for public and private property.

Imperative Need Number V

All youth need to develop a sense of the values of material things and
the privileges of ownership.

1.   To look forward with anticipation to live on the highest standard
     that they are capable of achieving.
2.   To learn fundamental processes and skills which will enable them
     to participate effectively in the economic system.
3.   To have experience in appraising the relative worths of material
     things.
4.   To be aware of readily available resources which aid and protect
     the consumer.

5.   To manage personal financial expenses involving a balance be-
       tween desires and resources.
6.   To practice respect for public and private property.

Imperative Need Number VI

All youth need to understand their natural and physical environment,
and they need opportunities for using the scientific approach in the solution
of problems.

1.   To gather facts and to think clearly about their meaning and
       their relationship.
2.   To differentiate between facts and opinions and between truth
       and fiction.
3.   To develop a wholesome curiosity about the nature of the earth
       and living things.
4.   To understand the importance of natural resources and their
       conservation.
5.   To grow in their understanding of the biological structure and
       functional processes of growth.
6.   To practice healthful and safe habits of living.

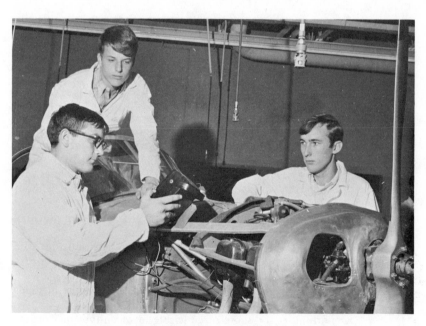

Fig. 5-1. All Youth Need to Develop a Sense of the
Values of Material Things (Tulsa Schools)

7.   To adjust their ways of living to the world of applied science and invention.
8.   To understand that cooperative living is imperative in a scientific world.

Imperative Need Number VII

All youth need the enriched living which comes from appreciation of expression in the arts and from experiencing the beauty and wonder of the world around them.

1.   Opportunities for expression in the arts and encouragement to take advantage of such opportunities.
2.   To discover and to develop special talents and abilities.
3.   Knowledge which contributes to appreciation and expression in the arts.
4.   Opportunities for experiencing and appreciating aesthetic values.
5.   Know how to use the principles of beauty in daily living.
6.   Expression in some of the arts as part of their leisure time activities.
7.   A growing awareness of the importance of the arts in community living.
8.   A sense of responsibility for developing and maintaining beauty in the community.

Imperative Need Number VIII

All youth need to have a variety of socially acceptable and personally satisfying leisure-time experiences which contribute either to their personal growth or to their development in wholesome group relationships, or both.

1.   Opportunities to engage in wholesome leisure-time activities with the opposite sex and to learn to react to each other without shyness or embarrassment.
2.   A wide range of leisure-time pursuits, and their own potential interests in and aptitudes for those pursuits.
3.   Skills and other forms of ability in leisure-time activities to a degree which promotes enjoyment and profit.
4.   Increasing attention to planning their use of leisure time.
5.   Respect for the ideal of safety and to learn and practice methods of promoting safety in leisure-time pursuits.
6.   Opportunities for unorganized leisure in which they may engage in casual talk and other informal activities.
7.   A discriminating use of leisure-time facilities.

Imperative Need Number IX

All youth need experiences in group living which contribute to personality and character development; they need to develop respect for other persons and their rights and grow in ethical insights.

1. To feel themselves acceptable to their peers and to have a sense of belonging and security in their environment.
2. To become increasingly emancipated from adult control and to retain the affection and support of one or more adults.
3. To grow in their ability to live harmoniously with others.
4. To develop skills and attitudes conducive to cooperative efforts for the common good.
5. Ample opportunities for the exercise of wholesome loyalties and responsibilities.
6. Experiences which give them status with their fellows.
7. Worthy outlets for their idealism and hero worship.
8. Group experiences of rich emotional import.
9. A system of values to which they refer when making choices and decisions, particularly in matters of conduct; they need to gain assurance in distinguishing between right and wrong.

Imperative Need Number X

All youth need to grow in their ability to observe, read, think, speak, and write with purpose and appreciation.

1. A growing concept of the purpose and value of language.
2. To understand and evaluate facts, ideas, rumors, superstitutions, opinions, and propaganda.
3. To read with understanding, for information, and for personal satisfaction.
4. To determine issues and problems that are meaningful to them personally for growth in understanding local, national, and world problems.

Individual Differences

Vast differences between students can be expected; and if instruction is good, an increased degree of difference will result. Capable students should progress more rapidly than slower ones. The teacher, then, must challenge the brighter students and, at the same time, allow the slower ones to grow. Although poor students may do better in industrial education classes than in other courses, success in industrial education usually goes hand-in-hand with general academic success. Mentally retarded or gifted children should be placed in special classes designed for them. (2)

The slow student needs much more attention, time, and praise from the instructor than the talented person. Continued failing experiences usually act to destroy self-confidence and make the individual unsure of his actions. The skillful instructor allows for proper balance between success and failure of all his students. A slow learner is also prone to emotional problems because of his lack of success in academic work. If an industrial arts course begins with purposeful activity, the slow learner with a mechanical aptitude may meet with success. It may mean an entirely new school experience for the student. He can also progress at his own rate and select challenging projects without much tedious planning. (2)

The majority of a class will be average students, and so it is up to the teacher to know each individual's strengths and weaknesses. In dealing with his pupils, the industrial education teacher should be fair and consistent, respect the contributions of each student, offer each a balance between success and failure, frequently evaluate the progress of each student, allow the student to engage in self-evaluation, direct individual study for bright and slow pupils, relate classroom work to the individual whenever possible, and maintain a proper balance between individual and group instruction. (2)

Purposes of a Course of Study

A course of study, according to Bakamis, is "a presentation of teaching materials together with suggested methods for their use." (4) It may be a sketchy outline of topics that assist a teacher in daily lesson delivery and a list of assignments and activities; or more intricate directions and suggestions can also be included. (5) Instruction, to be conducted properly, must proceed on some systematic basis. It is frequently stated that 50% of good teaching is careful planning. A far better course of study will be produced through the combined judgment of several teachers than one written by any single individual.

A course of study is particularly valuable to the beginning teacher. Faced with many responsibilities all new to him, a course of study can assist him in making daily plans, and can acquaint him with new procedures and routines. Also, such a guide helps to standardize the basic fundamentals within a degree of uniformity at different grade levels. (4)

An experienced teacher can use the course of study as a guide for the purpose of determining whether he is covering the essentials of the course. The supervisor can also use the guide to evaluate the teacher. (4)

Considerations in Making the Course of Study

Primary considerations in making a course of study are the background of the student and the nature of the school and the community. Included also are the attitudes of the community members toward the school curriculum, the opportunities in local industry, and future educational needs. Erickson identified these concerns:

Preliminary Considerations

1. Title page.
2. Acknowledgements and table of contents.
3. General statement of philosophy and viewpoint.
4. Objectives.

Basic Approaches in Organization

1. Student interest or need.
2. Projects or articles to be used
3. Sequence of tool processes.
4. Learning facts or accumulation of knowledge.
5. Future usefulness or adult needs.

Included in a Course of Study

1. The body of teaching content.
2. Suggested projects or activities.
3. Information and operating techniques.
4. Methods and instructional techniques.
5. Guidance and occupational information.
6. Safety instruciton.
7. Class organization and management. (5)

Course Outline

The following outline represents an attempt to present in some detail the steps that should be followed in developing a course of study in a particular field and is suggestive rather than exhaustive. The finished format should closely follow the outline. Any finished course of study should be typewritten and a carbon copy made.

1. Write the orientation section.
2. List the objectives for the course.
3. Prepare an analysis check sheet.
4. Determine the teaching units or major subdivisions of the course.
5. Determine and write out the purpose(s) or objective(s) of each unit. Consider this as each step is developed.
6. Develop the following for each unit.
   a. Activities included in the unit.
   b. Manipulative skills.
   c. New tools and equipment.

      d.   Related information.

      e.   Teaching aids.

      f.   References.

      g.   Method of approach to teaching the unit.

      h.   Evaluation.

    7.   Preparation of materials to be included in the appendix.

Of course, before the actual listing of objectives is begun, the instructor or committee must have developed a working knowledge of why public schools are an integral part of democracy; what part they have to play, and what goals they endeavor to reach. Going a step further, it should than be determined how the course fits into the functions of secondary education and the particular functions of industrial education. When these things are clear, it is time to state precisely and in unmistakable language the objectives of the particular course or the contributions it makes to the total educational picture.

There are numerous expressions or statements of the goals of education in a democracy. The ten imperative needs of youth are in many respects similar to the seven cardinal principles of education and other goals that have been stated from to time. They should serve to crystallize thinking on the desired outcomes of the education of American youth. The secondary school should provide educational experiences that will develop good living habits, interests, healthy attitudes, talents and abilities, good social behavior and competence, a vocational curiosity, and moral values. (3) Industrial arts develops these traits of personality through the actual use of tools and materials which trigger creative ability, expand knowledge in various fields, help use leisure time wisely, and aid the intelligent choice of a career in industry. (3) It is suggested that industrial arts teachers also review the general objectives of industrial arts as contained in the American Vocational Association Bulletin *A Guide to Improving Instruction in Industrial Arts* and the bulletin of the American Council of Industrial Arts Supervisors *Industrial Arts Education*.

With the above material thoroughly assimilated and a working philosophy clearly understood, the specific goals of a particular course can be determined. Before presenting sample statements of specific course objectives, together with suggestions and hints for their determination, several brief notes are offered to indicate the nature of such objectives:

    1.   The objectives for the course should serve as constant checks to indicate the extent to which the course is successful.

    2.   Beware of tradition for tradition's sake. The best antidote for this is to continually ask "why?" Everything that goes into the course of study should be justified.

    3.   Objectives should be stated in plain, simple language.

    4.   If there is difficulty in determining the objectives, consider what the students should expect to receive from the course.

5.   Consult many references or sources, but the finished product should represent individual thinking.
6.   The objectives should be a constant guide as the remainder of the course is developed.

Instruction Sheets

Four distinct types of instruction sheets are in use in industrial education programs. Each type serves a different purpose. The *job sheet* gives directions on how to do a job involving a number of operations. The *operation sheet* contains instructions for performing a basic manipulative operation. It is based upon learning principles rather than upon the performance of the operation on an actual job. The *information sheet* presents related technical or occupational information or facts to be learned. The *assignment sheet* serves a variety of purposes. It may be designed to direct reading, observation, or drill. It may also be in the form of a written test to check what the student has learned.

The following general rules for writing instruction sheets will be found useful:
1.   Condense information into a single sheet.
2.   Give information that applies directly to the job. Explain scientific terms when it is necessary to use them.
3.   Use plenty of drawings to supplement the instructions.
4.   Use the word instructor instead of teacher in all cases.
5.   When formulating questions, make them specific and understandable. Word them so that there can be no possibility of several, or evasive answers.
6.   Instruction sheets are for the use of the student. All material placed on the sheet should result in student thought.
7.   The steps should be a set of separate, numbered paragraphs to make each one stand out distinctly.

Job Sheet

The job sheet gives complete instructions for performing a trade job. It is the equivalent of the trade job ticket, work order, shop blueprint, etc. Some of the special points to include in job sheets are:
1.   In the aim, state the specific job to be done.
2.   Give a brief note about the job to explain its nature and purpose.
3.   List materials and equipment needed to perform the job.
4.   List all steps involved in solving the problem as set forth; arrange these in proper sequence.
5.   Instead of asking questions, give specific problems on this same subject. Give problems similar to the ones illustrated, but involving a new situation.

6.   Give an entirely different problem in which past experiences and judgment must be exercised.
7.   Provide directions for checking finished work.
8.   Illustrate adequately to clarify any anticipated difficulties.

Operation Sheet

Operation sheets are lessons in manipulative work, describing how specified jobs are performed. In most cases, such lessons will be demonstrated by the instructor, and before or after the demonstration the operation sheet will be used by the student.

1.   List all the steps in proper sequence.
2.   Write out the instructions for each step.
3.   List, with each step, any safety precautions that should be taken into consideration.
4.   Use a progressive approach to help clarify the procedure and make explanations more simple.
5.   Use correct and up-to-date terms.
6.   Call attention to where the operation unit will apply to other jobs, for every fundamental operation unit is used in many jobs of the trade.
7.   Ask carefully worded and clear questions. Questions should test the knowledge of why operations are performed in a certain way, and the application to other jobs in the trade or association to related technical knowledge.

Information Sheet

Information sheets are to be read and their contents assimilated as facts to be learned.

1.   State the title or aim clearly.
2.   Correlate the information presented with what the student has already learned.
3.   Use appropriate illustrations; the more the better, particularly when the subject is tools or equipment.
4.   Give references briefly and exactly as to page numbers, if supplementary reading is recommended.
5.   Do not crowd the sheet with too much text. Make the layout attractive.

Assignment Sheet

The purpose of the assignment sheet is to provide instruction to supplement that already received from the teacher. Accordingly, it may involve drill in manipulative operations, problem solving, research, and interpretation. However, some points common to all assignment sheets are as follows:

1. An assignment sheet should be self-activating; that is the assignment should be motivated by a brief introductory statement setting forth purpose and need for the work to be done.
2. In a problem-solving sheet, typical examples should be given.
3. When data is to be recorded, a suggested plan should be given.
4. When an experiment is to be made, the sheet should indicate the best procedure to follow.
5. Include effective illustrations to arouse interest and clarify what cannot be effectively described in the text.

Course Descriptions

A short course description should accompany the information on a particular course to furnish an overall perspective. A good form to follow uses the headings: Emphasis, Outcomes, and Characteristics of Course. *Emphasis* lists the major subareas and divisions of activity in the course; *Outcomes* outlines the skills, attitudes, interests, knowledge, and abilities that a student should gain from the course; *Characteristics of Course* gives a summary of the activities and experiences used in making the learning effective.

Functions of the Junior High School

Function I. Integration

1. To coordinate and integrate into effective and wholesome

Fig. 5-2. Students Need to Discover Their Specialized Interests, Aptitudes, and Abilities (Tulsa Schools)

behavior the skills, attitudes, interests, ideals, and insights presently or previously acquired.

2. To provide all students with a broad education in the basic knowledges and skills.

Function II. Exploration

1. To lead students to a discovery of their specialized interests, aptitudes, and abilities as a basis for decisions regarding educational and vocational opportunities.

2. To stimulate and develop a continually widening range of cultural, social, civic, avocational, and recreational interests.

Function III. Guidance

1. To assist students in making intelligent decisions regarding present educational and vocational opportunities and in preparing them for future educational and vocational decisions.

2. To assist students in making satisfactory mental, emotional, and social adjustment.

3. To stimulate and prepare for effective participation in learning activities to reach maximum development.

Function IV. Differentiation

To provide differentiated educational facilities and opportunities suited to the various backgrounds, interests, aptitudes, abilities, personalities, and needs of students.

Function V. Socialization

To provide increasingly effective and satisfying participation in an adjustment to the present complex social order.

Function VI. Articulation

To provide a gradual transition from preadolescent education to education suited to the needs and interests of the mature student.

Children of junior high school age face problems brought on by physiological, emotional, psychological, and social growth. They are in the early transitional age between childhood and adulthood. The rate of growth and maturity is great between the 6th and 9th grades. The teacher must recognize individual differences and know that the child is a person of potential value to society. Respect between teacher and student will be the result of such a relationship. Some of the problems of junior high school youth are:

1. Accepting his physique and a masculine or feminine role in life.

2. Achieving new relations with age mates of both sexes.

3. Achieving emotional independence of parents and other adults.
4. Achieving a means of economic independence.
5. Selecting and preparing for an occupation.
6. Developing intellectual skills and concepts necessary for occupational competence.
7. Acquiring desirable and socially responsible behavior.
8. Preparing for marriage and family life.
9. Building conscious values (aesthetic, religious, ethical) in harmony with an adequate scientific world picture.

Activities and Related Instruction

Activities, skills, and processes are all parts of instruction units. Among the activities a teacher must consider is the selection of an activity that contributes to the attainment of at least one major objective. Selecting or designing projects or activities within the students' abilities presents a challenge. Another activity which is very valuable in instruction is the well-planned and performed demonstration. Effective demonstrations must be provided for the class, small groups, and individuals. The utilization of past experiences plus class discussion tends to arouse the thinking of students and will create interest and enthusiasm. Having the ability to perform in industry or being an expert craftsman is not a sufficient guarantee that the teacher can demonstrate to others effectively. Ability to demonstrate comes from analysis of the problem and from an organization of the procedure plus a knowledge of those who are to learn from the presentation. There is no better way of building prestige among students than by the teacher's ability to prepare and present a skillful demonstration. This also applies to the use and care of hand tools and power equipment. To help students feel secure, the teacher should set up standards to be achieved. This will help students work more efficiently.

Written materials prepared by the teacher or purchased commercially also provide a most valuable teaching device. Materials for related information, both technical and general, may be classified as: (1) items that have a direct bearing on the efficiency of performing work; (2) materials that have to do with increasing the general scope of vision of the learner; and (3) materials providing occupational information and guidance.

Under the first of these classifications falls such knowledge as one would need for the best use and application of the principles of mathematics and science to the work performed, or to the understanding and reason for certain procedures or materials specified in connection with various assignments or jobs. This kind of related knowledge is essential to efficient work and to the development of an intelligent student.

Under the second classification is information that may not be considered essential for performance, but which is valuable in developing appreciation of the craft or the work performed, knowledge of the history of the industry represented, or an appreciation of the social and economic implications of the field.

Under the third classification, the teacher should see to it that the shop activities reflect those of industry and help the student to make a more intelligent future occupational choice.

Teaching Methods

The ultimate purpose of hiring a teacher, equipping a shop, and all the other aspects of industrial education effort is instruction. Methods are vitally important in making instruction effective and efficient.

I. Personal Characteristics – The teacher should always set an example of correct speech, conduct, appearance, attitude, and safe work habits. He should habitually be prompt, orderly, systematic, and neat. Students learn from example, perhaps more than they do by precept.

    A.   The teacher should approach his job with enthusiasm, a sense of responsibility, interest, curiosity, and a desire for personal satisfaction.

    B.   The teacher can help shorten the learning process by:

        1.   Knowing the subject.

        2.   Arousing interest.

        3.   Keeping explanations simple.

        4.   Putting across one idea at a time.

        5.   Showing the whole picture.

        6.   Keeping students thinking.

        7.   Using showmanship.

    C.   Students like to learn if:

        1.   They are given the right motivation.

        2.   They understand what is taught.

        3.   They get satisfaction from learning.

II. Lesson Planning – The lesson to be presented must be carefully planned so that the daily class becomes a complete unit. The lesson plan can be called the instructor's guide sheet or a blueprint for a class period.

    A.   Limit the lesson to a simple process, operation, or idea as much as possible. More complicated processes or ideas can be broken into simpler lessons and presented in parts.

    B.   The lesson plan can be made in the following arrangement:

        1.   Preparation.

            a.   Preparing learner's mind for new information.

            b.   Assembling equipment and supplies for demonstration.

  2. Aim — educational objectives.
  3. Presentation.
     a. Lecture.
     b. Demonstration.
  4. Summary.
  5. Testing and Drilling — question and answer period.
  6. Application — exercises and projects.
  7. Assignment and References.

III. Student should be given instruction sheets (job, operation, information, and assignment) for each lesson presented.

IV. Methods of presenting a lesson:

  A. The lecture is not very effective in teaching. If used, it should include numerous visuals and be kept short. Discussion of a text assignment may be a better approach.

  B. Demonstration is a most useful method of shop instruction.

  1. A teacher should talk directly to his students during a demonstration.

  2. Operations must be performed with a high degree of skill. Sloppy tool or machine operation by the instructor certainly will not induce high standards of skill in the student.

  3. As new tools and terms are introduced, they should be explained and defined.

  4. A negative view should not be presented to the students during a demonstration. For example, in use of a brace and bit, the students will see the brace turning backwards. The instructor should stand so that the students get a positive view of the operation with the brace turning forward. Mirrors can be used over the demonstration bench.

  5. The regular tools and materials used by the student should be used by the instructor in his demonstrations.

  6. All tools and equipment should be put in the best possible condition ahead of the demonstration.

  7. Students should be encouraged to ask questions at the end of the period rather than during the demonstration. Many questions will be answered by information presented later in the demonstration.

  8. Safety should be stressed at all appropriate places.

  9. The instructor should work on his own project and not a student's project.

  10. The instructor should ask questions to bring in student participation and to discover whether they are learning.

  11. Students should use their textbooks along with the demonstration.

      12.   Demonstrations should be kept to about 15 or 20 minutes.

C.   Use of visuals and teaching aids.
1.   Use the chalkboard.
2.   Use charts or blueprints or posters.
3.   Use visual education mediums; films, filmstrips, slides, transparencies.
4.   Use textbook pictures.
5.   Use models.

V. Outside Reading – It is very important in shop instruction units that the teacher know the subject. Perhaps some additional reading from a good text might be necessary for the teacher. He should give these references to the class for further study.

VI. Application – The student must be required to practice the lesson presented so that learning will actually take place.

A.   It is best to have a student carry out his practice of the lesson taught on the project he is making. Lesson sequence and project construction would need to be carefully integrated.

B.   Some practice operations could be asked of the student so that he could perfect his learning after a lesson is presented and before using on his take-home project.

VII. Textbook – Its usefulness is governed by how carefully it is selected and the student's grade level. All books should be effective and useful. If existing texts seem inappropriate, the teacher should ask to be furnished with textbooks of his own choice.

A.   Usually the text with numerous pictures and illustrations is more interesting to the public school shop student and more helpful.

B.   Texts can be used in conjunction with demonstrations.

C.   Texts usually include effectively prepared operation instruction.

D.   Questions from texts often are helpful in checking on student learning.

E.   Texts are valuable in teaching related information.

F.   Records must be kept on all textbooks so that they may be accounted for on inventories.

G.   Orderly and neat storage of textbooks is strongly advised. This simplifies checking of books and facilities for their use. A good textbook rack or case is an easy means of caring for textbooks.

VIII. References and Resources

A.   *Reference Books* are used to supplement the textbook. Reference books on wood furnishings and finishing in a woodshop are usually advisable because they give more complete information on finishing than the woodworking text.

B.   *Manufacturer's Operator Manuals* are published by manufacturers to explain the mechanism, operation, and repair of the machines they make. They are usually received when new machines are put into shops. Auto mechanics teachers may secure manuals on motor car operation directly from the auto manufacturer or through the department office.

C. *Trade Catalogs* listing tools, equipment, and supplies are very useful in the shop. They give excellent descriptions and drawings of the tools and equipment as well as price. They may be used by students in identifying tools, equipment, or material, and for consumer information.

D. *Magazines* are up-to-date sources of information for instruction. They can be secured from varied sources.

E. *Instructional Aids* are visual materials used by the teacher to strengthen the quality of the instruction and to make it more effective and memorable. They are classified as written material; projecturals (motion pictures, photographs, transparencies, filmstrips, slides); teaching aids (mock-ups, models, cutaways, and sample equipment); miscellaneous aids (tool panels, electrical identification panels, jigs, gages, and recordings); field trips; and guest speakers.

IX. Assignments — In order that some of the specific purposes might be achieved, the following suggestions are made for consideration:

A. A project or activity folder for each semester.

B. A sheet or card detailing work of a constructive or repair nature performed by the pupil outside of school hours.

C. Safety folder of notes, clippings, and pictures of industrial safety devices, programs, accidents, etc.

D. Assignments from textbooks for regular classwork relating to basic skills and technical information.

E. Handwork projects.

F. Clubwork or home projects.

G. Industrial or vocational readings and reports.

Principles of Teaching

All teachers must keep in mind the importance of the five senses in learning. Learning takes place within an individual when a new insight is achieved through communication between the teacher and the student.

Since teaching makes changes in learners, learning must involve the use of the mind. The teacher must, therefore, understand how the mind masters a new skill and how it deals with new information. Dr. C. A. Prosser characterized the mind as a mental switchboard that wires itself through experiences of thinking and doing. Experiences establish bonds, he found, which become strengthened through habit. The experience consists of stimuli from the environment and reactions to them. The instructor's job, then, becomes to establish desirable connections in the student's mind. Accepted laws of learning can be applied by the teacher to do this job well.

Professor Glenn Smith set down three laws of learning:

The first law is that the minds of students must be in a state of readiness to learn the things to be taught. There must be attention to, and interest in, the thing to be learned; otherwise much time of both the instructor and student is wasted.

The second law is that other things being equal, connections are strenghtened by use and weakened by disuse. This means that in setting up a training outline and in providing projects, exercises, and production work we must also be repetitive in skills sufficient to insure dependability. This may be another way of saying that one learns by doing, but the doing must first be guided by the instructor in the presentation step of the lesson through carefully planned demonstrations and the use of other appropriate tools of instruction.

The third law is that a state of satisfaction increases the effect of the lesson. This law of learning means that the good instructor sees to it that the student experiences satisfaction from desirable reactions or performances and an absence of satisfaction from undesirable performances. (8)

Project and Activities—Choice and Design

Projects and activities are the material objects around which industrial education activities are centered. They serve as a vehicle for teaching the student the skills and knowledge outlined in the course of study. As stated before, projects provide the means of learning by doing and furnish the educative experiences through which desired learning takes place.

Choosing the Project

1. Requirements of project choice:
    a. Contributes to achieving the objectives of the course, correlates student's learning with the course of study.
    b. Has interest for the student.
    c. Is within the student's ability.
    d. Presents a challenge.
    e. Is well designed.
    f. Can be completed within a reasonable time.
    g. Is economical.
    h. Presents, to the learner, some new industrial or craft process.
    i. Allows students to cooperate and work together on a common problem.

2. Methods of choosing project or activity:
    a. The teacher assigns the project.
        (1) The teacher makes certain by this method that all students cover the course of study completely, and it makes timing of demonstrations easier.
        (2) Assignment does not lend itself well to student planning since all plan sheets would be similar.
        (3) It does not meet individual needs or make provision for individual differences.
        (4) It is often difficult to sell a set of projects to the students.
    b. Choice from a group of projects.
        (1) Projects in the group must cover the same units of instruction and be of about equal difficulty.
        (2) Students can be required to make their own plan from a blueprint or a model of the project.
        (3) Student interest can be held more easily if he is allowed to select a project that is not in the group but fits into the group requirements.
        (4) Choosing from several projects takes more time.
        (5) Getting out materials is more of a problem with multiple choice than with the assigned method.
    c. Free choice of project
        (1) It is difficult to correlate the projects with units in the course of study.
        (2) It is easier to maintain student interest.
        (3) It works best at the junior high level.
        (4) It is an excellent chance to have the student make project plans.
        (5) Students will need direction and should be careful not to select from whim and then lose interest in finishing the project.
        (6) Instructors must see that students do not choose projects too difficult for their ability.
3. Sources of project design:
    a. Original design
        (1) This allows student self-expression.
        (2) Rarely does a student have any ability to create pleasing design, thus shop projects are apt to be of poor design and not too useful.
        (3) Requires much of a teacher's time to help students.
    b. Copying or adapting articles in existence either in school, at home, or in furniture stores.
        (1) A student makes his plan by copying from an article.
        (2) He can see ahead of time what the project looks like and

make a final choice better than if he had to choose from a blueprint.

(3)   A good design can be maintained in the project.

c.   Selecting from working drawings, blueprints, and pictorial drawings.

     (1)   They are obtained from design books, crafts magazines, other periodicals, furniture catalogs, and from complete plans furnished by manufacturers.

     (2)   The student makes his plans from the working drawing or blueprint.

     (3)   Design of shop projects should be good by using this source intelligently.

     (4)   Is easy for the instructor to check the student's plans.

     (5)   It gives the students practice in reading, visualizing, and using working drawings and plans.

     (6)   A wide range of designs is provided by this method.

     (7)   By using furniture catalogs to choose design, a professional design is facilitated.

Criteria for Projects

Criteria for selecting projects:

1.   Must be timely.
2.   Appeal to the interest of the student.
3.   Be challenging.
4.   Provide for student participation in planning and in execution.
5.   Embody good design, good construction, and good finish.
6.   Involve some of the operation and information units to be taught.
7.   Lead to other interests.
8.   Within the range of available tools and equipment and individual's price range.
9.   Lead to greater efficiency through the mastery of new skills and information.
10.   Be useful.
11.   Contribute to the objectives of the course of study.
12.   Afford practice.
13.   Embrace available material and time.
14.   Introduce new instructional materials.
15.   Incorporate new operations. (1)

Design

It is recommended that the simple fundamental principles of design be taught as a basis for the projects developed by the individual students since design is implicit in all phases of work.

   I.   Qualities of a good industrial project:
       A.   Must be of service to the community or individual.
       B.   Must be made of durable material.
       C.   Should possess beauty of proportion, outline, and color.
  II.   Steps in designing.
       A.   Structural design.
           1.   Questions of: How high or how long in relation to width.
           2.   Influenced by: Knowledge of tools and materials, use of object.
           3.   Proportion: An object should have a ratio of 1 to 3, 3 to 4, 3 to 5, 7 to 10, etc.
       B.   Outline design.
           1.   Enrichment of structural outline (Example: carving parts, adding lines, hammering, etc.)
           2.   Division.
               a.   If an object is divided in two horizontal divisions, there should be dominance — in either the upper or lower section.
               b.   If an object is divided into three horizontal divisions, the dominance should be placed in the center with varying widths in the upper and lower thirds.
               c.   If an object is divided into two vertical sections, the division should be equal in area and similar in form.
               d.   If an object is divided into three vertical divisions, center should be larger, with the remaining divisions of equal size.
           3.   Enrichment.
               a.   Should be subordinated to and supported by the structure.
               b.   Should add grace, lightness, unity, and variety to the design.
               c.   Curves are:
                   (1)   Necessary for the effect of lightness.
                   (2)   Natural support of weight.
                   (3)   For force.
                   (4)   For variety.
       C.   Surface design.
           1.   Must be a need.
           2.   Related to the structural contours.
           3.   Appropriate to the material.
           4.   Show unity.
           5.   Present a center of interest.
           6.   The dominating section of the subject. (7)

Teacher-pupil planning is one concept of project planning in which the teacher and pupil plan together the procedure for a given job. Individual initiative, creative thinking, and reasoning is required by the pupil in such a planning activity. The teacher should set the stage so the pupil will enter into his work with interest and enthusiasm. Complete participation on the part of the pupil will not be evidenced if the project and planning is dictated. The ability to think through the design and construction of a project, estimate its cost, and prepare a plan whereby the project can be made is a definite asset. Such experience contains immediate educational values as well as useful knowledge for future needs. It is problem-solving similar to those in life situations.

Teacher-pupil planning in large classes at the beginning of the course presents many problems. An effort should be made in group planning at this initial stage with individual planning of suggested projects to follow. Later independent planning of projects might follow, depending upon the pupil.

Vocational Guidance

A vocational guidance program is essential if young people are to find occupational fields for which they have ability and qualifications. Placement of graduates of the vocational program and follow-up studies of their progress is another responsibility of the school.

The classroom teacher may be able to offer specialized counseling to young boys in junior high school and to interpret industry to students, parents, counselors, and administration. He has the responsibility of helping students discover abilities by providing a wide range of activities and tools, materials, and processes. Further development is achieved in elective courses in the secondary school. As students advance in the high school vocational programs, they should develop definite career interests. The teacher can then provide information about specific opportunities, apprenticeship programs, junior colleges, and the qualifications needed for managerial and entrepreneurial careers. (6)

Safety in the School Shop

The general safety aims should be:
1.   To develop a safety consciousness in teachers and students.
2.   To create a desire to work and act in such a way so that accidents will be reduced both in and out of school.
3.   To develop safe working conditions in the home, in public, and on the job.
4.   To reduce accidents in the shop. (9)

School safety instruction should include shop dress, regulation of shop routine, and proper use of machines, tools, and other equipment. Demonstrations for the use of equipment can be individual or group and knowledge of safe practices may be tested by examination or use under careful supervision. The teacher should always set a good example for his students and should know procedures to take in case of an accident. (9)

The shop should be safe with respect to lighting, ventilation, sanitation, travel, storage space, and conditions of building and mechanical equipment. The following precautions should be taken:

A.   Conditions of shop equipment:

1.   Shops, auxiliary spaces, school and personal equipment should meet the state building codes and standards. New or repaired machines should not be used until properly guarded. When machines are out of order or when repairs are to be made, the current should be shut off by placing the switch box lever in the off position, disconnecting the power in the central control panel, or by pulling the connecting plug. Disconnecting the electrical power with the push button or switch normally used to operate the machine is not sufficient.

2.   Hand tools and equipment should be in good condition at all times; that is, they should be well sharpened, with handles properly secured. Mushroomed tools should not be used.

3.   Flammable materials should be stored in fireproof cabinets and used in accordance with local and state codes.

4.   Laboratories, shops, and classrooms should be clean and in order. No stock, machine parts, supplies, or refuse should be on the floor. Tools and supply rooms should be in order.

5.   Instructor must never be out of the shop while machines are running or can be run.

6.   Machines must be properly and fully guarded at all times.

7.   Operator zones should be established around each machine. This can be done by painting a line on the floor; only the student operating the machine should be allowed inside the zone.

8.   Machine cutters and saws should be kept sharp at all times. Dull cutters are dangerous.

9.   No major electrical or plumbing repairs or alterations should be made by the teacher.

10.   Safety cans should be provided for disposal of oily or paint cloths.

11.   Properly designed spray booths should be provided in shops where finishes are to be sprayed.

12.   Floor areas where machine operator stands should be covered with nonskid material.

13.   Every shop should have an adequate first aid kit.

14. Safety inspection should be made of the shop periodically. Use a shop safety inspection sheet as a guide, such as the National Standard School Shop Inspection Check List.

B. Instruction and guidance in safety:
1. Students below the 9th grade and also immature 9th graders should not be allowed to use the band saw, the circular saw, the jointer, or the shaper.
2. Insist on the strictest discipline and obedience from every pupil who is allowed to operate machines. Deny the privilege of operating a machine to a student whose conduct and character make him unsuitable for safe machine operation.
3. The instructor should consciously and effectively make safety instruction the outstanding feature of every shop lesson or demonstration.
4. Students should never be allowed to run machines while wearing loose or floppy clothes. A properly fitting shop apron is recommended with sleeves rolled up. Neckties should be removed and long hair properly covered.
5. Operators must always shut off the power and wait until the machine comes to a complete stop before inspecting work, changing machine setup, cleaning machine, or oiling it.
6. Only one student at a time should be allowed to run a machine. Persons must not gather around and talk to an operator.
7. A student should not be allowed to operate any machine unless he has had definite instruction as an operator and can demonstrate his ability before the instructor. A safety test on any machine can be given the student with permission to use the machine based on successfully passing the test.
8. Protect the hands with gloves when handling large sheets of metal.
9. Visual aids can be used to teach safety, both for hand and power tools.
10. A student who is not feeling well should not be allowed to run a machine.
11. Use goggles in operations hazardous to the eyes; they are required at all times in many states.
12. Detailed safety instruction should be developed for all equipment.

C. Teacher's responsibilities in the event of an accident:
1. An accident is an injury that requires a doctor's care or absence from school for ½ day or more. It should be reported immediately.
2. Render first aid promptly.
3. Normally the school district is in no way liable for any expenses

incurred in treating an injured student. All expenses for treatment of the injured student must be paid by the parents.

4. The shop teacher can be sued personally for damages resulting from injuries incurred in a school shop, if he is found negligent. The instructor, therefore, should be zealous in discharging his responsibility for shop safety by being sure that his equipment is in safe condition at all times, properly guarded, and that reasonable discipline and adequate safety instruction is maintained at all times.

References

1. *A Guide to Improvement of Industrial Arts in Oklahoma Schools.* Oklahoma City, Okla.: State Department of Education, 1965.

2. *A Guide to Teaching Industrial Arts,* Minneapolis: Minneapolis Public Schools.

3. *Aims, Purposes, and Procedures of Education in the Public Schools of Utah,* Salt Lake City, Utah: State Department of Instruction, May, 1946, and June, 1957.

4. Bakamis, William A., *The Supervision of Industrial Arts.* Milwaukee: Bruce Publishing Company, 1954.

5. Erickson, Emanuel E., *Teaching the Industrial Arts.* Peoria, Ill.: Chas. A. Bennett Co., Inc., 1956.

6. *Guide for Industrial Arts Education in California.* Sacramento, Calif.: State Department of Education.

7. *Industrial Arts and Vocational Education.* Tulsa, Okla: Tulsa Public Schools.

8. Smith, Glenn, Lectures on Trade and Industrial Education, Oklahoma State University.

9. *What do You Know About Your Tulsa Schools?* Tulsa, Okla.: Tulsa Public Schools, 1960-1961.

Chapter 6

Shop Management

A student personnel organization helps reduce the amount of personal attention that the instructor must give to routine details, thus allowing him to devote more time and energy to the teaching part of the job. It contributes directly to educational values in industrial education subjects because it provides opportunities for developing the meaning of individual and group effort; opportunities for directing, supervising, and aiding in the activities of others; means of working cooperatively or harmoniously for the common good; and familiarizes students with an organizational system of the type commonly used in industrial plant management. Assuming responsibility tends to develop character and leadership. Also, students learn to respect authority and to understand the problems that confront the employer and employee in life situations. It provides opportunity for students to observe qualities of one another, such as ambition, dependability, honesty, and obedience. Furthermore, in such realistic situations, students can demonstrate cooperation, tolerance, perseverence, purposefulness, self-control and self-direction.

The experiences gained by students as they participate in a pupil-personnel organization are at least as educative as anything provided for in the strictly constructive activities of the shop.

Personnel Organization

The personnel organization is an important factor in meeting the objectives of industrial arts. Its three basic functions are: (1) to train for leadership, followership, cooperation; (2) to explore industry; and (3) to relieve the instructor of certain routine duties. The plan may be organized by the instructor or developed from within the group. The success of the personnel system depends on its being accepted by students and on complete cooperation between officers and the instructor.

A personnel organization plan should fit the conditions in which it is employed. An important objective of any such plan is to give students some idea of job relationships in industry, so the type chosen should bear some relationship to the industry represented by the shop organization. For example, the personnel plan for the general metal shop should be typical of plans commonly found in the metal industries.

Students are quick to recognize those positions in a shop organization which can be assumed by members of the class and should develop their plan from within the group. A totally new organization does not need to be developed each semester, but each class should be given the opportunity to review and revise the system used by previous classes. There should be a definite assumption of responsibility by each class officer. It is wasted effort to designate a student as superintendent and then not give him any responsibility. Authority should be exercised by each officer in keeping with the responsibilities designated to him by the committee of class members.

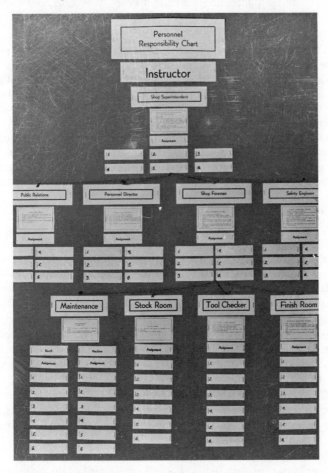

Fig. 6-1. Typical Personnel Chart

The personnel plan should be more than a mere cleanup schedule. It should at least have three major objectives:

1. To train students in leadership and followship. This means that all students must be given an opportunity to exert leadership and to act as cooperative followers. Many students need to be pushed into being officers by the instructor.

2. To provide an exploratory situation which to some extent parallels the personnel system of industry. This cannot be accomplished if the school organization is concerned only with keeping the laboratory in order.

3. To relieve the instructor from certain routine tasks such as giving out supplies, keeping certain types of records, and attending to ventilation, so that he is able to give more time to demonstrations and other types of instruction. (2)

To accomplish these objectives, students must feel that the plan has a purpose and that they are important to its proper functioning. Officers should be changed when they have received the ultimate educational possibilities of a given position. Keeping a student in an office after he has mastered all the details connected with its operation, simply because he is effective, tends to discourage other students who may need the experience.

Officers may be given an opportunity to meet and discuss problems of the personnel organization during class hours with the instructor to give advice and suggest improvement. Frequent meetings of this type are morale builders. Weaknesses can be noticed early and proper measures can be taken in time.

Briefly, the officers of the class should be charged with the following general responsibilities: (See Fig. 6-1.)

Shop Superintendent – oversees the entire personnel system, checks cleanup, dismisses class, receives ideas and suggestions from class members, keeps a list of needed materials and supplies, keeps a Responsibility Chart up-to-date, and confers with the instructor on matters pertaining to the welfare of the class.

Safety Engineer – checks all machine guards, sees that all students perform their work according to prescribed safety regulations, sees that all health and safety precautions are observed, keeps a constant check on first aid supplies, reports an injury immediately, and reports any safety suggestions or hazards to the instructor.

Shop Foreman – oversees all cleanup personnel, makes substitutions for absent cleanup members, improvises and receives ideas for improving cleanup procedure, checks all cleanup, and reports to the superintendent when it is satisfactorily completed.

Personnel Director – checks roll, keeps the planning center in good order, checks over project files at the end of the period, checks library books and magazines out to the class, and keeps a supply of plan sheets and job sheets.

Public Relations Director — responsible for display cases within the shop and show cases out of the shop area, writes any articles for the school paper, and confers with the instructor on items of school and community relations.

Tool Clerk — checks all tools at the end of the period and reports any missing, keeps track of all Tool-Out Sheets, inspects all tools and keeps them in working order, and keeps tool boards and tool cabinets in good order.

Finishing Manager — takes care of finishing supplies; keeps a constant check on all paint, varnish, and shellac; keeps finishing cabinet and bench in neat and proper order; and reports any needed finishing supplies to the superintendent.

Stock-Room Director — issues materials and supplies as requested by the instructor and keeps supplies in order.

Maintenance Director — instructs students in cleanup routine, sees that each student performs his duties as assigned, and reports to shop foreman at the end of the period.

Meeting a New Class

It is of great advantage to a teacher in beginning a school year to gain control of the class. Every teacher has a different technique, but certain basic principles have proven valuable to all teachers. The following principles may be varied according to grade level and type of shop organization:

1. The instructor should dress neatly; a shop coat is recommended.
2. He should write his name on the board and inform students of its correct pronunciation. A name card in the lapel may be used. An instructor can get better acquainted with the students if he describes his educational background briefly.
3. Work stations may be assigned, although this might be postponed until enrollment is stabilized.
4. A tour of the shop is worthwhile, especially in cases where there are areas for different types of work, special room for lumber, finishing room, storage lockers, washup basins, drinking fountains, etc.
5. A preview of the year's course may be given briefly, stressing the project or activity side of the subject. Show samples of things to be made. Discuss the course and what purposes are to be achieved by both the teacher and the students. Explain the entire field of industrial arts and vocational education.
6. Explain student personnel organization and shop housekeeping. (2)

Supplies and Equipment

Instructors are often obligated to collect sufficient funds at the beginning of the school year to assure that the resale supplies used will be paid for when the project is completed. The instructor should not collect money in excess of an estimate of student needs. The following are suggested procedures for handling finances:

1. Receipts should be issued to each student for the amount he puts on deposit or pays directly toward purchase of materials he will use or has used.
2. Use one receipt book for collection of resale supply money only.
3. Deposit all resale money collected in the school treasurer's office. A receipt is issued by the treasurer's office for each deposit of resale money.
4. Deposits of resale money should be made as often as possible.
5. Deposits may be made directly in the treasurer's office or by personal check through the school mail.
6. On specified dates, report to the central departmental office all resale collections on blanks provided. Final report should be made at final checkout at the close of school.
7. All resale receipts, used or unused, are to be turned in to the department office with final checkout at the close of the school year.
8. Any money deposited by students and not entirely used must be refunded.
   a. Enough undeposited resale money should be kept on hand for such purposes.
   b. Each student should sign a receipt in triplicate.
   c. A report should be made to the department when such refunds are made. (2)

Department Budget

Five sources furnish finances for supplies and equipment:

Resale Fund is provided by the money the student pays for the materials used in projects.

Board Fund is provided by the school district. It is used for miscellaneous instructional supplies.

Maintenance and Repair Fund is provided by the school district for purchase of machine and tool parts and maintenance labor needed to put broken equipment into good operational condition. The shop teacher can do minor repairs but more extensive labor is done by the maintenance department.

Replacement Fund is provided by the school district for purchases of replacement equipment. This includes both hand tools and power equipment. Requisitions for new and used tools and machinery to replace broken and worn out equipment are to be made from this fund.

New Equipment Fund is set up by the school district for additional equipment. For example, the shop does not have a spotwelder and one is needed. It would be requisitioned from the new equipment fund. (2)

Recommendations for Economy

The following suggestions will assist in meeting needs with economy:

1. Plan work carefully for the year and order only materials necessary to carry out the program.
2. Increase pupil planning and related work in regard to projects. Require a bill of materials with cost calculated. The student should list operations to be performed, and sketch items to be made and topics to be studied.
3. Calculate prices carefully. Charges for materials should be reviewed at least annually, with approximately 20% to 25% added for waste. Study the per capita cost as listed in the yearly report. Compare similar shops as listed in the yearly report. Talk with others to see how they manage resale items and supplies by the board.
4. Model projects should be available for use and display as new areas are introduced.
5. Use scrap pieces for small projects.
6. Saw stock for beginning projects slightly oversize to allow for working to size. This reduces waste considerably.
7. Increase demands for workmanship.
8. Seasonal projects such as kites, boats, and production items that will add to the program. Know the students and the community and adapt projects to their particular needs.
9. Home repairs offer many possibilities. Encourage pupils to bring broken toys, chairs, etc. to school to be repaired by them as a shop project. Nothing will sell industrial arts to the home better than this.
10. Salvaged materials can be utilized, depending upon the area of work being offered.
11. Supplies furnished by the board constitute a large part of shop costs. Sandpaper, emery cloth, files, small drills, etc. should be stored in such a manner as to conserve supply as well as for ease in issuing. The supply room should be in order at all times.
12. Routine attention to lubrication of all power equipment will cut

down maintenance and replacement costs. In the event of
breakage of tools due to deliberate misuse, the pupil should pay
the damages (for his character's sake if not for economic
reasons).

13.   An inventory of equipment and supplies should be made from
time to time in addition to a daily check of the tool and supply
cabinet. Compare tool loss with others in the annual report. Plan
to use the slow moving stock or let the office know what might
be exchanged with some other shop instructor. (1)

Class Administration

The importance of safety measures must be kept in mind during the
entire year. Explicit instructions, proper safety devices, remaining present
while equipment is used – all will reduce the possibilities of accidents. If
accidents do occur, a complete written report must be submitted to the
principal. (1)

Inventory should be checked at the beginning of the year. The instructor should check items charged with those received. Requisitions should
be made for funds to buy supplies. No direct funds should be used. Reports
should be made at the end of the year indicating loss of tools and damages to
equipment. (1)

A suitable course of study should be a part of every teacher's plans for
the year. It serves as a guide for the teacher's daily preparation. (1)

A variety of instructional methods should be employed in the industrial education program. Of course, the instructor must demonstrate various
operations and processes correctly and clearly. He must relate lesson topics so
that students may build on past skills and knowledge, and he should make use
of a variety of visual aids. He must also help students plan projects according
to their abilities and interests.

Closing Facilities

After inventory has been taken and proper forms filled out, equipment
should be oiled and stored for the summer months. Saws, blades, and stones
should be removed from power machines and all machines dismantled where
appropriate. A list of repair work should be made for the summer maintenance crew.

References

1. *Industrial Arts Education – Organization and Administration.* Albany, New York: State Department of Education, University of New York, 1960.
2. *Handbook for Instructors and Vocational Education.* Tulsa, Okla.: Tulsa Public Schools, Bulletin 6.

Chapter 7

Staff Improvement

The industrial education department staff is determined by the enrollment of the school and the number of industrial education facilities provided. The addition of facilities would be determined by the growth of the enrollment and the changes in the community's educational needs.

An industrial education teacher should be provided for each shop or drafting room. In some of the larger schools, it is advisable to have an additional teacher on the staff for a larger-than-anticipated enrollment in the program. In school districts providing a planning period or preparation period for the teacher, classes of the additional teacher could be scheduled in the shops or drafting rooms of teachers during their planning or preparation period.

Prospective Staff Members

The election of staff members is the responsibility of the school board with the superintendent selecting and nominating the candidates. However, he should seek the recommendation of the supervisor or department chairman because such persons know the conditions under which the new teacher will work and are more acquainted with the technical qualifications required for each particular assignment.

The person selecting prospective teachers should know the sources of supply. Placing industrial education teachers from different colleges in a given school provides a greater variety of training experience and the industrial education program will profit. The elements which compose the total qualifications of a desirable industrial education teacher are: educational background, professional training, personality, technical knowledge, mechanical skill, professional attitude, and both teaching and industrial experience. Basing the selection of teachers solely on grades is a common error, for the ability to teach and inspire may not be reflected by academic success. Letter and oral recommendations are also very important. References should be required from more than one person in a position to evaluate the character of the applicant.

Teacher Selection

The classroom teacher is an educator as he attempts to transmit the cultural heritage, an administrator or manager as he directs and controls the classes, and a statesman when he acts as a citizen to further his personal philosophy. There is no formula for selecting a teacher that will evaluate and reconcile all these categories. The junior high teacher must have a great deal of competence, more breadth, and understand adolescents. The senior high school teacher must specialize in one area but have a substantial knowledge of all areas. (7)

Responsibilities of Industrial Education Staff

A. The industrial education instructor as a teacher should:
1. Have a sound philosophy of education.
2. Have a basic philosophy of industrial education.
3. Be able to establish and maintain a good shop organization.
4. Promote interest on the part of the student.
5. Have the ability to develop instructional materials.
6. Be technically skilled.
7. Understand and be able to apply analysis techniques.
8. Have character and a good personality.
9. Understand human behavior.
10. Be able to evaluate student progress.
11. Have a professional attitude.
12. Practice guidance.
13. Understand and be able to use the proper methods of teaching.
14. Display leadership.
15. Be able to maintain good discipline.
16. Experiment with new ideas.
17. Recognize and handle individual differences.
18. Practice and exemplify good health.
19. Develop and carry on good teacher-pupil relationships.
20. Promote good public relations.
21. Maintain high student morale.
22. Be able to express himself effectively.
23. Be able to accept responsibility.
24. Make wise use of leisure time.
25. Be able to adjust to varying situations.
26. Be able to evaluate himself and make adjustments where needed.
B. The industrial education instructor as a member of the staff must:
1. Become acquainted with other staff members.
2. Be cooperative.

3.   Be a participating member of the group.
4.   Be professional.
5.   Be ethical.
6.   Exercise good leadership.
7.   Respect authority.
8.   Have an understanding of the total school program and state laws and regulations.
9.   Be open minded.
10. Show personal interest.
11. Develop self-reliance.
12. Promote guidance and counseling programs.
13. Possess good personal qualities.

C.   The industrial education instructor as a member of the community must:
1.   Set an example.
2.   Take part in community activities.
3.   Present a good personal appearance.
4.   Exercise good judgment in community issues and problems.
5.   Assist school public relations.
6.   Establish personal integrity.
7.   Help clarify school policies and programs.
8.   Know community history and resources.
9.   Promote adult classes.
10. Establish industrial identity.
11. Promote leisure-time activities.
12. Understand the world community.

Professional Organizations

It is important that a teacher belong to one or more professional organizations so that he may gain a feeling of belonging and may become aware of changes in his field.

Teacher-Profession Relationships

A professional person:
1.   Keeps informed about best practices in his field.
2.   Belongs willingly to his professional organization — local, state, and national.
3.   Contributes his time and talents to the organization.
4.   Accepts responsibility in the professional organization.
5.   Helps to make possible a democratic approach to school administrative authorities through teacher organization channels.

6. Speaks proudly of the importance of the service of education to society.
7. Maintains efficiency by reading, studying, and traveling.
8. Dignifies his profession.
9. Becomes recognized professionally.

Purposes of AIAA and AVA

Professional organizations at the national level are the American Industrial Arts Association and the American Vocational Association.

The American Industrial Arts Association is the only national or international professional organization concerned primarily with the promotion and improvement of industrial arts as general education. Objectives of AIAA:

1. To make industrial arts more fully available to the boys and girls in the schools.
2. To serve the interests of the teachers and supervisors of industrial arts.
3. To give industrial arts a voice and a participating role in the national and international level.
4. To provide the opportunity for high school and college teachers and supervisors to work together on common problems affecting industrial arts.
5. To provide services which will benefit individual members and their schools.

The function of the AVA as *AVA Bulletin* defines it is:

To present a united front on the national level for all phases of vocational and industrial arts education. It is recognized, however, that each field has its own needs and problems, and so the association is divided into several divisions, as follows: Agricultural Education, Business and Office Education, Distributive Education, Home Economics Education, Industrial Arts Education, Trade and Industrial Education, and New and Related. (9)

The Association's program and policies are determined by its membership through its elected Executive Committee. The officers are selected by the total membership through mail ballot.

Personal Professional Growth

Professional growth is influenced by the attitude of an individual teacher toward self-improvement and toward a contribution to the overall status of the profession. Such an attitude is reflected in the concern of the individual for group growth, morale, and discipline; and the group's concern for individual growth, morale, and discipline. (6)

Professional growth is motivated by such internal factors as job satisfaction, better status, acceptance by a group, teaching effectiveness, salary increases, and promotions. External influences are provided by others, especially members of the professional group. (6)

Inservice activities which contribute to job improvement result in professional growth. Examples are participation in professional organizations, conference and convention attendance, advanced study, work in school and community affairs, and contributions to professional publications. (6)

Evaluation of Teachers

Erickson formulated seventeen points to consider in evaluating teachers:
1. Is enough time being spent on the work for which the salary is received?
2. Is the working time correctly apportioned among the various teaching activities?
3. Is the work being carried out according to a previously prepared plan?
4. Is the teacher skilled in mechanical arts?
5. Is the teacher's first interest in industrial arts?
6. What results are being accomplished?
7. In what condition is the equipment?
8. Are new ideas invited and put into practice?
9. Is the teacher becoming acquainted with new means for evaluating student work?
10. Is the shop library being used?
11. Is related and technical information being applied?
12. Are personal contacts being made?
13. In what condition are shop records?
14. Is the teacher's health being considered?
15. What is the relationship with fellow workers?
16. What is the relationship with the administration?
17. What professional growth is being experienced? (5)

Evaluation As a Means of Inservice Growth

A. Why should staff be evaluated?
1. Individuals need to know their strengths and weaknesses in order to have a better basis for personal improvement.
2. Schools and the public need to know how effectively assigned functions are being carried out.

B. Who should evaluate?
1. Formal evaluations must follow organizational lines of authority and responsibility.
2. Some provision should be made for evaluation by peers and persons served.
3. Informal evaluation is constant by all persons contacted. Persons alert to responses by individuals secure constant evidences of acceptance or rejection, approval or disapproval.
C. Basis for evaluation:
1. Evidences of students' growth and achievement.
2. Attitudes and participation in professional educational organizations.
3. Understandings of child development, the nature of society, and national and world affairs.
4. Evidence of meeting personal needs of school personnel.
   a. Increased emotional stability
   b. Sense of security
   c. Sense of belonging
5. Growth in knowledge and skills: instructional, managerial, professional.
D. What should be done with evaluation:
1. Used by individuals to see themselves as others see them.
2. Used by administrators for retention and promotion.

Measurement and Evaluation

Evaluation is determining the value; thus, educational evaluation is judging the value of teaching or learning. Measurement is counting or expressing something numerically, but implicit in its use is the assumption that appropriate and dependable quantifiable information is available. One reason for taking a measurement is to get data for evaluation. Good measurement contributes to intelligent evaluation.

Teachers generally accept the use of a definite, objective rating sheet prepared with the cooperation of the teaching staff and with participation by at least two persons in four definite ratings of the teacher under consideration. Ratings of this type are often viewed as a privilege, not an imposition. The teacher on probation should expect it as a basis for improvement, and the teacher desiring promotion should request it also.

Self-Appraisal Questions

General Questions

1. Do you believe that you have a desirable influence on students in the development of character?

2. Do you teach students or shop work?
3. Do you realize that a nervous disposition of the teacher reacts on the students to make them "jittery?"
4. Is your voice at normal pitch at all times?
5. Do you profit by criticism or resent it?
6. Do you spend some time after school hours on professional improvement making your employment a profession?
7. Do you subscribe to a professional magazine?
8. Do you belong to and take part in professional organizations?
9. Do you seat students with impaired hearing or impaired vision in the front row?
10. Does your principal trust you with administrative responsibilities within the school?
11. Do you take part in community activities?

Class Management

1. Do you receive the respect of the students?
2. Are you firm but kind and sympathetic?
3. Are students permitted to scuffle in class?
4. Do students talk in normal tones, or do some occasionally yell out?
5. When you talk to the class do some occasionally have to face the light from the window?
6. If you notice several students simultaneously making identical errors in manipulation, do you call the class to attention and correct them all in a group demonstration?
7. Do you stop occasionally and look over the classroom to be sure that all are working?
8. When you call the students to attention, does it take longer than 20 seconds after the signal before you can begin?
9. Is your bulletin board display changed regularly and does it contain interest-catching materials?
10. When you notice a waning of interest in a student, do you question him about his favorite subject, extracurricular activities, and out-of-school interests so that you may suggest a project associated with his interest?

Instructional Content

1. Do you have a convenient written plan for each course so that in your absence a substitute may know where you begin the day's work?
2. Do you visualize your subject by explaining the relation of the subject content to life and its occupations?

3. Have you a good library and planning center? Is it used, and for what purpose?
4. What new units have you recently added to the instructional content?
5. Which units have you dropped?
6. Have you compared your teaching with that of other teachers?
7. Do you have lesson plans?

Demonstrations

1. Do your demonstrations require over 15 minutes?
2. Do you select students to give demonstrations?
3. Is each demonstration previously prepared for?
4. Do you have a demonstration repeated by a student to those who have been absent?

Projects

1. Are projects selected upon the level of the student's abilities?
2. Do you first consider the interest of the students?
3. Are projects well designed?
4. Are you and the students proud of each project when it is completed?

Exercises

Have you reduced your exercises to a minimum using only those in which drill is necessary before students attempt actual performance on valuable stock?

Instruction Sheets

1. Are your assignments definite, concise, and well written?
2. Do students plan their procedures on a sufficient number of jobs so that you are assured they can think for themselves?
3. Is the reading level of all instruction sheets within the ability of the average reader in your classes?

Discipline

1. Do you send more than one or two students each year to the principal's office to be disciplined?
2. Are you sure the students like you?
3. Can you jest with them and yet control the class?
4. Is your discipline authoritarian or is it aimed toward student self-discipline?

Testing

1. Are objective tests given periodically?
2. Do you use a progress chart and keep it up-to-date?
3. What proportion of the class time do you allocate for manipulative work in contrast to class study and recitation?
4. Is your grading flexible enough that you recognize individual capacities and results?
5. Do you properly weigh the marks in the same proportion?
6. Do you employ a rating scale for marking manipulative performance?

Housekeeping

1. Have you visited modern industrial plants to notice that unusual attention is now given to the appearance and orderliness of the plant?
2. Do you use student assistance in keeping an orderly shop?
3. Do you stack unfinished projects or boxes on top of cabinets?
4. Are there pieces of short stock standing in corners to prevent proper sweeping of the floor?
5. How thick is the accumulation on your desk top?
6. Do you insist on supplies and scrap pieces being kept off the floor or out of the aisles as a safety measure?
7. Are you ashamed to have anyone look into the drawers of your desk or supply cabinets?

Equipment and Supplies

1. Does each class clean off all equipment and put all tools and supplies away, leaving the shop in a good and orderly condition?
2. Do you have a place for supplies and keep them there?
3. Do you have a definite work station for each student?
4. Does each student have separate duties for keeping the shop orderly and caring for supplies, tools, equipment, and other instructional materials?
5. Are all machines in good working order?
6. Are individual benches numbered and the tools for each station likewise numbered?
7. Do you insist on keeping the bench tops free from heavy scratches, hammer marks, paints, drill bit holes, knife cuts, and nails?
8. Are safety zones painted on the floor about dangerous machines and hand tools?
9. Have you given instructional materials on safety?
10. Do you know your liability in case of an injury to a student? (8)

Program Planning

The U.S. Office of Education supplies the leadership necessary for program planning in vocational education. Nationally, appraisals of existing programs are made while stimulating states to do constructive program planning. The appraisal includes a survey of the value of the program in preparing a labor force, the progress that is being made in revising old plans and in preparing new ones in the light of new developments in science and technology, and consideration is given to modification of programs conducted under various national vocational education acts. With careful evaluation and planning, available vocational services can be effectively utilized by all students.

I. Why planning is important:
    A. Planning insures that the situation has been examined, that needs and resources have been analyzed, and that certain problems will be remedied.
    B. Planning insures an orderly sequence of professional activity.
    C. Planning that is done cooperatively makes coordination easier.
II. Principles governing supervisory planning:
    A. The supervisory program should be the result of cooperative planning.
    B. It should be based on facts concerning the needs of persons and the material setting.
    C. The supervisory program should include provision for its own testing and evaluation.
III. Steps in planning programs:
    A. Evaluate achievement, behavior, and growth of pupils at various stages of development by means of suitable instruments and procedures.
    B. Analyze the teacher-learning situation in relation to pupil growth and learning or failure to grow and learn.
    C. Introduce new procedures or policies which might result from scientific experimentation or philosophic analysis.
    D. Select through group discussion definite problems, difficulties, and needs as objectives of the improvement program.
    E. Evaluate the effectiveness of the program in the light of anticipated objectives, by reputable means of appraisal, to determine what improvement has been achieved.
IV. Common characteristics of an acceptable supervisor plan:
    A. A statement should be made of the situation out of which the problem grew, of the survey techniques used, and the needs and problems revealed.
    B. A set of clear, definite, and achievable objectives should be

made. These should be integrated with long-time objectives of education.

C.   Provide an outline of the possible means to be used in obtaining objectives.

D.   Provide a list of criteria or checks for evaluating the degree of success achieved by the supervisory program.

V.   Some suggested specific objectives:

A.   To develop understanding of the theory and practice of unit organization of teaching materials.

B.   To develop understanding of the theory and practice of creative activity.

C.   To continue work on the construction or reorganization of curriculum material such as course of study for drafting.

D.   To develop a more unified theory of supervision.

E.   To develop cooperatively an analysis sheet for use by teachers, principals, and supervisors in the study of instructional practice.

F.   To improve the teaching of fundamental skills.

G.   To train teachers in the use of diagnostic tests.

VI. Some suggested techniques in supervisory programs:

A.   Planning conferences with individuals and groups, study groups, and workshops.

B.   Extension courses, summer-school work, and leave of absence for study or travel.

C.   Cooperatively developed bulletins.

D.   Individual or group research.

E.   Committees to examine student interests, attitudes, problems and needs.

F.   Committee work on curriculum improvement.

G.   Visiting teachers in local or outside schools.

Program Evaluation

Assuming a recognition of the need for teacher growth and an acceptance of an inservice program as the best means of attaining that growth, the following attempts to provide a framework to evaluate such a program in terms of organization, aims and purposes, areas, and results.

I.   Organization

Is the organization principal- or administrator-initiated and dominated, or is it an outgrowth of a felt need on the part of the staff and democratically and cooperatively set up through voluntary participation?

II. Aims and Purposes

A.   Is there cooperative effort to the end that teacher growth may be furthered by means of group thinking, discussion, planning, decision, and action?

B. Is there a problem inventory in terms of professional, school, and community needs?

C. Are problems selected to challenge the cooperative efforts of the whole group or selected groups?

III. Areas

A. Does the program more clearly define and effectively implement the function of the teacher in the modern school as it seeks to meet the needs of a greatly changed and rapidly changing society?

B. Does it produce a better understanding of the nature of child growth and development?

C. Does it lead to more effective utilization of modern devices and aids (mechanical, psychological, and social) as a means of facilitating the learning and growth processes of children?

D. Is time given to discovering and utilizing community resources?

IV. Results

A. Has more effective teaching resulted?

B. Is there greatly improved teacher morale?

C. Is there evidence of the discovery and releasing of unique talents and abilities of individual teachers?

Teacher Visitation

Classroom visitation, as already pointed out in Chapter 2, should be based on "coordination and service." Every contact between supervisor and teacher should operate to coordinate the program of instruction and provide service for the individual teacher.

Other purposes of classroom visitation can be outlined:

1. To discover the educational practices of the teacher.
2. To learn the good and promising characteristics of the teacher.
3. To discover the needs of the teacher.
4. To stimulate the teacher to do a better job of teaching.
5. To discover if the teacher is taking suggestions.
6. To develop confidence in the supervisory program.
7. To know if the pupils are receiving the best possible instruction. (1)

Insights and skills needed by the supervisor:

1. Understands the needs of students.
2. Ability to identify the levels of learning.
3. Understands the problems of approach.
4. Is aware of the kinds of experimentation that may be conducted.

5. Has ability to assist but not dominate.
6. Can evaluate effect of teaching methods and materials on learning.
7. Understands the teacher-pupil relationships developing in class.
8. Is familiar with all types of instructional materials.
9. Can select and evaluate pertinent material.
10. Has ability to see the relation of class instruction to the total instructional program.
11. Recognizes new instructional practices.
12. Understands the pattern of learning in class.
13. Understands how to evaluate behavior.
14. Understands the effect of classroom procedure on development of specific objectives.
15. Understands the general principles of learning.
16. Recognizes the use of principles of learning.
17. Sees relations of class procedure to educational theory.
18. Defines causes of instructional problems.
19. Evaluates the importance of administrative policies as a cause of instructional problems.

Orientation of New Teachers

Some type of orientation is necessary to assist teachers in becoming acquainted with the school system in which they are to teach. The type of orientation provided can either increase or retard the effectiveness of the contribution of the new teacher to the school and the community. All concerned benefit by a well-planned orientation program that explains the school policies and specific obligations.

Organization charts are useful as a part of an orientation program so that teachers can see at a glance the particular relationships that exist. The importance of lesson plans has been stressed as a part of the typical preparatory program. Each school organization, however, will have its own carefully developed curricula. Generally there will be up-to-date·courses of instruction which staff members use in preparing the overall program and daily routine. The importance of daily lesson planning cannot be minimized. Department chairmen or supervisors have the responsibility of assisting new teachers in establishing procedures for this important phase of teaching.

The first demand upon the time of a new teacher can well be for the purpose of becoming acquainted with people with whom he will work and live and with the general conditions that will affect his duties and opportunities. A new teacher should spend time laying foundations for acceptance in the system and in the community as a new citizen and neighbor. A member of the teaching profession joins and contributes his time and efforts to those professional and social organizations where he can do the most good for the most people.

New teachers will safeguard their own interests as well as those of the school by obtaining copies of inventories and listings of supplies. From these inventories, they should proceed to satisfy themselves that all items listed have actually been turned over to them. With the inventories of the past year in the new teacher's hands, he can proceed intelligently to locate the equipment that will be under his care and put it through such servicing as may be required. Attention should be called here to the fact that some school systems have maintenance departments and certain policies are established for repair and maintenance of equipment.

The success or failure of a new teacher may often be attributed directly to his ability or inability to maintain class control. The teaching of subject matter and the formation of acceptable attitudes must never be departed from within the classroom or especially within the framework of general education. New teachers should concern themselves with preventive discipline, leaving the corrective discipline for those better prepared to handle the duty.

Conferences and Workshops

Individual conferences are planned to help individual teachers and are not preceded by a classroom visit. They may be suggested to answer a question raised by a teacher or grow out of problems. Committee conferences in which a teacher presides have definite advantages in developing a democratic system. The supervisor who regards meetings with his school staff as being important has begun to make supervision effective. (2)

Workshops related to problems in the teacher's daily work may be planned, organized, and conducted by teachers; have broadly representative memberships; and be quite informal with greater emphasis on promoting good human relationships. However, they are not a continuous, sustained program of professional activities and often fail to make or carry out provisions for careful follow-up of activities initiated.

The supervisor is interested in promoting the organization and use of workshops as a regular feature of the program of supervision. Among attending members there should be no passive on-lookers.

The *Encyclopedia of Modern Education* describes a workshop as:

an experience-centered study undertaken by a group of mature persons. The group takes as its starting point the interests and needs of its members, and subgroups are formed to insure a profitable interchange of opinion, knowledge, and experience. Consultants, rather than instructors, serve these groups, placing specialized resources at their disposal both in group discussion and the exploration of individual problems and plans. The characteristics of this simple, informal and functional organization are its flexibility and its relevance to the specific tasks which the members wish to undertake more skillfully and with clearer vision after the workshop period. (14)

Means of Improving Instruction

1. Help the instructor to become adjusted to this new situation and show him how to keep records and make reports properly and efficiently.

2. Help the instructor to develop effective methods of selecting suitable students.

3. Help the instructor to plan lessons and show him how planning will make his job easier and more effective through demonstrations and informational lessons.

4. Help to prepare, obtain, and use instructional materials and teaching aids.

5. Help the instructor make assignments and keep records of student progress.

6. Show the instructor how to give related information on the job when needed.

7. Help to improve teaching methods by determining whether a lesson is going over, emphasizing and summarizing points, determining and recording the extent to which trainees have acquired skill and knowledge.

8. Help the instructor to identify individual and group needs:
    a. What information may be given to the class as a whole.
    b. On what basis subgroups may be formed.
    c. When and how to form informal groups in order to minimize this need for individual instruction.
    d. When individual instruction is necessary and how to give it. (Caution against the tendency of new instructors to do the job for the student.)

9. Help instructor improve his class management by:
    a. Appointing student assistants for routine tasks.
    b. Improving his methods of record keeping and reporting.
    c. Improving his methods of checking tools and materials.

10. Check functional values of the instruction, suggest revision of content and method, if necessary, and help the instructor to select and obtain suitable instructional jobs.

11. Help instructor with problems relating to individual students
    a. How to *draw out* the diffident student.
    b. How to subdue the *wise boy*.
    c. How to adjust or eliminate the *misfit*.

12. Get the Advisory Committee to visit the class and make suggestions to the supervisor for the improvement of the functional value of the instruction.

Inservice Study

Inservice programs provide new teachers with a feeling of security in their new environment, can be interesting and varied experiences that stimulate better teaching and often are an avenue through which they can gain recognition and thus feel more worthwhile as individuals.

The idea of inservice projects is to upgrade the work of longtime teachers and to help those new in the system. The inservice period gives teachers time to develop their own experiments and projects which can be used later in classroom teaching, and it is another way in which teachers get caught up on new areas in their profession.

Developing an Inservice Program

Step 1. Organize a faculty group for inservice growth.

Step 2. Determine the functions of a planning body for the inservice programs.

Step 3. Discover the relation of the principal to the planning body.

Step 4. Determine the place of outside consultants in the inservice program.

Step 5. Determine the degree to which participation should be voluntary or required.

Step 6. Settle the question of college credit or local credit for the inservice program.

Step 7. Seek principles of group dynamics essential for a successful inservice growth program.

Step 8. Discover the place of community groups in inservice growth programs.

Step 9. Evaluate the place of the spearhead approach (limited experimentation of a single problem attack) in inservice programs.

Step 10. Determine the relation of summer study work and travel programs to inservice study.

Step 11. Solve the problems created by the new teacher and the contribution he makes to the inservice program.

Step 12. Identify the problems of the school and those of the individual teacher.

Assumptions

1. The effectiveness of any supervisory program is dependent upon a good teacher-supervisor relationship.
2. The effectiveness of communication is largely determined by the existing relationship between supervisor and teacher.
3. Bulletins—a one-way track—will not get the job done.
4. In order to establish this good relationship and provide for effec-

tive communication, it is important that there be appropriate opportunities for individual meetings and large and small group conferences at frequent intervals. Problems:

a.   How may this be accomplished without resorting to a burdensome number of teacher's meetings after school and without asking some number of teachers to come to the office?

b.   What are effective means for initiating a program of democratic action on a city-wide basis?

c.   Should teachers be encouraged and stimulated to read materials in group processes and have reviews and discussions?

d.   What suggestions would you offer to principals and teachers in acquiring better understanding of group participation?

5.   Teachers can be motivated to participate more freely in meetings.

6.   Leadership emerges from the group.

7.   There are times when group leaders should be selected by an advisory committee of which the supervisor is a member.

8.   It is advisable to encourage leaders to make some preparation, particularly in the beginning, until confidence and assurance in group action are acquired.

9.   In planning for group meetings, leaders should make preparations for discussion.

10.   It is important that a group designate a recorder and an evaluator.

11.   It is important that participants in the group be informed by the evaluator as to what role each member is taking in group reaction.

12.   The services rendered by the various departments — guidance, tests and measurements, research, personnel, etc. — can be utilized to provide for more effective supervision.

13.   Plans for special helps for new teachers should be made.

14.   Classroom teachers should participate in the planning and organization of departmental meetings.

15.   Suggestions should be solicited from teachers on methods of making visits profitable to teachers.

16.   The chairmen of subject committees may be appointed by the supervisor or may be chosen by the whole group.

17.   The supervisor needs assistance from the group in assisting in integrating intellectual points of view (verbal statements, high-sounding words, etc.) and actual practice.

18.   Other teachers, as well as the supervisor, can assist a teacher in

modifying behavior (classroom practices) to keep somewhat close to ideas.

19. When a project is well under way, it may be used for study and experimentation.
20. Study groups can be too divorced from reality.
21. Need and desire are essential to growth and change.
22. Teaching may become so routine and humdrum that the teacher who ought to feel the most need to improve may become the most complacent and satisfied with the way in which teaching is done and the techniques used.

Staff Morale

Kimball Wiles listed 29 suggestions for improving conditions of staff morale.

1. Take the lead in working for good salaries and working conditions for the staff.
2. Work to secure attractive classrooms and school grounds.
3. Keep the staff informed of actions that are being taken in their behalf.
4. Provide tastefully-decorated, comfortable teacher's rooms.
5. Try to keep all teachers well supplied with up-to-date materials.
6. Be willing to help teachers work out difficulties with pupils, parents, and other teachers.
7. Be willing to work with a teacher in solving a problem caused by mistakes.
8. Work to increase the friendliness and group feeling in the staff.
9. Respect and accept the special contribution of each staff member.
10. Submit proposed individual schedules to the total group involved or to a scheduled committee for suggested improvements before issuing them officially.
11. Recommend the organization of a teacher welfare committee.
12. Establish inservice training to build necessary skills for next steps in program improvements.
13. Give staff members the opportunity to grow and advance.
14. Promote from within the ranks when possible.
15. Let people know when they are doing good work.
16. Show confidence in the ability of the staff.
17. Respect a teacher's analysis of the teaching he is doing.
18. Listen to the opinions and proposals of all staff members.
19. Consult with teachers before action is taken that will affect them.

20.   Keep the staff informed of policy changes originating outside the unit that will affect them.
21.   Widen the participation in policymaking.
22.   Plan work together instead of issuing directives on how it should be done.
23.   Give teachers a part in establishing deadlines for work.
24.   Avoid action that will make the teacher feel less important.
25.   Disregard status lines in helping teachers of the school group settle an argument.
26.   Decrease, as far as possible, the regulations governing faculty action.
27.   Seek to decrease school regulations affecting private lives of teachers.
28.   Check frequently on indices of teacher morale.
29.   Plan with staff members the way a job assignment is to be executed. (10)

There are ten basic employment needs according to Keith Davis, professor of management at Indiana State University:

1.   Employees need and depend upon good leadership.
2.   They want to know goals, where they stand, and all the forces affecting their environment — they need to be informed.
3.   They need to be treated with human dignity.
4.   They need incentive and opportunity to grow and progress.
5.   They want independence and freedom in the conduct of affairs.
6.   They want to avoid personal conflict.
7.   They need a relative degree of security and safety.
8.   Employees want working conditions and comforts comparable to their associates.
9.   They need to accomplish a feeling of achievement in work that contributes to social needs.
10. They want to be treated fairly. This means that action will be consistent and in accord with the total situation, not just with the law. (3)

References

1.   Bakamis, William A., *Improving Instruction in Industrial Arts.* Milwaukee: Bruce Publishing Company, 1966.
2.   Briggs, T. H., and Joseph Justman, *Improving Instruction Through Supervision.* New York: The MacMillan Company, 1952.
3.   Davis, Keith, "What Do Workers Want?" Bloomington, Ind.: Indiana State University (An Unpublished Study).
4.   *Encyclopedia of Modern Education.*

5. Erickson, Emanuel E., *Teaching the Industrial Arts.* Peoria, Ill.: Chas. A. Bennett Co., Inc., 1956.
6. *Guide for Industrial Arts Education In California.* Sacramento, Calif.: State Department of Education.
7. *Improving Industrial Arts Teaching.* Washington, D. C.: Department of Health, Education, and Welfare, June, 1960.
8. *Industrial Arts and Vocational Education.* Tulsa, Okla.: Tulsa Public Schools.
9. *Your Professional Organization.* Washington, D. C.: American Vocational Association.
10. Wiles, Kimball, *Supervision For Better Schools.* New York: Prentice-Hall, Inc., 1950.

Chapter 8

Good School-Community Relations

Good public relations must be based upon sound administration and effective teaching. A good job of education merits publicity and community approval, but citizens must be informed of problems along with achievements. Doing a good job and telling the community about it bears fruit — in getting cooperation in planning, conducting, and financing effective instruction. Industrial education programs are fully effective only when they have the active support of citizens and groups in the community. Programs must be continually publicized, explained, illustrated, interpreted, emphasized, and dramatized. There are many "publics" — many groups — each with its own attitudes and prejudices, its own potentialities for helping to further the objectives of vocational and industrial arts education. (3)

Interpreting the Program to the Administration

In interpreting industrial education programs to the school administration, it is necessary to examine the philosophy of the school and analyze the program of industrial education.

A school philosophy emerges from group action. It should be the product of the critical thinking of many persons under optimum conditions of communication. Such a philosophy, to be effective, should be a personal conviction of all those concerned with the instructional program and a motivating force in all that is done for children and youth in the school. With this philosophy as a basis, the interpretation of a program of industrial education to the administration is made much easier. Of course, the philosophy should be generally accepted in the school system, and the program of the industrial education program should be consistent with it. The supervisor's first responsibility, then, in implementing a philosophy of education based on respect for the individual, is to practice such a philosophy in his relationship with co-workers.

The administration should understand (1) that the basis of the industrial education curriculum is modern industry, building and construction; (2) that the industrial education curriculum has developed over the years with

154

the selection of skills and information adaptable to school shop and drafting rooms; (3) that industrial education is an integral part of the school curriculum rather than a special subject; and (4) that efforts are being made to coordinate industrial education instruction with other departments of the school.

It sometimes happens that industrial education teachers associate only with those who already understand their phase of education, thus isolating themselves from the larger educational community. If such a withdrawal has taken place, it is time for action to incorporate the industrial education staff as an integral part of the entire faculty of a school system. It is difficult to talk of being an integral part, while operating separately from the rest of secondary education.

Good relationships develop from mutual respect and understanding. Keep both ends of the street open. How well do you know what other personnel in the school system are doing? How can you learn from them and how can you help them? Be interested in their jobs and they will be more ready to interest themselves in your phase of the program. Gaining support from the administrator in the school can be done only by continuous, patient, and sincere effort. This involves more than invitations to them to visit classes — it involves going to them, recognizing their contributions, asking them for help, and in turn offering to be of service to them.

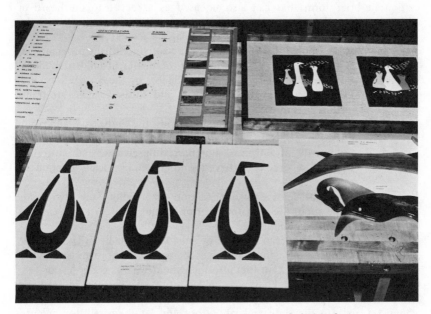

Fig. 8-1. An Informal Display in the Lab—Suitable for
In-School Public Relations (Tulsa Schools)

With these points in mind, interpreting a program of industrial education to the school administrator is more effectively done. Supervisors generally work under a dual delegation of responsibility. One delegation of a supervisor's responsibility is direct from the superintendent. The second delegation is from members of the superintendent's staff. The superintendent delegates responsibilities to members of the staff, who in turn delegate responsibilities to supervisors.

The superintendent of schools is a most important public relations control for the entire school system. The public relations program will be considerably handicapped if he is not included in the overall plan. In the same way, the principal of a school is the keystone in a building's public relations program.

When developing an administrator's understanding and recognition of the industrial education program, remember that they are busy people. Schedule conferences and reports so they do not conflict with their rushed schedules, and remember that it is impossible to sell a whole program in one afternoon. The right approach is regular, steady action, perhaps with a time-table prepared an entire year in advance. (3) Involve administrators in planning for long-range objectives. Ask for their help as curriculum work is proceeding. People involved in the planning state are far more understanding of the final decision. Provide the superintendent and/or principal with information in brief form that can also be used as a report to the board of education. Keep the administrator's office files continually supplied with the usual legal reports and the following public relations media:

1. A scrapbook of publicity about the activities of the program.
2. A summary of the laws relating to vocational industrial education and how the school system benefits by them.
3. Periodic write-ups on how social and cultural values are transmitted by industrial education.
4. Taped or recorded programs from the industrial education classes.
5. Comments of citizens (plumbers, housewives, and auto mechanics) recorded as they attend a school social function or evening class.
6. Written memos explaining actions in handling any complaints made about the department or presenting information in cases of unjustified complaints.
7. Marked articles in issues of professional magazines. (3)

Before accusing an administrator of being uncooperative, carry on a self-evaluation: Have you kept him informed about what is going on; do you know what he is doing, and have you helped him take a personal interest and feel a personal responsibility for the successful outcome of a program? Invite administrators into the shop and laboratory and let them talk to students. Invite them to industrial education meetings at local, state, and national levels. The state vocational staff can help with good relations by sponsoring activities which will help to broaden understandings of the underlying philosophies and procedures of all fields of vocational education and gain recognition for the advantages of education which includes provision for occupational competency. It is still up to you to prove to the administrator that the program is worthy of support.

Working with Other Supervisors and Administrators

A supervisor should be competent in his assigned area and understand the contributions made by all departments and grade levels to the total educational program. Good working relationships result from:

1.   Working toward general agreement in interpreting and implementing the education philosophy of the school.

Fig. 8-2. Facilities Planned with Corridor Display Space Are
Helpful Adjuncts in Student and Community
Relations (Tulsa Schools)

2.   Knowing and understanding the other supervisor as an individual.

3.   Being willing to work with and share in the problems and responsibilities of other supervisors.

4.   Aiding the supervisory group to grow professionally through the exchange of information about trends, departmental philosophies, methods, procedures, and resources.

5.   Holding a follow-up conference after a visit to a building when either the principal or the supervisor feels that one is needed.

6.   Serving as a consultant to a principal in the placement of teachers, curriculum changes, instructional problems, and physical facilities needed in the building.

7.   Serving in an advisory capacity on such matters as sectioning, scheduling, class load, etc.

8.   Consulting principals about exhibits, fairs, tours, and contests.

9.   Aiding in arranging for teachers to take part in interschool visitation.

10.   Keeping the principal informed about new trends in the supervisor's area.

11.   Helping develop a continuous program of evaluation.

12.   Helping establish and utilize lines of communication.

13.   Participating in special school and PTA programs when requested and when it seems advisable.

14.   Helping identify and develop leadership in the school staff.

15.   Working with the principal to encourage instructional research with individual and small groups.

16.   Cooperating with the guidance counselors in the school system, for they need help in learning more about industry and the contributions that it makes to education.

Public and Professional Relationships

Interpreting industrial education to the lay public and professional colleagues, as well as assuring inter- and intra-professional relationships on a constructive and wholesome basis, is a continuing problem. However, it has received a minimum of professional attention in relation to its probable significance to progress. There is room for some sheer creativity in this area of responsibility. The following outline, while to some extent peripheral, points out the nature of the problem:

I.   Understanding the community

    A.   Since each community has its own personality, the problems peculiar to each community must be discovered and analyzed and definite means developed to meet them.

    B.   Significant facts about the community are vital to all and particularly to the beginning teacher new to the school.

    C.   The parents and relatives of pupils form the largest adult community group vitally interested in the schools. The teacher and the school should take the initiative if there are any barriers or tensions to be broken down between teacher and parent.

    D.   Mutual understandings are achieved through participation in cooperative enterprises carried on by both the school and other areas of community life.

    E.   Community information requires analysis, condensation, and interpretation for use by staff members.

II.   Understanding the world community

    A.   The exchange of educational materials cannot be neglected. Professional materials are essential. Among other sources, books, pamphlets, and periodicals dealing with the community are provided by the Institute on International Affairs and by the National Congress of Parents and Teachers.

    B.   State departments of education, colleges, universities, institutes, and foundations have a wealth of material for the seeker of information.

    C.   Art and music speak a universal language. Their study and promotion lead to appreciation and respect for their creator. Literature expresses the soul of a nation and is a sound basis for understanding.

III.   Community work

    A.   Attempts to establish good public relations are often facilitated by participation in community organizations, special projects, and charity campaigns.

    B.   Informal contacts often develop a sound basis for understanding and authority.

Promoting Good Community Relations

Programs of public relations are often restricted to the production of materials for publication, the production and presentation of materials for fairs and exhibits, and the production of radio and television programs. The most successful means of interpreting a program is founded upon personal integrity, initiative, and a genuine friendliness toward everyone in the community. These attributes should characterize all who work in the program. Persons especially interested in the industrial education program are taxpayers, public officials, students, parents, representatives of newspapers, members of civic groups, and fellow teachers. (3)

The interpretation of any program takes place as one works with the various divisions of the school administration. The program must be educationally sound and meet the purposes of public education as subscribed to by the administration. The worth of any program is reflected by the students, the teachers, and the supervisory and administrative staff.

The industrial education public relations program can utilize a variety of promotional techniques:

1. Featuring industrial arts in school assemblies.
2. Demonstrating processes in display cases.
3. Sponsoring PTA demonstrations.
4. Holding an industrial arts night for visitors to watch students at work.
5. Allowing fathers to work with sons on special occasions.
6. Working with professional organizations.
7. Speaking to civic groups.
8. Having guest speakers for the class. (1)
9. Sponsoring annual exhibits.
10. Using the local newspaper, radio station, and television to advertise.

Effective publicity is the result of a variety of promotional activities and messages and attractive design, color, and taste in displays. (1)

Fig. 8-3. Publicity Given to Industrial Gifts Is a Splendid
Opportunity for General Program Information to
Reach the General Public (Tulsa Schools)

The Supervisor's Role

Every person who has a supervisory function has an important role in public relations. Supervisors are responsible for maintaining communication channels between themselves and other persons with whom they work. Through cooperative planning, provision should be made for opportunity for growth and development of all persons participating in the school program.

1. The supervisor should help the members of his department to realize that school-community relations start in the classroom.

2. He should strive to create a climate that will encourage teachers, students, parents, and other personnel connected with the school to seek counsel and assistance.

3. He should endeavor to improve the partnership concept between parents and teachers in meeting the educational needs of children.

4. For the greatest efficiency of the school system, the supervisor

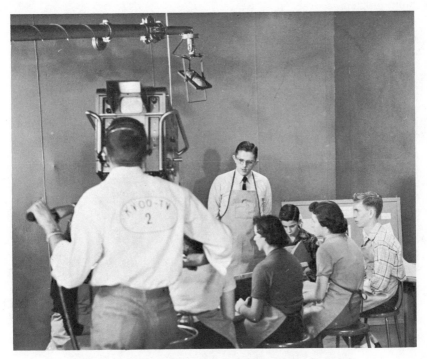

Fig. 8-4. Publicity Should Be Natural, Interesting, and
Activity-Centered (Tulsa Schools)

should make provision for utilizing cooperative planning, interpretation, and evaluation of the entire program.
5.   He should always be ready and willing to give credit to anyone
      for any program or any task well done.
6.   He must keep informed on recent trends and developments in his
      field and provide information for coworkers.
7.   He should work closely with all school personnel to establish a
      cooperative plan of public information and interpretation of the
      program of instruction and services of the school.
8.   He should be a participant in community activities.

Working with the Public to Improve the School Program

Educators need to work with the public to create better understanding
between schools and the home, to contribute to the improvement of the
learning situation, to give the teacher more effective working conditions, and
keep the public aware of the improvement and progress made in the instructional program.

General good will and adequate lay and professional support of schools
comes about through participation by laymen in the evaluation of school

Fig. 8-5. Recognition Programs and Awards Are Important in
School-Community Relations (Tulsa Schools)

policies and public awareness that pupils learn at various rates and are taught on their ability levels.

Some effective techniques of working with the public are:

1. Making visitors to the building feel welcome.
2. Making buildings available to character-building education groups.
3. Showing appreciation of what character groups are trying to do.
4. Meeting with parents of children in each group or section in the early year, to explain the school program through short talks, exhibits, demonstrations, etc., and conducting question and answer discussions.
5. Giving correct information concerning the schools.
6. Utilizing the PTA in the interpretation of the school program.
7. Regular communications to parents, such as superintendent's quarterly letters. (2)

References

1. *Bulletin to Members of the American Council of Industrial Arts Supervisors,* Washington, D. C.: American Council of Industrial Arts Supervisors, October, 1959.
2. *Summary of Principal-Supervisor Inservice Conference.* Tulsa, Okla.: Tulsa Public Schools, 1954.
3. *Your Public Relations.* Washington, D. C.: American Vocational Association, 1954.

Chapter 9

The Industrial Teacher

As a Manager of Learning Experiences

The effective industrial education teacher knows that good teaching involves careful organization. His demonstrations are well planned before class begins. He knows that if the pupils are expected to learn, he must present the lesson in a way that can be understood by all the class members. His class procedure is organized so that each pupil is given responsibility in shop administration. At appropriate periods, these assignments are changed. By these means, each pupil develops a team spirit and learns to take responsibility.

A good teacher has an effective system of tool and material storage and distribution. Each piece of equipment has a definite place and everything is kept in order. He is concerned with safe practices. In teaching, he emphasizes safety in his demonstrations and while he works. He sees that all tools and equipment are used properly.

The resourceful teacher recognizes the value of a good shop library and maintains a collection of recent printed materials related to his field. He often refers students to this material and encourages them to seek solutions to their problems through proper references. He is alert to the need of self-improvement. He keeps in touch with industry to make sure that practices he teaches conform to those used in modern industry. He returns to college at intervals to learn new philosophies and keeps himself informed with books and periodicals dealing with his specific field. (4)

Functions, Responsibilities, Duties

The functions, responsibilities, and duties of a teacher fall into four main headings: to himself, the student, the school system, and the community.

To Himself

A. The teacher needs to have faith in the school program as a whole and in his specific job.

164

B. He needs to be a good person keenly alive to the world around him.

C. He must constantly grow professionally.

To Students

A. The teacher must never lose sight of the seven cardinal principles of education: health, command of the fundamental principles, worthy home membership, vocational education, civic education, worthy use of leisure time, and ethical character.

B. He should provide experiences for boys and girls that will lead to their developmental growth in the various subject matter areas, and to their continuous growth in becoming better social beings.

To the School System

A. The teacher should inform himself of established policies, conform to them, and support them.

B. He should be experimental in his teaching and share his experiences.

To the Community

A. The teacher needs to accept the fact that the schools belong to the public.

B. He should make an effort to work closely with parents.

C. He should help to keep the community correctly informed about the objectives, methods, and policies of the school, and keep the individual parent informed as to the progress of the student.

Inservice Growth in Understanding of Children.

Through the school's program, the teacher assists children to grow mentally, physically, emotionally, and socially toward and into adult citizenship of worth in society. Some of the ways this may be done are by:

1. Establishing rapport among individual pupils and the teacher.
2. Adapting the curriculum and materials to the social and individual needs and capabilities of the students.
3. Modifying methods and procedures in accord with the expanding knowledge of human growth and development.
4. Establishing codes of conduct suitable to the nature of the student and his growth level.
5. Establishing a sense of belonging.
6. Understanding causes of behavior.
7. Building intelligent teacher reactions upon insights.

The teacher should keep pace with the scope of scientific knowledge about child growth and development. He should be familiar with research findings regarding:

1. Physical growth and physical processes that underlie child behavior.
2. Influence of affection and climate of love in a child's home.
3. Impact of the family cultural background.
4. The role of the student in society and in the peer group, and the stages through which he grows into the adult world.
5. Importance of the child's experience background — his actual knowledge and skill; how he uses his knowledge; and his attitudes, values and goals from day to day.
6. Emotional factors — what makes a student happy or unhappy and how he defends himself.

Through an understanding of the child and how he grows and matures, the teacher is able to adjust his program or his teaching methods. As he better understands the child, he will be better able:

1. To improve and expand the course of study to include activities and experiences within the interest and grasp of the individual student.
2. To apply appropriate methods in dealing with the students in their learning experiences and reactions.
3. To handle discipline more easily by searching for the causes of behavior.
4. To better analyze group situations.
5. To improve the relationships between pupil-teacher, pupil-parent, and pupil-pupil.
6. To help students with worthwhile activities which they can do with an emphasis on intrinsic rather than extrinsic values.
7. To provide opportunities for a child to develop his own understanding of his reponsibilities as an individual and a member of the group.

Relationships with Other Teachers

Good relationships with other teachers, both within the industrial education department and outside of it, are important. Feelings of belonging, of working together, are enhanced when people are united in a common cause. Some general policies of the individual teacher would include:

1. Recognize accomplishments of fellow teachers and tell them so.
2. Refrain from adverse criticism of the methods of fellow teachers except when comment is requested by a school official for purposes of school improvement.

3.   Refrain from blaming the previous teacher for inadequate preparation of students.
4.   Avoid letting jealousy of a good teacher adversely affect personality.
5.   Avoid unkind gossip.
6.   Have a respectful attitude toward the subject matter and work of other fields.
7.   Refrain from interfering in arguments and quarrels between teachers and students.
8.   Avoid criticism of an associate before students and other teachers.
9.   Cooperate with all colleagues in the school.
10. Participate willingly in the activities of the school.
11. Have an open mind and tolerate different ideas.

Organizing Teaching Steps

After determining the desired outcomes of a course of study, the next and equally important step is selecting the course content through which

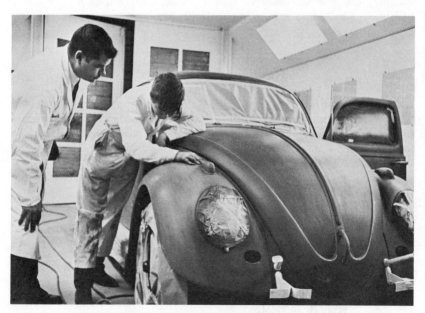

Fig. 9-1. A Planned, Orderly Sequence of Operations Is
Necessary to Accomplish the Defined Job

objectives can be reached effectively. It is through the presentation of subject content that the objectives of education are realized. Any course of study must be planned to fit a particular situation. In addition to the general objectives, some factors to which it must be adapted are listed below:

1. Age of the students.
2. Background and abilities.
3. Grade level.
4. Length of class period.
5. Duration of course.
6. Facilities of school.
7. Personality and ability of the teacher. (2)

Having once determined the course content, the operation units should be listed in a logical teaching order. When they are matched on an analysis chart they can be listed conveniently on an operation sheet in the order performed in constructing the project. The list of operation units should offer some suggestion of the procedure in making the project. One of the steps may contain two or more of the learning units and an operation unit. While listed only one time, it may be employed several times in the completion of a project.

The student's experience in a particular field affects the size of the teaching unit. The unit must be simple enough to be within his grasp, but difficult enough to inspire his best efforts. (2)

Relations with Students

In common with any good teacher, the industrial arts instructor should be familiar with the background of each student, should strive to rehabilitate students, show a genuine interest in their accomplishments, and help each one succeed in new shop experiences through individual help. Under the instructor's leadership, each student should grow. (9)

Each teacher should apply the following principles in his relationship with his students:

1. Individualize teaching.
2. Find out students' capabilities and talents.
3. Refrain from the use of sarcasm.
4. Avoid embarrassing a student before the group.
5. Create an atmosphere of friendliness and helpfulness.
6. Provide for democratic participation of students.
7. Establish and maintain a good shop organization.
8. Promote interest.
9. Maintain good discipline.
10. Express himself effectively. (5)

Student Evaluation

The improvement and progress of students should be carefully determined. Evaluation is important for the following reasons:
1. To determine the degree of advancement made by students.
2. To learn the difficulties experienced by learners.
3. To motivate the learning process.
4. To motivate the teacher. (8)

The grade a student earns on a project or activity may be determined:
1. Arbitrarily, by the teacher putting a grade on student records.
2. Through careful analysis of quantity of work accomplished, quality of work, effort put forth by the student, knowledge gained and applied, proper attitude toward equipment, work, and fellow students. Mathematically these ratings might be weighted as: Quantity = 20%, Quality = 25%, Effort = 20%, Knowledge = 20%, Attitude = 15%.
3. With students participating in the evaluation, ratings may be made by the student who made the project, the student foreman, the student who graded the related information test, and the teacher.
4. By testing. An essay test may be given at the close of unit, but an objective test is more effective. Tool naming tests can be given periodically, and tests can involve matching pictures and names of machines and tools. Oral tests are somewhat more difficult to apply. (8)

An efficient grading system should consume a minimum of the teacher's time; be based on a wide scope of student response and attainment; and ratings should be frequent, uniform, and permanent. Appropriate periods are at the completion of projects and at the end of a unit, though grade cards may be issued each 6 or 9 weeks. The final grade is a composite of all the subject matter grades and citizenship. (8)

Self-Evaluation

In a modern program of supervision, the evaluation of the pupil or teacher will be completed through the use of anecdotal records, check lists, inventories, interviews, and batteries of tests designed to measure various aspects of the individual's physical, social, emotional, and mental growth. All these methods will not be used, but as many techniques as necessary will be used to accomplish the goal. Getting teachers to use the techniques is not easy. Many teachers are content to continue doing what they have done for years, while others are not interested in improving simply because it involves changes in methods, techniques, and points of view.

The basic problem frequently is stimulating a desire in teachers to evaluate methods and learning. Success is easier when one teacher has been able to do it. For example, if a teacher discovers, with the help of a supervisor, that his students do not always attain the level of achievement of which they are capable, then the supervisor is able to start the teacher examining causes. Once the causes are eliminated, teaching and learning are improved. (3)

Self-analysis involves the following considerations:

Attitude Toward Self
1. Do I react favorably to suggestions from others?
2. Do I ask for suggestions from others?
3. Do I find it difficult to assume responsibility in making decisions?
4. Do I feel it my responsibility to continually improve the efficiency of my work?
5. Do I find it difficult to evaluate my work and the work of others in an objective manner?
6. Do I know how to listen?
7. Am I quick to point out the faults and mistakes of others?
8. Am I tolerant of the opinions of others?

Attitudes Toward Others
1. Do I try to maintain an open mind?
2. Do I publicly recognize the contributions of others?
3. Am I guilty of racial, political, or religious prejudices?
4. Do I forget grievances easily?
5. Do I conduct myself in contacts with the lay public in such a way that they recognize my position in the community?
6. Do I deal with people in ways which emphasize their dignity and self-respect?
7. Do I avail myself of every opportunity to discuss problems with coworkers before reaching a decision?
8. Do I feel it necessary to defend the personnel or program of my department when questioned by others?

Attitude Toward Work
1. Do I recognize the importance of the contributions that can be accomplished through my work?
2. Am I hesitant to take a new assignment because of the accompanying responsibility?
3. Do I seek opportunity to discuss common professional problems with coworkers because I can learn from others?
4. Do I plan my work?
5. Have I set up goals toward which to work?
6. Do I continually examine new books and materials and tenta-

tively try them in selected areas in an effort to bring the best practices to students or coworkers?

7. Do I check myself and evaluate my work periodically?
8. Do I like the type of work I am doing?
9. Do I clearly understand my professional duties and responsibilities?

Emotions

1. Do I have a tendency to blow up easily?
2. Am I at ease in discussing matters with my superiors?
3. Do I become nervous and irritable under tension?
4. Do I allow worries or disturbances of a personal nature to affect my work? (5)

Supervisors also need to carry on a regular self-evaluation, for they are prone to the same sorts of weaknesses and blind spots as teachers, administrators, and other workers. Table 9-1 may be helpful.

Table 9-1
SELF-ANALYSIS CHART FOR SUPERVISORS

(Check the appropriate column at the right; U — Usually, O — Occasionally, R — Rarely)

		U	O	R
1.	Am I receptive to suggestions?			
2.	Do I ask for suggestions from others?			
3.	Do I weigh all available evidence before making decisions?			
4.	Do I assume responsibility for my decisions?			
5.	Do I improve my efficiency by keeping up to date professionally?			
6.	Do I understand my professional duties and responsibilities?			
7.	Do I plan and evaluate my own work?			
8.	Do I evaluate the work of others in an objective manner?			
9.	Am I able to help others correct shortcomings and mistakes without giving offense?			
10.	Am I able to disregard petty grievances?			
11.	Do I try to maintain an open mind?			
12.	Do I give credit to others for contributions and work well done?			
13.	Do I show respect for the dignity and personality of each individual?			
14.	Do I allow racial, political, or religious prejudices to affect my professional relationships?			

	U	O	R
15. Do I let personal likes and dislikes influence my professional relationships?			
16. Do I practice democratic processes in my professional activities, such as curriculum revision, teacher's meetings, etc.?			
17. Am I willing to take an extra assignment if it is within my capabilities?			
18. Am I willing to admit it when I don't know?			
19. Do I show poise and self-control in dealing with people?			
20. Can I accept change when change is needed?			
21. Do I examine new books, materials, and methods and try them in selected areas in an effort to bring about the best practices?			
22. Do I show enthusiasm for the work I am doing?			
23. Am I able to control my emotions under tension?			
24. Am I at ease in discussing matters with the superintendent?			
25. Do I allow worries or disturbances of a personal nature to affect my professional activities?			
26. Can I take criticism impersonally?			
27. Can I disagree without becoming disagreeable?			
28. Do I have patience to explain things thoroughly?			
29. Do I exhibit a sense of humor?			
30. Do I cultivate a distinct, pleasing voice?			
31. In group situations, do I monopolize conversation or discussion?			
32. Am I a good listener?			
33. Do I speak disparagingly of my coworkers?			
34. Am I sympathetic to the problems of teachers and other coworkers?			
35. Do teachers give the impression of feeling better after talking with me?			
36. Do I see my work in its relationship to the total school program?			
37. Do I reflect credit on the schools in my contacts with the public?			

Liability Laws

Shop teachers should have some liability protection. It may be a diligently planned and executed safety program, individual liability insurance, or group liability protection. The financial loss due to liability in cases of proven negligence can be catastrophic, and the shop teacher may be sued for damages if a student is injured in a shop accident. (7)

In fixing liability for school accidents, the decision is based on individual negligence. The teacher of a school shop or an average citizen are held equally accountable for negligence.

Accident Reports

Accident reports are written records of accidents that have occurred within the teacher's jurisdiction and these should be made and filed with the school administration immediately after the accident occurs. The shop teacher should know:

1. If printed forms are available.
2. If minor cuts, burns, and bruises are reported.
3. Where the reports are filed.
4. The extent of the teacher's responsibility.
5. Whether explanation of witnesses should be included. (1)

Insurance

The individual teacher should take the responsibility of obtaining information about liability insurance. These questions should be kept in mind:

1. Does the district cover teachers with liability coverage?
2. What is the extent of the coverage provided by the district?
3. Where can the teacher get information about insurance he should have?
4. What constitutes negligence? (1)

Precautions

All shop teachers should take certain liability precautions. The following eight principles should be considered by any teacher:

1. Teachers and the school district are liable for breach of contract.
2. Teachers can be held liable for failure to exercise adequate supervision over the pupils in the classrooms.
3. Teachers can be held liable for injuries inflicted by corporal punishment of students.
4. The teacher may be held individually liable for injury or damage caused by a pupil while he is on an errand for the teacher.
5. Teachers can be held liable if they fail to exercise reasonable supervision over the students and an injury results.
6. Teachers can be held liable for allowing students to use personal automobiles for school purposes.
7. Some states protect teachers with *save harmless laws* requiring a

district to pay the cost of any lawsuits for the negligence of a teacher.

8. Teachers and supervisors responsible for patrol operation should insist upon legal protection against consequences of their negligent acts. (6)

References

1. *A Guide to Developing Administrative Policy in Industrial Arts Education.* Los Angeles: Los Angeles County Schools.
2. *A Guide to Improvement of Industrial Arts in Oklahoma Schools.* Oklahoma City, Okla.: State Department of Education, 1965.
3. Adams, Harold P., and Frank G. Dickey, *Basic Principles of Supervision.* New York: American Book Company, 1953.
4. Diamond, Thomas, "Teacher's Letters," *School Shop*, February, 1957.
5. *Handbook for Instructors of Industrial Arts and Vocational Education.* Tulsa, Okla.: Tulsa Public Schools.
6. Hamilton, Robert R., *Legal Rights and Liabilities of Teachers*, Laramie, Wyo.: School Law Publication, 1956.
7. Hoffman, Shelton Barstow, "Legal and Moral Problems of Shop Teacher Liability," Greenville, Ill.: Greenville College (An Unpublished Study).
8. *Industrial Arts and Vocational Education.* Tulsa, Okla.: Tulsa Public Schools.
9. *Organization and Administration of Industrial Arts Education.* Columbus, Ohio: State Department of Education, 1959.

Chapter 10

Local, State, and National Agencies

The need for strong, dynamic professional organizations at the local, state and national levels has never been more apparent and vital, not only to the profession, but to the welfare of our citizens and to the nation itself.

United, vocational educators make up a potent force in our democratic society. Our professional organizations are facing great challenges and great opportunities, and our profession will maintain its rightful place in education only if we, as members of professional organizations, communicate with people as yet uninvolved and successfully secure their help in promoting, improving and protecting our programs.

With the passage of the Smith-Hughes Act more than fifty years ago, a very strong administrative structure for vocational education was created at the federal level. Through the federal-state-local partnership, vocational funds were administered in such a way as to carry out the intent of the law, which primarily was that of preparing people for work. The program was administered by the Federal Board for Vocational Education (consisting of the Secretary of Agriculture, the Secretary of Commerce, the Secretary of Labor, the Commissioner of Education, and three members appointed by the President and confirmed by the United States Senate). Such a structure provided for the necessary lines of communication between education and the various occupational areas to the end that people and jobs were brought together through the process of vocational education.

When the Federal Board was dissolved in 1933, the administration of vocational education was delegated to the U.S. Office of Education, a part of the Federal Security Agency. It has since remained within the structure of the U.S. Office of Education although it has undergone a series of shifts and changes which has resulted in situations in which persons responsible for vocational education no longer reported directly to the U.S. Commissioner of Education.

The federal administrative structure and the lack of visibility for vocational education at the national level have become prime concerns of the American Vocational Association. Two major studies conducted by high-level committees have made recommendations concerning the administrative level for vocational education and call for upgrading the administrative level so that more visibility could be provided for the program. (1)

The necessity for strong leadership for vocational education at the national level has become even more apparent in our present era of educational change, social unrest, and economic expansion.

The AVA has a vital responsibility to the affiliated State Associations to aid their efforts. It must have the resources to give guidance and counsel, when requested, to strengthen the voice of vocational education at the state level. More comprehensive field services must be provided.

The image of education, and industrial education, at all levels is changing. Society has an increasing awareness of the need for all types of vocational education. There must be a concerted effort to inform the public continually of the role and benefits of vocational education. Industrial educators must maintain contact with a growing number of organizations concerned with vocational education at the national level. Professionally, the AVA is available to assist the activities of State Associations in promoting public relations.

The Division of Vocational and Technical Education of the U.S. Office of Education, as the federal agency in cooperative arrangement for the national program of vocational education, has the following responsibilities:

1. Cooperating with state boards in the administration of national acts.
2. Examining plans submitted by state boards and approving such plans if in accord with the provisions and purposes of the acts.
3. Making studies, investigations, and reports for the purpose of assisting the states in the establishment of vocational schools and classes, in providing instruction in commerce and commercial pursuits, and in the vocational fields for which federal funds have been made available.
4. Certifying annually whether the several states have accepted and are using the provisions of the federal acts in accord with regulations. (5)

Division of Vocational Education

Under the Federal Vocational Education Acts, the Division of Vocational and Technical Education provides assistance to the states in the several fields of vocational and technical education. Most of the activities of the office require close cooperation with the states. The functions of the division can be outlined as follows:

A. Functions for which the entire responsibility for both planning and operation rests with the Division of Vocational and Technical Education.
1. Administering the national program of vocational and technical

education under the provisions of the Federal Vocational and Technical Education Acts.

2. Working on the national and interstate levels with public and private agencies and groups on activities relating to vocational and technical education.

B. Functions for which the states have the chief responsibility for both planning and operation, but in which the Division of Vocational and Technical Education cooperates.

1. Identifying the instructional needs of individuals and communities on the basis of occupational opportunities and trends.
2. Planning, organizing, supervising, and administering vocational and technical education programs.
3. Developing instructional materials and suitable standards for facilities for vocational students.
4. Selecting and training instructors, counselors, supervisors, administrators, and other professional personnel.
5. Improving and developing instructional and guidance procedures in vocational and technical education.
6. Evaluating vocational and technical education programs. (5)

Organization

An organizational chart of the U.S. Office of Education and a detailed chart of the Bureau of Adult, Vocational and Library Programs, division of Vocational and Technical Education, are shown as Figs. 10-1 and 10-2. Dr. Marshall Schmitt in the Demonstration Projects Branch, Division of Plans and Supplementary Centers in the Bureau of Elementary and Secondary Education, is the individual in the Office of Education with responsibilities for industrial arts. In the Division of Vocational and Technical Education there is no one assigned to work with the industrial arts programs.

It was the intent of the Congress of the United States in passing the Vocational Education Amendments of 1968 to make vocational education available to all people in all communities. The organizational form in the Office of Education is now function-oriented rather than related to the program specialists that previously consulted with State Departments of Education and provided much needed leadership. Many of the State Departments of Education may be duplicating this organizational pattern without analyzing the true function of supervisory and leadership persons.

State Supervision

Patterns of the fifty states vary widely, though there are probably more similarities than differences. The following sections of the Oklahoma Policies and Procedures Manual will provide some insights:

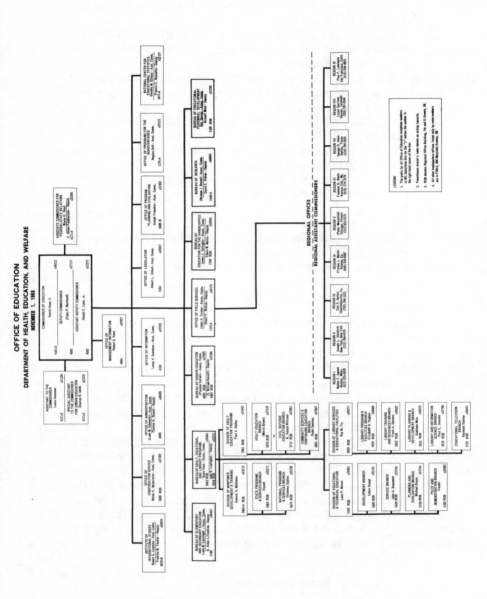

Fig. 10-1. Partial Chart of the U.S. Office of Education

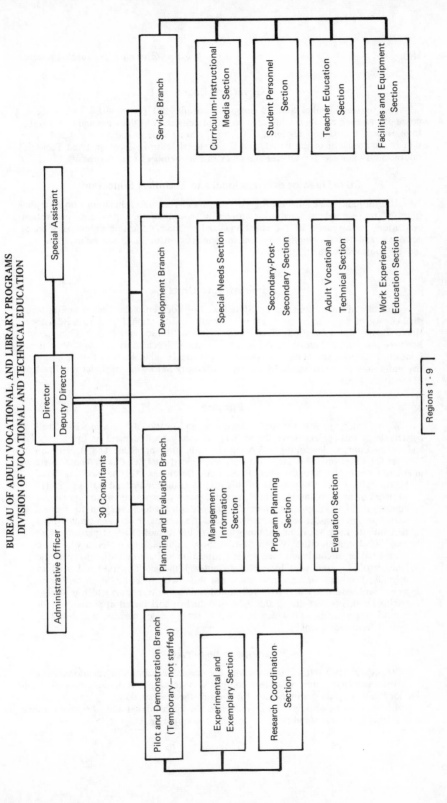

**BUREAU OF ADULT VOCATIONAL, AND LIBRARY PROGRAMS
DIVISION OF VOCATIONAL AND TECHNICAL EDUCATION**

Administrative Officer

Director
Deputy Director

Special Assistant

30 Consultants

Regions 1 - 9

Pilot and Demonstration Branch
(Temporary—not staffed)

Experimental and Exemplary Section

Research Coordination Section

Planning and Evaluation Branch

Management Information Section

Program Planning Section

Evaluation Section

Development Branch

Special Needs Section

Secondary-Post-Secondary Section

Adult Vocational Technical Section

Work Experience Education Section

Service Branch

Curriculum-Instructional Media Section

Student Personnel Section

Teacher Education Section

Facilities and Equipment Section

Fig. 10-2. Bureau of Adult, Vocational and Library Programs

Governing Board

The thirteen-member State Board of Vocational and Technical Education is composed of the seven members who serve on the State Board of Education and one member from each of the six congressional districts. The State Superintendent of Public Instruction is the President of the Board, and the State Director of Vocational and Technical Education is the Executive Officer and an ex-officio member of the Board.

State Director of Vocational and Technical Education

The full-time State Director for Vocational and Technical Education who is responsible for the general administration, direction, coordination, supervision, promotion, evaluation, improvement of the vocational and technical education programs, services, activities, and for the application and implementation of the State policies and procedures approved by the State Board.

Administrative Units

The administrative units of the State Board of Vocational and Technical Education shall consist of divisions in the fields of Agricultural Education, Distributive Education, Home Economics Education, Trade and Industrial Education, Health Occupations, Business and Office Education, Technical Education, Special Services, Area Vocational Education Schools, and Manpower Development and Training. Each of these administrative units shall be administered by a State Supervisory Staff working under the direction of the State Director.

Purpose

We are entering a scientific-technological age in Vocational Education. How well we participate in this age and serve the welfare of mankind will depend on our ability for and imagination in developing a Vocational Education program. The Declaration of Purpose for Vocational and Technical Education clearly defines this challenge as stated in Public Law 88-210, 88th Congress, H. R. 4955, December 18, 1963, Section 101.

Section 101. It is the purpose of this title to authorize Federal grants to States to assist them to maintain, extend, and improve existing programs of vocational education, to develop new programs of vocational education, and to provide part-time employment for youths who need the earnings from such employment to continue their vocational training on a full-time basis, so that persons of all ages in all communities of the State – those in high school, those who have completed or discontinued their formal education and are preparing to enter the labor market, those who have already entered the labor market but need to upgrade their skills or learn new ones, and those with special educational handicaps – will have ready access to vocational training or retraining which is of high quality, which is realistic in the light of actual or anticipated opportunities for gainful employment, and which is suited to their needs, interests, and ability to benefit from such training.

Persons to be Served

Secondary: High school students who are enrolled in approved vocational courses.

Post-secondary: Those who have completed or left high school and who are available for full-time study in preparation for entering the labor market.

Adults: Persons who have already entered the labor market and who need training or retraining to achieve stability or advancement in employment.

Special: Persons who have academic, socioeconomic, or other handicaps that prevent them from succeeding in the regular vocational programs provided for in the three above paragraphs.

Objectives of Instruction

Vocational instruction will be designed to fit individuals for employment in a recognized occupation. Such instruction will include vocational or technical training or retraining for (1) those preparing to enter a recognized occupation upon the completion of instruction and (2) those who have already entered an occupation but desire to upgrade or update their occupational skills and knowledge in order to achieve stability or advancement in employment. Vocational instruction supported by funds allotted under Section 3 of the 1963 Act shall be designed only to fit individuals for gainful employment. All students receiving vocational instruction in preparatory classes under the State Plan will have an *occupational objective which is a matter of record.* Their objective may be either a specific, recognized occupation or a cluster of closely related occupations in the occupational field.

Occupational Orientation of Instruction

Instruction Related to Occupation: The instruction will be related to the occupation for which the student is being trained. Instruction shall be of high quality, which is realistic in the light of actual or anticipated opportunities for gainful employment, and which is suited to the needs, interests, and abilities of the student in order that he may receive the greatest benefit from such training. Instruction related to the occupation for which the student is being trained means instruction which is designed to fit individuals for employment in a recognized occupation and which is especially and particularly suited to the needs of those engaged in, or preparing to engage in, such occupation. Such instruction shall include classroom instruction and field, shop, laboratory, cooperative work, or other occupational experience.

Instruction Necessary to Benefit from Training: Where necessary the State Board will provide instruction which is designed to enable individuals to profit from instruction related to an occupation for which he is being trained by correcting whatever educational deficiencies or handicaps prevent him from benefiting from such instruction. Such instruction will be provided in courses which are an integral part of the vocational education program in which the student is enrolled.

Standards for Establishing Vocational Education Programs in Secondary Schools

Vocational Agriculture and Vocational Home Economics: Applications for new programs of Vocational Agriculture and Vocational Home Economics may be considered for establishment in any public high school having an ADA of 80 students in the upper four grades. A minimum of 30 students voluntarily enrolled in a full-time program of Vocational Agriculture is recommended. A minimum of 30 students voluntarily enrolled in a full-time program of Vocational Home Economics is recommended.

Business & Office Occupations, Distributive Education, and Trade & Industrial Education: Applications for new programs in Business & Office Occupations, Distributive Education and Trade & Industrial Education may be considered for establishment in any public high school having an ADA of 100 students in the upper three grades.

Business & Office Education – A minimum of 30 and a maximum of 50 students voluntarily enrolled in a full-time cooperative office education program is recommended. A minimum of 15 and a maximum of 25 students voluntarily enrolled in a half-time cooperative office education program is recommended.

Distributive Education – A minimum of 30 and a maximum of 50 students voluntarily enrolled in a full-time Distributive Education program is recommended. A minimum of 15 and a maximum of 25 students voluntarily enrolled in a half-time Distributive Education program is recommended.

Trade & Industrial Education – A minimum of 10 and a maximum of 15 students voluntarily enrolled, with an allowance over beginning of three in full-time Air-Conditioning-Plumbing, Appliance Repair, Auto Body, Auto Mechanics, Barbering, Brick Masonry, Cabinetmaking, Carpentry and Machine Shop programs is recommended. A minimum of 10 and a maximum of 18 students voluntarily enrolled, with an allowance over beginning of three, in full-time Commercial Art, Drafting, and Vari-Typing programs is recommended. A minimum of 12 and a maximum of 23 students voluntarily enrolled in a full-time Cosmetology program is recommended.

Requirements for Vocational Education Teachers
Adult Program(s)

In order for a secondary vocational education teacher to receive reimbursement for teaching a vocational adult class, such teacher must first conduct or sponsor an organized vocational education class for adults (non-reimbursed). When the above requirement is met, any full-time vocational education teacher may receive reimbursement on a dollar-for-dollar matching basis, not to exceed a total of $5.00 per hour for teaching an adult education class(es). Where reimbursement is desired, prior approval must be given by the State Supervisor in charge of adult education for all vocational education classes for adults. Reimbursement must be requested by the local Board of Education at the end of the course.

Evaluation

In the evaluation of local programs of Vocational Education, a determination of needs for Vocational Education with reference to existing programs should constitute a very important phase of evaluation. In theory a positive correlation should exist between the occupations for which training is provided in the local school and the opportunities for employment and placement of former students and graduates and/or the inservice, employment training needs of adults. Valid information relative to persons in need of training and the job opportunities which exist, as well as accurate placement and follow-up records on students, are essential and required and should receive major consideration in the evaluation of vocational education programs at the local level. Similar information on the State level should be used in establishing, continuing, or terminating programs of vocational instruction.

In accordance with the provisions contained in the 1963 Vocational Education Act and the Rules and Regulations pertaining thereto, evaluation of the program of instruction will be made "periodically on the State level and continuously on the local level with the results being used for necessary change or improvement in the program through experimentation, curriculum improvement, teacher training, and other means." The implementation of evaluation on both the State and local level is a responsibility of the administrative and supervisory staffs of the divisions of vocational education.

The local schools should initiate evaluation programs and continuously make such evaluations to meet the changing needs which may occur; however, the State program will be evaluated on the basis of the extent and degree of evaluation at both State and local levels.

On the basis of the evaluative criteria which may be considered as applicable, each Division of Vocational Education should implement the necessary and required evaluation of local vocational education programs in their respective occupational areas.

Committee for Surveys and Evaluation

This committee will review applications for the establishment of Vocational Education programs, evaluate programs upon request from the division and/or superintendent of schools and recommend action to be taken. (3)

State Responsibility

The responsibility of the State Department of Education, as the educational agent of the state, is the creation and stimulation of better opportunities for learning. State departments vary in the extent to which they can or should assume leadership responsibility, but preparation and improvement of professional personnel, basic instructional programs, instructional and professional materials, dissemination of effective instruction practices, evaluation of instructional programs, and emerging and experimental programs are generally important. (5)

The State Superintendent of Schools, the education leader of the state, is responsible throughout the state for implementing the leadership, regulatory, and operational function of the State Department of Education. His administrative leadership responsibilities include planning, implementing, coordinating, and evaluating activities. Provision must also be made for adequate consultative services, effective public relations, and necessary research studies. Supplementing these activities are the leadership functions exercised by the professional staff personnel. Organized, responsible leadership is necessary to insure that the organization and future development of industrial education will be in line with conditions and needs of the individual. (2)

Somewhat typical of state structures in industrial arts is the organization in Oklahoma. The State Advisory Committee for Industrial Arts was originally appointed by the State Department of Public Instruction in the spring of 1937. The members are now selected by the Oklahoma Industrial Arts Association. This committee has carried on a number of studies, has prepared courses of study in several industrial arts subjects, and has prepared a safety bulletin for school shops.

Membership of the State Advisory Committee

1. Two representatives from classroom teachers in small cities.
2. Two representatives from classroom teachers in large cities.
3. A supervisor of industrial arts in a large city.
4. A supervisor of industrial arts in a small city.
5. Two teachers of industrial arts in state junior colleges.
6. Nine heads of industrial arts departments in state colleges.

7.   Two representatives from the graduate schools of state universities.
8.   The State Supervisor of Trade and Industrial Education.
9.   The State Director of Teacher Education.
10. The Director of Instruction, State Department of Education.
11. The President of the State Industrial Arts Association.
12. The President of the State Council of Industrial Arts.
13. The Secretary-Treasurer of the State Industrial Arts Association.
14. The Supervisor of Industrial Arts in the city where the meetings are held.
15. Life members of the State Industrial Arts Association.
16. District officers of the State Industrial Arts Association.

State supervisors of industrial arts and vocational subjects are in key positions to interpret industrial arts and vocational education programs to the people. Duties entail responsibility for developing programs of instruction in industrial education designed to meet the needs of the students in each community, working cooperatively with school superintendents, supervisors, and local school personnel. (2)

Job Outline or Description of a State Supervisor of Industrial Arts

A state supervisor must maintain professional relations with others in the state department, secondary school inspectors, certification bureau, field supervisors, and itinerant teacher trainers. He must work with local school administrators, trustees, superintendents, and principals. It is important that he develop effective communication and liaison with leaders of industries in the state, personnel in industrial trade associations, labor leaders, and with educational leaders of the legislature.

A supervisor must keep up his professional growth, being particularly alert to trends in instruction, curriculum studies, and changes in industry.

The supervisor will work with many persons as he assists in the solution of current problems. His activities must include regular services to the instructional staff, administrative functions, inservice training, upgrading of physical plant, and public relations.

Services to Instructional Staff

1.   Notices of new professional books.
2.   Notices of new text or reference books.
3.   References on related informational materials.
4.   Occupational reading lists.
5.   Descriptions and illustrations of new and interesting projects seen about the state.
6.   Description of instructional aids used in the state.

7.   Manipulative tips picked up on visits.
8.   Information received at conferences and conventions.
9.   Reports on significant projects in industrial arts.
10. Information about new industrial products appearing on the market.
11. Promotion of safety practices in the school shop.

Administrative Functions

1.   Organize office services so that they may be of the most help to the efficient functioning of the state program.
2.   Coordinate work with other supervisory groups of the state.
3.   Assist administrative officers in the promotion of programs.
4.   Consult and approve service for the planning and development of new shops.
5.   Advise and stimulate the organization of experimental and demonstration centers.
6.   Sponsor a continuous program of research which will serve as a basis for solving industrial education problems.
7.   Assist and advise in the reorganization and modernization of existing departments.
8.   Develop long-term programs of work.

Inservice Education

1.   Cooperate with programs of training.
2.   Promote orientation of new teachers in their field and in their professional organization.
3.   Counsel individual teachers.
4.   Arrange for meetings of teachers to observe ideal plants and instruction.
5.   Arrange for meetings to observe new processes or present new material.
6.   Hold small conferences.
7.   Encourage measures for professional improvement of the teachers.

Physical Plant and Equipment

1.   Assist in the remodeling of existing plants.
2.   Assist in the planning of new shops.
3.   Assist in equipping shops.
4.   Upgrade existing shops and promote good housekeeping.
5.   Promote shop safety.

Instructional Supervision

1. Visit and supervise the instruction in centers where industrial education programs are set up.
2. Prepare for and assist teachers in preparing instructional materials and visual aids.
3. Work with curriculum committees.
4. Make general evaluations of the work being done in the various school programs.

Promotion of Programs

1. Initiate and develop legislative interest.
2. Advise officials in regard to certification standards and regulations.
3. Exhibit interest in the formulation of salary schedules.
4. Encourage the preparation and evaluation of textbooks and other instructional materials. (4)
5. Promote industrial arts for elementary grades.
6. Acquaint school officials with the philosophy, aims, and purposes of the program.

References

1. *AVA Like It Is.* Washington, D. C.: American Vocational Association.
2. James, H. M., "Responsibility of the State Department in Improving Education," *Industrial Arts and Vocational Education*, September 1961.
3. *Policies and Procedures.* Oklahoma City, Okla.: State Board of Vocational and Technical Education.
4. *Suggested Responsibilities of a State Supervisor of Industrial Arts.* Washington, D. C.: American Vocational Association.
5. *Vocational Education, Bulletin 1.* Washington, D. C.: U.S. Office of Education, 1958.

Chapter 11

New Supervisors

Leadership is any contribution to the establishment and attainment of group purposes. It may be exercised by the supervisor or by any member of the group. Two types of leadership exist — the official leader and the leader who emerges from the group. An *official leader* may take any of at least three approaches to his job: He may think it is his function to dominate, control, and operate the group; he may try *working on* a group; or he may believe it is his function to *help the group* carry out its purposes. If the supervisor believes it is his function to help a group form and execute purposes, he may work within it. The *leader who works within the group* helps release the full ability of the members and this is the only defensible method. (4)

How Does a Supervisor Begin?

A supervisor may have been promoted from the ranks, or he may have come from an outside position.

If a man is promoted from the ranks, the staff knows his strengths and weaknesses. He has been a member of the group and this relationship must not change. His biggest problem will be exercising leadership from a different position in the group. When a supervisor comes from outside the group, first impressions can do much to win acceptance or to build hurdles that must be overcome. (4)

Knowing where to start is difficult. If a supervisor thinks of his job as one of helping his staff, he will start with the problems that they have. In this way, he is able to demonstrate that he is sincere in his desire to help develop the program already in operation, even though the problems may be unimportant from the supervisor's point of view.

The leader helps to set the pattern and tone of work in the department. A department grows in unity, strength, and effectiveness as individual members find satisfaction for their desires. In exerting leadership for program improvement through the staff, the supervisor must understand these desires and do all he can to promote the type of staff environment and operation that will fulfill them. Morale is the mental and emotional reaction of a person to his job. The important element in morale is what the individual (teacher)

187

feels and believes, and it is the leader's job to guide these feelings and beliefs in the proper directions. (4)

Self-Improvement

A chief ingredient in giving and receiving help effectively is self-improvement. Six areas in which self-understanding and self-improvement can be very rewarding to the supervisor are:

1. Understanding the concept of self.
2. Sharpening perceptions in human relations.
3. Clarifying perceptions of one's job and the situation in which one operates.
4. Attaining professional breadth and depth.
5. Allowing habits to contribute to personality.
6. Setting reasonable levels of aspiration. (5)

The leadership of an industrial education department is a most important factor in the development of a worthwhile program for the youth in the schools. The fundamentals involved in a supervisory job description generally include three factors. The first is the *administrative role* as department chairman, supervisor, or head teacher. The second group of functions identify the *supervisory role* in which he must serve, and the third role is that of *leadership service.* (2)

Management or administrative functions are the area to which many supervisors and chairmen give first attention. Such items as inventory, preparation of budget, and the utilization of school facilities must be handled efficiently and these functional details should serve the department and faculty to permit the most effective use of staff time for instructional purposes. When a proper balance is struck, the necessary information is available without burdensome clerical duties by educators. (2)

In order to achieve good *personnel relationships*, the department chairmen need to concern themselves with the recruitment and selection of teachers, salary ratings and promotions, and the problems of teacher welfare in the working situation and in community relationships. Every contact in the school system is inexorably intertwined with the work of the total department. (2)

The *curriculum* is the implementation of a basic philosophy which is reflected in the scope of course offerings in industrial education. Curriculum may be identified as an administrative function, but the supervisor's leadership while maintaining administrative control is certain to be tested. The democratic process must operate at its best in the area of curriculum. When administrative decisions must be made, the leader cannot evade the responsibility. For example, reconciling class schedules and class size with the needs and resources of the school system is an administrative responsibility. (2)

Evaluation is the supervisory survey of the entire program, the instructional services being offered, and a review of the records of student and teacher evaluation. It is the time when the question of "How are we doing?" must be answered. (2) Such questions as the following should be answered in the evaluative process:

1. Do all boys have an opportunity to take courses in industrial education?
2. Does the program include work in electricity-electronics and power mechanics?
3. Do students use textbooks and are they responsible for out-of-class assignments?
4. Is there an overemphasis on the making of projects? Is too much attention given to displays and exhibits?
5. Are students learning to read and make all kinds of drawings, house plans, graphs, charts, maps, and so forth?
6. Do the woodworking experiences in the program include modern methods of home construction, bending and laminating wood, patternmaking, as well as basic hand and machine woodworking?
7. Does the metal shop include experiences in machine shop, welding, foundry, and forging, as well as bench metal and sheet metal?
8. Is good design and problem solving stressed?
9. Are students learning about industrial procedures and methods, or how industry does the job?
10. Does the industrial arts program strengthen the application of math and science?
11. Are industrial arts students learning about occupations?
12. Is there a classroom area in which the students can sit down for audio-visuals and demonstrations?
13. Is there a course of study on file in the office for every program that is offered?
14. Is the school shop expected to do school repairs?
15. Is an adequate budget available for equipment, tools, and materials? (1)

The problem-solving workshop is an effective means of bringing staff together and creating a working unit. Such questions as the following may provide a basis for organizing short-term groups:

1. How should we evaluate teaching?
2. How can we use the potentials of the group in teaching and learning?
3. How can we improve individual conferences?
4. How can teachers determine problems real to students?
5. How can teachers learn problem-solving techniques?
6. What is the role of the teacher in modern programs?

7. How do teachers maintain a sense of security while making changes?
8. How can teachers evaluate student growth?
9. How can teachers do pupil-teacher planning?
10. What are the implications of democratic procedures for classroom practices?
11. How can teachers evaluate their own growth?

The Supervisor Develops Relationships

There are numerous other factors of the job, many of which are specific and peculiar to industrial education. After reviewing all of the musts of supervision, an individual needs to make certain resolutions:

1. Accept responsibilities, both from your superiors and on the job.
2. Give everyone in your department an opportunity to advance if he is willing to pay the price in intelligence and hard work.
3. Emphasize the human side of your job; build morale and work attitudes for your department and school system.
4. Recognize that your job is the key to successful organization and operation.
5. Maintain a creative attitude and use a logical approach to every problem.
6. Have enthusiasm for change, courage to accept new ideas, daring imagination, and sincerity of conviction.
7. Cooperate with others to make their jobs as easy and pleasant as possible.
8. Have high standards and enough strength to stand on your own feet.
9. Have the courtesy to treat others as you would like to be treated.
10. Realize that by building the school organization you enhance your own stature.

Supervision might be defined as a cooperative activity for the improvement of instruction and the coordination of the program. Supervisors, strictly speaking, are leaders of a group cooperatively seeking to improve instruction. They are concerned with materials of instruction, including course content and teaching aids; methods; training and upgrading teachers; evaluation of instruction; tools and equipment; and physical conditions. They are leaders with respect to coordination and synchronization of curriculum with student and community needs and maintaining desirable relationship with the entire school personnel, with school patrons, civic and community leaders. When supervisors inspect, help, visit, or confer with power to act, they have had administrative authority delegated to them. Otherwise, their findings, suggestions, and assistance would have to be administered by another person.

Supervisory Responsibility

Leadership must be different if education is given the task of improving the whole society in the same sense that it improves the whole child. In a society where increasing numbers are participating in all aspects of living, leadership in education must conform to the social trend and provide for continuing and effective participation by staff, students and public.

The school can perform its functions only as all education workers improve their vision, increase their knowledge, and refine their human relations skills. Educators must see more clearly the relationships between education and the general welfare in moral and spiritual values, economics, politics, and aesthetics. Teachers must gain greater knowledge of the nature of our society and the people who compose it, and refine their skills in working with other educational workers, with laymen, and children.

The greatest hope for the improvement of society lies in cooperative group action. Educators and community leadership need to plan together what is to be done to improve the educational program. This will involve planning together and acting separately; planning together and acting together; and coordinating the planning and acting of separate groups.

In the dynamics of working with groups, it is necessary to involve the total group in the study, whether it be centered on the improvement of the education program or the improvement of the people. Also, it is important that the group work on something large enough to see results.

The supervisor also needs to focus some attention on the school building unit with its faculty, pupils, and community, relating the central service division to that effort by contributing to the success of each school and by helping to meet the individual needs of persons that cannot be met in the normal process of working on school unit problems common to all teachers in the school.

Evidence of progress will be necessary to keep groups functioning. A continuing evaluation of the changes that have been made in the school program and the growth that has taken place in the faculty, using some point as a baseline, will help to keep morale up.

Personnel Relations

One of the functions of supervision is the creation of a wholesome climate in the school. Some schools are happy, hard-working, enjoyable situations. Some, on the other hand, are disagreeable places which everyone dislikes and avoids as much as possible. In the first type of school, everyone likes each other and each enjoys his assignments. In the second type of school, there is little in common and members of the staff get away from their situation as soon as they can. Much of the difference lies in the way the supervisor works with people and sets the stage for relationships of others.

One of the best ways for a supervisor to help create a good working climate is to respect the personality of all individuals with whom he comes in contact. This has many manifestations. It involves being concerned about people and their problems, being willing to place their desires ahead of his own, giving full consideration to their ideas and suggestions, creating the type of meetings in which each member of the staff has an opportunity to voice his opinions, encouraging activities of a social nature that will help to build friendly relationships, providing working conditions that are comfortable and attractive, and such things as showing courtesy and maintaining an even disposition. A supervisor must have a warm, sincere, humble personality.

Supervisors must have a deep faith in the worth of each individual in the school and a firm belief in the developing potential of each individual. This faith is the key to the creation of the type of climate in which all will grow. It is the foundation of good human relations. (4) The leader should always remember to:

1.   Let each person know how he is getting along.
2.   Let each know what is expected of him.

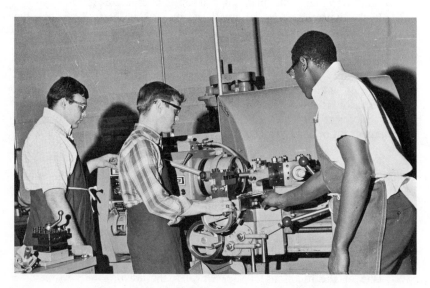

Fig. 11-1. A Good Working Climate Is Important in the
Achievement of Learning

3.   Commend good performance.
4.   Give credit when due.
5.   Make the best use of each person's abilities.
6.   Acknowledge that improving requires an accepting attitude if the teacher is to accept and work toward change.

When handling a problem, fairness and justice should be the objective, with the impact of personalities kept to an absolute minimum. The supervisor must:

1.   Get the facts.
2.   Review the record.
3.   Find out what policies, rules, and customs apply.
4.   Talk with individuals concerned.
5.   Get opinions and feelings.
6.   Fit the facts together.
7.   Consider their bearing on each other.
8.   Determine alternate and possible actions.
9.   Consider objectives and effect on individual, group, results.
10.   Take action.
11.   Check results.

Supervisory Conferences

Individual Conference

1.   The conference must be planned to help a given teacher.
2.   The conference may or may not be preceded by a classroom visit.
3.   The conference may have been suggested by a question raised by the teacher.
4.   The conference may have grown out of some problem the teacher has been working with for some time.

The Committee Technique

Conferences in which a teacher presides have definite advantages in the direction of developing a truly democratic atmosphere. The quality of a small conference depends upon the attitude of the principal members.

When the supervisor has come to regard meeting with his staff as a chief means of effective supervision, he has made a long stride toward making it just that. No matters are too trivial to be taken up. Agenda should be fluid to allow ideas from the floor.

To pass up until later, matters of pressing nature to the staff members, is to pass up forever certain opportunities for school improvement.

You should never vote on matters of belief. It is better to drop the subject until people are in accord.

The supervisor or teacher, as he works with people, should be able and willing to set the stage for action in which the atmosphere is permissive for growth.

Try to keep both ends of the street open by taking an interest in what others are doing, and how you can help them or how they can help. Developing mutual respect and understanding with the administrative staff pays dividends and helps to keep the lines of communication open.

Make it a practice to sit down with both new and old administrators and explain the various phases of industrial education. Involve administrators in helping to make long-range plans (for approximately five-year periods). These plans need to be discussed with administrators, department chairmen, and teachers. Such goals will help the program and put into operation a number of programs that would never materialize otherwise.

A supervisor should have facts available to present to the board of education, to the superintendent, or to anyone else, if he is called upon for further information to explain his plans. The superintendent is the key to any such plans. If he is in agreement and understands the overall plan, the supervisor's requests will generally receive approval.

Much time should be spent in working with principals. In the junior high schools, an exploratory program of industrial arts requires constant counseling on the part of the supervisor to make scheduling of the various areas possible. In new schools, with large enrollments, it is not always possible to follow scheduling as recommended; schools with small enrollments may present similar problems.

Programs of vocational industrial education require more time to interpret, plan, and put into operation than those in industrial arts. A need must be shown; students who are interested must be found and selected before a principal will consider such a course.

Overcrowded conditions in senior high schools have required shop and laboratory facilities to be used for industrial arts courses where principals feel more students may be served, thus making it difficult to schedule trade and industrial classes. Considerable effort must be put forth in explaining and showing, through facts and figures, the possibilities of vocational courses which will meet the needs of many students, and which are approximately the same in student class hours in the use of facilities.

In presenting information on industrial education enrollment to each of the senior high school principals and making proposals for future scheduling of such courses, department chairmen in each of the schools and the industrial education staff must understand the plans.

One of the greatest deterrents to developing a growing, dynamic program of industrial education is one poor program or instructor in a school. To help with such a situation, work closely with the personnel department in the recruitment and selection of teachers. The requirements for industrial education teachers are such that department chairmen, or supervisors, have a unique opportunity to help in teacher selection.

Work with the various members of the central staff and try to be prompt with answers to any requests they make. For example, as plans and equipment lists are requested for new industrial education facilities, try to have such plans or lists in the office before anyone else, and in so doing have established good relations with those concerned.

Make it a point to take administrators on visits to various classes, and in instances where a new class is being proposed in a school, take the principal to a school where such a class is in operation.

Another means of interpreting industrial education to the administration is in encouraging and helping industrial education teachers to become counselors and principals. As teachers in the department have been placed in such positions, it makes interpreting the program to students and staff easier.

There are at least three important factors which pertain to interpreting industrial education programs to the administration. One must explain, first, the changes which are taking place in the nature of the goals and methods of our industrial education classes; second, the increasing importance being attached to the need for public understanding; and third, the evolving and expanding meaning of democracy.

The most successful means of interpreting a program is founded upon common sense, personal integrity, initiative, and a genuine personal attitude of friendliness toward all persons in the community. Those persons especially interested in the industrial education program are administrators, taxpayers, public officials, students, parents, representatives of newspapers, members of civic groups, and fellow teachers.

The most important public relations devices that can be used are a sound industrial education program and YOU. Make the industrial education public relations program YOUR public relations program.

The program must be educationally sound and meet the purposes of public education as subscribed to by your administration. The worth of any program is reflected by its product, the children; by the teachers, and by the supervisory and administrative staff.

How does your administration feel about your program of industrial education? Do they understand its purposes in the overall curriculum of the school? Have you done a good job of interpreting industrial education to the school administration?

Disciplinary Problems

There are times when the administrator may encounter situations where an individual cannot be controlled by staff self-discipline. Even though the principal or supervisor may be striving for such self-discipline, he cannot permit the morale of the staff to be endangered because one person does not wish to be controlled by the self-imposed rules and regulations of the staff. When such a situation arises the administrator must recommend disciplinary action.

If the executive action is required in disciplinary cases the administrator must be able to distinguish between the authoritarian approach and the "democratic" approach. In the authoritarian approach, a breach of discipline occurs when the administrator's rules and regulations are violated. On the other hand, if a teacher fails to comply with the rules, policies, deadlines, etc., of the group he is actually hindering the accomplishment of the purposes of the group, and any discussion between the offender and the administrator must be on this basis.

Before any disciplinary action is taken, the administrator must get all the facts. This can usually be accomplished by one or more conferences with the teacher. Once the administrator ascertains that all the facts are presented and that there really is a breach of discipline, an effort must be made to determine the reason for the teacher's behavior.

Unsatisfactory behavior on the part of the teacher is usually a result of: definite conflict with an individual or individuals within the staff; resentment of some act or acts by the administrator; lack of recognition by the group or administrator of his efforts.

Every effort must be made to discover the reason for the behavior. The administrator must study his own behavior to determine if his actions were the cause of this breakdown of discipline. He must be as objective as possible and should at no time during the discussions show any unnecessary display of authority. By maintaining a calm, objective attitude and by sincerely seeking the facts and possible solutions he can impress upon the teacher his interest in the teacher's growth and his desire to maintain staff self-discipline.

Following the teacher-supervisor-principal discussions, the teacher may agree that he has violated the group-established purposes or rules and that he is willing to mend his ways; or he may refuse to agree that a mistake was committed. He may even reject any solution proposed by the supervisor. If the teacher agrees that he was in the wrong and shows that he is interested in rectifying his mistake, the supervisor should attempt to work out a mutually satisfactory course of action. This may mean that other members of the staff may be called upon to help find a solution to the existing problem.

On the other hand, the teacher who refuses to accept the solution poses a very unpleasant problem. In a situation of this type it may be necessary to suspend, transfer, or dismiss him. The administrator, however, should not resort to recommending any of these extreme measures until all avenues for helping the individual return to a voluntary acceptance of his responsibilities to the staff have been thoroughly explored. The final recommendation should be made in terms of what is best for the industrial education program. In cases where there is agreement on facts but disagreement on whether an action has been undisciplined the administrator should bring in other members of the staff to help make the final decision. Decisions made will be in the form of a recommendation to the responsible administrator.

References

1. "Administering Industrial Education," *Industrial Arts and Vocational Education*, May, 1961.
2. *Industrial Arts In Education.* Washington, D. C.: American Industrial Arts Association, American Council of Industrial Arts Supervisors, April, 1961.
3. Mathews, Chester O., "Self-Improvement of Supervisors," *Educational Leadership*, May, 1959.
4. Wiles, Kimball, *Supervision for Better Schools.* New York: Prentice-Hall, Inc., 1950.

Chapter 12

Trends in Industrial Education
That Affect Leadership

National attention is focused on vocational education as never before in history. The nation is taking a serious look at the process and product of vocational education. Industry, education, labor, economists, sociologists, urban planners, civic leaders, public relations firms, and many other groups, individuals, and organizations are seeing vocational education as a process for solving some of the human, social, and economic problems of our time.

The evidences of unemployment and occupational shortages also accentuate the emphasis now being given to vocational education programs. In September 1968 the unemployment rate dropped to 3.6 percent, but there were still serious pockets of unemployability and unemployment.

Vocational education must be ready to accept responsibility for training people for work. Recent experience in some of the manpower and other emergency training programs has shown that the individual suffers when education and training are treated as separate and apart.

Our schools are unique public institutions having custody of youth until they are well into their mid-teens. Thus, it is logical that our schools should be the institution to help all youngsters understand that education can be meaningful and can lead to career opportunities. On the other hand, our schools must be prepared to justify such promises. Too many of our schools are resigned, if not contented, to be mere custodians of our youngsters. Our society can no longer tolerate resigned, contented, or custodial education institutions.

Vocational education is the bridge between man and his work. Millions of people need this education in order to earn a living. Every man wants to provide for his family with honor and dignity and to be counted as an individual. Providing for an individual's employability as he leaves school, and throughout his work life, is one of the major goals of vocational education. Vocational education looks at a man as a part of society and as an individual. Never before has attention to the individual as a person been so imperative.

Vocational-Technical Education

Vocational education has meant different things to different people.

There are those who insist that all education is vocational. They argue that being able to read, write, and do simple calculations is necessary in most present-day employment; therefore, reading, writing, and arithmetic are vocational education subjects. The importance and necessity of skills in these subjects cannot be denied. Certainly vocational educators would be the last to minimize their importance to workers. In the sense that education is preparation for and aids in adjusting to life, and work is a major factor in everyone's life, *all* education *can* be thought of as vocational preparation in a broad general sense. (Perhaps education might be improved greatly if it *were* considered realistically as preparation for and an aid in adjusting to gainful employment.)

There are also those who believe that vocational education is confined to training of the hands. They visualize vocational education simply as practicing certain routine physical manipulations. Of course, development of manipulative skills is important. It is a basic *part* of any vocational course. The development of the routine skills of an occupation is not, however, the only aspect of vocational education. A realistic up-to-date view is wider in scope.

Vocational education has come to be accepted as that phase of education designed to improve the proficiency of an individual in a specific occupation. It is either preparatory for specific employment or supplementary to the work of those already employed in a specific occupation. It is not restricted to boys and girls in secondary schools but is provided for any youth or adult who needs and can profit from vocational education.

On all fronts . . . business, industry, agriculture, even the home . . . automation has advanced. The world of work and problems of preparation for it, access to it, and successful performance in it have become even more complex. Out of the changing social and economic environment of the past two decades have emerged clearer concepts of career, both in terms of occupation and higher education. From these concepts we can draw operational principles and design a system of legislative and administrative changes necessary for achieving vocational education for all.

For many occupations, the technical content has increased dramatically. Whole job categories have disappeared. Skills deemed essential in the past have become obsolescent. Most jobs today and for the foreseeable future require more complex understandings, less physical skill, more knowledge at the entry level, and greater versatility.

The need for more trained people to fill the jobs is already apparent and will continue to grow . . . and grow . . . and grow!

Too many young people have been allowed to leave the high schools each year, untrained and uneducated, yet society expects, and they expect to find jobs. America is faced with an alarmingly high rate of unemployment among young people . . . unemployment not because they are too lazy to work, but because they do not have the skills of modern technology.

We need to prepare young people for the fulfillment of participating in a meaningful way in the world of work. We need to prepare them for the vast range of occupations needed to keep a rapidly expanding economy operating.

Our goal should be a marketable skill for every youth and adult. This should be the goal of every school throughout the nation. Vocational education is the right of every young person and adult; it must be available to all in all kinds of education settings. Its programs must take into account the mobility of our population and the talents of our students. The curriculum cannot be based on immediate local needs alone.

We are on the verge of an educational revolution. This revolution in the making is bringing vocational education to the front as a leading force in the total education scheme. Vocational education has come of age; it is gaining increased respectability and recognition as the fields respond to the social needs of the times.

Enrollment in vocational education courses increased by nearly a million during 1967-68 to a total of more than seven million, and federal spending for such programs rose above the $257 million mark, a $23.7 million jump over the previous year's outlay.

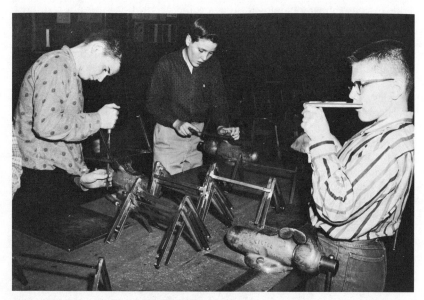

Fig. 12-1. Mass Production Experiences in Industrial Arts Provide
Insights and Understanding of Industrial
Methods and Organization

Trends in Industrial Arts

Our present-day society is highly organized and complex due, in part at least, to the rapid advancements in the sciences, engineering, and technology. Consumer demands for better things have made the production line an integral part of the culture. Mass production has put most of the objects used in modern living within the income bracket of most of American families, resulting in the highest standard of living in the world and more leisure time for recreation and hobbies than any other nation.

This great industrial progress has brought about many changes in educational programs in this country, especially in industrial arts, because industry has become a basic element of culture and because a prime purpose of industrial arts has become to provide youth a greater understanding of industry.

Industrial arts education, along with vocational education, is receiving more and more attention from educators these days with about 75 percent of U.S. secondary schools offering industrial arts courses, taught by some 40,000 teachers to approximately 4.5 million students.

It is essential that a high standard of craftsmanship be maintained in industrial arts. Considerable time must be spent with students to instill in them a sincere appreciation for good workmanship. However, this appreciation, if developed, will have a carry-over value in personal life, as well as in many phases of industry. To be sure, the change from the classroom to industry is great. In school, a student is able to take raw materials and painstakingly convert them into a useful object or a thing of beauty. When the project has been completed, there is a personal satisfaction in having created a work of art. The outcomes brought about through this type of education may be classified for convenience as knowledge, skills, attitudes, values, appreciation, and special abilities. The division of labor in modern industry seldom affords this type of experience; however, the patterns of behavior established in school enable the graduate to adjust himself to the group efforts of a company. He has participated in group efforts; he has learned the meaning of skill; he appreciates the perseverance required to become adept; and he has had an opportunity to develop a standard of quality performance.

Rapid technological changes have made it imperative for the industrial arts teacher to keep informed of new developments, for the technological advances should be reflected in the curriculum. Automation and nuclear energy are two good examples of vastly changing areas and should be considered in the periodic revision of industrial arts programs. (6)

We in industrial education are aware of the tremendous progress being made in America's industry. These changes have forced many changes in the curriculum. The tremendous expansion and modification of existing materials and the development of new and exotic materials has placed a new emphasis on the study of industrial materials, their use, and the processes of industry. The list is almost endless, and serves to emphasize the need for changing our industrial education curriculum. This change cannot be accomplished with the addition of new courses. It must be a reevaluation of what is being taught and the establishment of new instructional patterns based on changes within industry which utilize the basic knowledge needed for introductory instruction and the valuable content selected from existing programs.

Several curriculums being recommended for the schools seem to fall into a pattern of four areas; (1) *Industrial Communications*—including drafting, graphic arts, photography, computerized drafting, and industrial design; (2) *Materials and Processes*—either an integrated or a separate study of industrial materials and the processes used to form these materials into useful products. This includes wood, metals, plastic, and adhesives; (3) *Power Mechanics*—including sources of power, transmission through fluids, mechanics and electricity and uses such as transportation and aerospace; and (4) *Electronics*—including the study of electronic circuitry, instrumentation, and devices used in the home and industry.

In order to continue the movement toward this type of an updating pattern or toward any of the new curriculum patterns suggested by the American Industry Project, the Industrial Arts Curriculum Project, and other research and development programs, an organized process of change is needed. In industrial education this process requires three considerations: (1) *innovative curriculum*, (2) *educational media*, and (3) *inservice education.*

To get started on local innovations in industrial arts, ideas must grow out of enthusiastic teachers' concern for individual students.

Industrial Arts Curriculum Project

The Industrial Arts Curriculum Project is committed to the design, engineering, field testing and evaluation of curriculum materials for a two-year sequence in junior high school industrial arts. The first year of the sequence encompasses "Construction"; the second year will cover "Manufacturing." These two courses provide a study of the ways in which man modifies his environment—constructing on site and manufacturing in plant. Field testing involved more than 15,000 students.

Unique in the structure of Industrial Technology is the concept of psychomotor activity—the combination of mental learning reinforced with manual doing. Stress is placed upon the "how and doing" in addition to the "why and what." As a result, students are provided clarification and reinforcement of the concepts they study in the daily lessons.

American Industry Project

The American Industry Project proposes to substitute for conventional industrial arts courses a curriculum which emphasizes understanding of the spectrum of American Industry rather than skill development.

Industrial arts traditionally has accepted the challenge of giving its students an understanding of industry. But industry is finding it increasingly necessary to retrain its people, apparently because they do not have this understanding.

A structure of industry was identified, built around 14 major concepts—energy, processes, materials, production, management, marketing, personnel and industrial relations, purchasing, research, physical facilities, financing, public interest, transportation, and communication.

Subsequently, preliminary sets of subconcepts were identified. For example: under the major concept of energy would be forms of energy, harnessing energy, storage and transmission of energy and using energy. Under forms of energy would be mechanical, chemical, thermal, electrical and atomic.

The next step was fashioning the kind of curriculum that would enable students to see more effectively the relationships between the classroom work and the real world of industry. It would give the student knowledge and understanding that would enable him to solve problems related or created by industry as well as to think with a wider perspective. Otherwise society's interests would not be served as they must be.

A Good Program in Industrial Arts

The leaders of industrial arts education have two main objectives in mind: first, to bring the curriculum into focus with a modern industrial and technological society, not just today's, but tomorrow's too; and second, to unify industrial arts with the rest of the school's program. These objectives can be satisfied in many ways. One interesting example is the correlation of industrial arts with science. Recently, new efforts have been made to go beyond mere emphasis on design and workmanship, to correlate scientific principles with construction and to seek an educational application of the finished product. Thus, the students might build meterological instruments in which construction and application are tested as a unity of study. Strong evidence of this trend is to be found in some of the school-centered science fairs.

The unique and substantial contribution that industrial arts makes to a nation's educational program and its economic development is a fact too seldom understood by the teaching community and very rarely understood by the general public. Each member of the profession should understand the value of his field and work in his own way to impress his fellow teachers, students, parents, administrators, etc. with the contribution of industrial arts to achieving the goals of American education.

Specialization in Society

A general education through the high school is no longer a reasonable guarantee of job security and income progress, for the labor market is saturated with people who are so educated. An old-fashioned jack-of-all trades is obsolete and the need is for the master of one. In almost every profession, the expert receives *premium compensation.* For example, contrast the Orthodontist with the Dentist, the Tax Attorney with the General Lawyer, the Flooring Expert with the Carpenter, and the Carburetor Specialist with the Auto Mechanic.

Specialization is ever increasing and will likely continue as machines and devices become more complex, more automated. This underscores, of course, the plight of the individual who has no trade, no profession and no special talent. In tomorrow's labor market, the unskilled worker will be at a much greater relative disadvantage than he is today. Occupationally, there will be a greater need for specialized personnel in tomorrow's complex world. At the same time, intelligent consumption will demand a greater general orientation to technically sophisticated products and services if man is not to become the servant of his machines. Trends toward urbanization and population centers of unprecedented size and complexity will place ever-increasing stress on interpersonal relationships. (7)

Technical Education

A technician performs a wide variety of tasks since he fills the gap between the engineer and the skilled craftsman. Technicians work in manufacturing, distribution, sales, or servicing and so must have knowledge along with skills. Some of the more important groups of technicians include those working in electronics, instrumentation, drafting, chemistry, etc. Programs of technical education can start in the high school; however, they are usually two-year college degree courses.

It will be increasingly difficult to tell exactly the demarcations between industrial arts and vocational-industrial education and between vocational-industrial and technical education. For example, an industrial arts program in auto mechanics may be offered in a school to all students, but there might be an auto mechanics program for those students who wish to become skilled repairmen. There might also be a two- or four-year program in transportation technology. (7) Transitions from program to program will need to be facilitated; surely there would need to be provision for students to move from one to another.

Educational programs for technical occupations may take several forms within the next few years. No one can successfully predict where the leadership necessary for an education area of this magnitude will come. After the

National Defense Act of 1958 was passed, technical institutes through the United States and Canada established a pattern of college-level educational services designed for engineering technicians. These institutions, by virtue of established reputation and professional leadership, will undoubtedly continue to turn out technicians of high quality. An increasing number of schools of engineering are currently developing on-campus and satellite programs in fields of technology closely related to professional engineering. In all probability, these institutions will develop services patterned after accredited technical institute programs now offered at several state universities throughout the country.

Some states are developing separate vocational and technical schools while others are offering joint vocational-technical education in comprehensive high schools and community colleges. Each state must determine how it should best organize and conduct its program of vocational and technical education to meet the needs of industry and its citizens within its own educational philosophy. (7)

Occupational Trends

The many changes taking place in the economy and industry will have significant influence on industrial education by creating new occupations. To illustrate, the space age has created thousands of new opportunities in atomic energy, air transportation, and automation. As opportunities become more complex, there is a need for the further development of placement services. There must be the closest possible link between teachers, counselors, and placement personnel with agencies and organizations that are in a position to assist in the task of placing trained persons. (7)

Changes in the Labor Force

Occupations are now quite different from those of former years and further changes can be expected in the future. For example, 50 years ago more than 30% of all workers were on farms compared with fewer than 10% today. A gradual shift has been underway from blue collar to white collar occupations. The greatest growth in recent years has been in the professional, technical, and clerical occupations. Professional and technical occupations are expected to grow more rapidly in the future. There will be great demand for employees in all areas of health service, residential construction industry, the service industries, and the wholesale and retail trades.

CHANGE IN EMPLOYMENT 1968-1980

Occupational Group	Change
Professional and Technical	50% Increase
Proprietors and Managers	22% Increase
Clerical and Sales Workers	32% Increase
Skilled Workers	23% Increase
Semiskilled Workers	10% Increase
Service Workers	40% Increase
Unskilled Workers	No change
Farmers and Farm Workers	33% Increase

It may be observed in the above table that there is no change in the number of unskilled workers, and there is decrease in the number of farmers and farm workers. Chief gains in the numbers of workers are in areas requiring specialized training or unusual resources.

Occupational Surveys

At a vocational education conference in Philadelphia, Robert Heilbroner reported that in an examination of today's labor force, 9 million professional and technical workers are expected to increase 40% by 1975. In 1966, there were 8 million managers and proprietors, and the increase is approximated at 25% by 1975. This means that almost one in four of the labor force in 1975 will be in professional, technical, managerial or proprietary positions. These two categories accounted for one in ten of the labor force at the turn of the century. At the bottom of the employment pyramid, he found that during 1965 three-quarters of a million youngsters dropped out of school. Of the 26 million new workers in the decade ahead, it is anticipated that 7,500,000 will be dropouts. In some ghetto neighborhoods, the unemployment of teenagers ranges from 40% to 80%. Thus, although there is much talk of a need for a retraining and upgrading at all levels of the labor force, there is most urgency for an effective training program for the bottom of the pyramid. (8)

Educational Outlook

In the 1970's the American labor force is expected to rise to 100 million. 87 million will work full time, 26 million will be young workers, and 30 million will be women. A panel of consultants on vocational education considered the educational needs of all nonprofessional workers. Many now at work will need training to keep pace with new methods, materials, and opportunities, and others will require retraining as their jobs disappear due to automation or economic change. The local-state-federal vocational and technical program can provide appropriate training and retraining for them.

The 26 million young workers who will start work in this decade must adapt to the needs of the changing economy. Those students now in elementary schools who will not go on to college or who will drop out must secure occupational competence through on-the-job training and apprenticeships, public and private technical institutes in vocational and general high schools, the armed services, individual study and work, and (most likely) especially through a public program of vocational and technical education. The 30 million women who will hold full time jobs will also need marketable skills. Public vocational and technical programs can help these women improve skills and gain new ones.

The local-state-federal program of vocational and technical education was inaugurated in 1917 with the Smith-Hughes Act. Subsequent legislation expanded and extended the original programs. Enrollments in vocational education for fiscal years 1960-1967 as listed by U.S. Department of Health Education and Welfare, were as follows:

Fiscal Year	Total Enrollment	Percentage Increase
1960	3,768.149	
1961	3,855,564	2.3
1962	4,072,677	5.6
1963	4,217,198	3.5
1964	4,566,390	8.3
1965	5,430,611	18.9
1966	6,070,059	11.8
1967	6,880,000*	13.3

*Projected

The major concern of the Panel of Consultants in 1968 was the strengths and limitations of local-state-federal programs, including implications of automation, technology, population mobility, discrimination organization, and the administration of the programs. The panel recommended that vocational education must:

1. Offer training opportunities to the noncollege graduates who will enter the labor market in the late 1960's and the 1970's.
2. Provide training for the millions of workers whose skills and technical knowledge must be updated, as well as those whose jobs will disappear due to increasing efficiency, automation, and economic change.
3. Meet the critical need for highly skilled craftsmen and technicians through education during and after the high school years.
4. Expand vocational and technical training programs consistent with employment possibilities and national economic needs.

5.　　Make educational opportunities equally available to all, regardless of race, sex, scholastic aptitude, or place of residence. (5)

The panel also concluded that the Federal government must continue
to work with states and local communities to develop and improve the skills
of its citizens. In place of the occupational categories specified in existing
statutes, the panel recommends that the local-state-federal partnership increase support of vocational and technical education for high school students
preparing to enter the labor market or become homemakers, youth with
special academic or socioeconomic problems or other handicaps that prevent
them from succeeding in the usual high school vocational education program,
youth and adults who have completed or left high school, full-time post-high-
school students preparing to enter the labor market, youth and adults
unemployed or at work who need training or retraining to achieve employment stability. Adequate services and facilities must be provided.

To assure quality in all vocational and technical education programs,
the panel recommended the following:

1.　　Institutions of higher education, especially land-grant colleges
and state universities, should provide for the professional growth
of vocational and technical teachers.

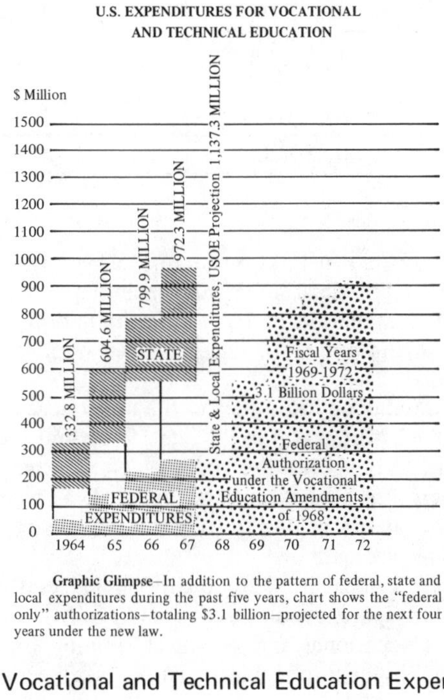

**U.S. EXPENDITURES FOR VOCATIONAL
AND TECHNICAL EDUCATION**

Graphic Glimpse—In addition to the pattern of federal, state and
local expenditures during the past five years, chart shows the "federal
only" authorizations—totaling $3.1 billion—projected for the next four
years under the new law.

Fig. 12-2. Vocational and Technical Education Expenditures

ENROLLMENT IN VOCATIONAL EDUCATION CLASSES, BY LEVEL OF PROGRAM
Fiscal Years 1963-1968

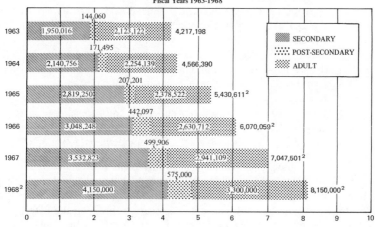

¹Projected Data

²Includes Special Needs¹

LEVEL OF PROGRAM (MILLIONS)

Frame of Reference—This protrayal of gains in vo-ed enrollment since the passage of VEA '63 captures the impact of stepped-up federal support. Recently announced USOE projections foresee the totals climbing to 9,600,000 by 1970 and to 14,000,000 by 1975.

Fig. 12-3. Vocational Education Enrollment

TOTAL EXPENDITURES FOR CONSTRUCTION OF AREA VOCATIONAL SCHOOLS
Vocational Education Act of 1963 and Matching Funds
Fiscal Years 1965 to 1968

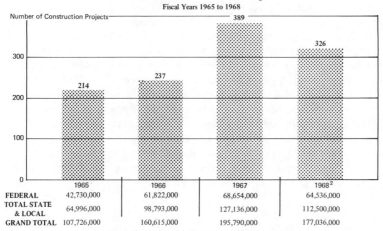

Number of Construction Projects — 389

	1965	1966	1967	1968²
FEDERAL	42,730,000	61,822,000	68,654,000	64,536,000
TOTAL STATE & LOCAL	64,996,000	98,793,000	127,136,000	112,500,000
GRAND TOTAL	107,726,000	160,615,000	195,790,000	177,036,000

¹Projected Data

Physical Plant Perspective—Also earmarked for substantial expansion under the new law is this four-year pattern of growth in expenditures for area-school physical facilities.

Fig. 12-4. Expenditures for Area Vocational Schools Construction

2. Basic educational material laboratories should be established in appropriate institutions and financed and coordinated through the Division of Vocational and Technical Education of the U.S. Office of Education.
3. State and national leadership of guidance services for programs should be supported and coordinated at the national level by the Division of Vocational and Technical Education.
4. Research and development in vocational and technical education should be encouraged, supported, and coordinated at the national level. The results of this research and development should be made available on a nationwide basis. (5)

Adults must have educational opportunities because they already constitute a considerable part of the great number of unemployed and are in need of a type of education that will fit them for useful life. For retraining to be done on a full-time basis, it would be necessary to broaden the offerings in the schools beyond the three or four types of work usually found in the school shop. Area schools scattered over the country drawing students from a wide area might be designed as centers for training in one or more types of work not commonly found in most high schools and in which there is a demand for workers. If this were done, all trainees could be directed to the center where training for the occupation selected by the trainee were offered.

The retraining of technologically displaced persons is a matter of national concern. One suggestion has been that these programs should be a direct responsibility of the Federal government. If this arrangement were in operation, it would be possible for individuals to cross state lines to another state where the most applicable training is available. The U.S. Department of Labor already determines when or where a surplus or a shortage of labor exists and those occupations in which training should be provided. A cooperative effort could insure that when the supply of workers exceeded the demand in any field, training for that occupation would be eliminated. (1)

As a result of existing federal programs, more adults appear to be attending some form of organized educational activity than in former years. Stimulated by increased educational offerings, state subsidies, and other factors, large numbers of adults are attending part-time day and evening classes, as well as full-time programs. Many of the adult courses are vocational in nature. Some cities have reported that their programs reach 10% of the total population of the city in one form or another.

Federal Programs

Basic to the purpose of the vocational acts are six fundamental ideas which may be briefly summarized:

1.   The programs of vocational education are geared to immediate and future needs on a local, state, regional, and national basis.
2.   Programs to be offered under terms of the act prepare students for employment in a great variety and range of jobs. Training includes the entire occupational spectrum, excluding only those jobs which the Commissioner of Education determines as professional or which require a bachelor's degree.
3.   All citizens must have access to education and training that is of high quality and realistic in terms of opportunities for gainful employment.
4.   Vocational education programs are conducted in any type of school or educational institution. This provision includes comprehensive specialized vocational-technical, and technical high schools; junior, community, public and private colleges; and universities. Vocational programs may be conducted in private schools under contract with the state board or local educational agency.
5.   Special emphasis is placed on periodic evaluation of goals and progress. The states are required to evaluate their programs and vocational services continuously in the light of labor-market needs and the needs of all groups in all communities of the state.
6.   Research and development, long tools of successful business and industries, are assigned an important place in the future of vocational education. (3)

Pilot and Exemplary Programs

There is a great need for pilot and exemplary programs to determine the effectiveness of vocational education and work experience for those who drop out of school, for the aging, and other special groups. After such pilot programs are operated for a period of time, a careful evaluation should delineate the successful approaches, activities, and programs so that full-scale efforts may be launched to bring these persons to appropriate competency levels. There is likewise a need for the further development of research and experimentation in all types of vocational education.

A continuation and extension of current vocational education programs will not meet all of the needs for vocational education. Special types of vocational education are needed for such groups as the handicapped, migrant farm workers, the unemployed, and the underemployed.

For example, a vocational education and training program for handicapped and disadvantaged has been initiated in the Tulsa, Oklahoma, schools. The comprehensive program encompasses teacher training, pilot projects, and appropriate curriculum necessary to meet the needs of youth, fourteen years of age or older, who are not served by any present Tulsa vocational program.

The largest project in the program is Career Exploration (orientation to the world of work) in the junior high school. Teachers in this project are certified in Industrial Arts, Home and Family Living, and Business Education. The Career Exploration part of the program includes four mobile units for these junior high school students, providing experiences in a wide variety of occupational areas in (1) construction and manufacturing; (2) power, transportation, and service; (3) business, clerical, and sales; and (4) home economics and health. High school vocational projects for handicapped and disadvantaged youth include courses in such areas as building and construction, home and community jobs, household maintenance and community services, checker-cashier training as well as such assistance as counseling, guidance, and placement. Expected result of the program is an increase in the social vocational knowledge, a positive attitude toward the world of work, and eventual gainful employment.

Vocational education programs have been operated for over half a century. Service studies, appraisals, and research have been a means for organizing, developing, and improving them over the years. Programs for the future can be assembled and analyzed using the basic facts and information gathered and contributed to the attainment of the proposals suggested. (7)

Research in Vocational Studies

The following facts indicate the need for a study of the vocational education programs:

1.   Approximately 50% of the students who graduate from high school go immediately into the labor market.

2.   One of the major reasons why approximately 25% of those who enter high school drop out before graduation is that they do not have enough chance to develop "salable" skills.

3.   The minimum beginning age for employment has been pushed up and the long-term trend seems to be in that direction. Many employers are unwilling to hire workers below the age of 18 years, and some state laws enforce this higher age level.

4.   At present, the high schools fail to serve adequately a large number of students neither destined for college nor for skilled occupations.

Emerging Federal Role in Vocational Education

Responding to a variety of needs and situations, the Federal government has enacted legislation to create a variety of new programs which are significant to industrial education. In essence, this legislation continues the traditional approach of categorical aid. Consequently, the supervisor and administrator must be familiar with the purposes and specific applications of the various programs. Brief summaries of these programs are included in the following paragraphs.

The purpose of vocational education as stated in the Vocational Education Act of 1963 follows: ... so that persons of all ages in all communities of the State ... will have ready access to vocational training or retraining which is of high quality, which is realistic in the light of actual or anticipated opportunities for gainful employment, and which is suited to their needs, interests and abilities to benefit from such training.

Vocational education is on the threshold of great expansion. To accomplish the purpose of the Vocational Education Act of 1963 and the Amendments of 1968, vocational education is serving more people and is changing to meet the actual and anticipated opportunities for employment. Current projects in research and demonstration are validating many of the practices used, disproving some, and revealing new ones.

It is no longer an academic question whether vocational programs should be expanded, remain as they are, or dropped. Technical developments and social change have set the stage for development and expansion. It is up to the vocational educator to meet this challenge.

Today, and in the years ahead, successful vocational educators must keep abreast of, give support to, and be a part of new developments in their field.

1968 Amendments to Vocational Education Act

Following is a brief summary of the provisions of the Vocational Education Amendments of 1968: (2)

1. **Authorization of Appropriations**

    Authorizes $355 million for FY 1969, $565 million for FY 1970, $675 million each for FY 1971 and 1972, and $565 million for FY 1973 and each succeeding fiscal year. Ninety percent of these funds shall be for (Part B) grants to states for basic vocational education programs, and 10 percent for (Part C) research and training in vocational education.

    For each of fiscal years 1969 and 1970, $40 million is authorized for programs for the disadvantaged and the handicapped. Also, there is authorized such sums as may be necessary to pay the cost of the development and administration of state plans, advisory councils, evaluation and dissemination.

2. **National and State Advisory Councils**

    Establishes a National Advisory Council on Vocational Education; requires each state desiring to receive a grant to establish a state advisory council. State councils shall be appointed by the Governor or, in the case of states in which the members of the state board are elected, council members shall be appointed by the state board.

3.   **State Vocational Education Programs (Part B)**
     Authorizes grants to the states to assist them in conducting vocational education programs for persons of all ages in all communities of the states. Programs must insure that education and training for career vocations are available to all individuals who desire and need such education and training.

4.   **Research and Training (Part C)**
     Authorizes the Commissioner to use 50 percent of the sums available under this Part to make grants to and contracts with institutions of higher education, public and private agencies and institutions, state boards, and local education agencies to support research and training in vocational education, experimental and demonstration programs, and to meet special vocational education needs of new careers and occupations. The remaining 50 percent of the sums authorized shall be used by the state boards for (a) paying up to 75 percent of the costs of the state research coordinating unit, and (b) grants to colleges and universities, and other public or nonprofit private agencies and institutions to pay 90 percent of the costs of programs for research and training, experimental and pilot programs, and for dissemination of information about the result of these programs.

5.   **Exemplary Programs and Projects (Part D)**
     Authorizes the Commissioner of Education to use 50 percent of the sums available to the states under this Part to make grants to or contracts with state boards or local education agencies (or other organizations and institutions which can make an especially significant contribution to the purposes of this Part) to pay all or part of the costs of creating a bridge between school and earning a living for young people, who are still in school, who have left school either by graduation or by dropping out, or who are in post secondary programs of vocational preparation, and for promoting cooperation between public education and manpower agencies.
     The state board may use the remaining 50 percent for making grants to or contracts with local educational agencies or other agencies and organizations to pay all or part of the costs of developing and operating exemplary occupational education programs.
     Authorizes appropriations of $15 million for FY 1969, $57.5 million for FY 1970, and $75 million for 1971 and 1972.

6.   **Residential Vocational Education (Part E)**
     Authorizes appropriations of $25 million for FY 1969, $30 million for FY 1970, and $35 million each in fiscal years 1971 and 1972, for the Commissioner to make grants to state boards, colleges and universities, and public education agencies for the construction and

operation of residential schools to provide vocational education for youth 15-21.

Also authorizes appropriations of $15 million each for fiscal years 1969 and 1970, for grants to the states to provide residential vocational education facilities.

The federal share of the cost of planning, constructing, and operating residential vocational education facilities may not exceed 90 percent of the costs in any fiscal year.

7. **Grants to Reduce Borrowing Costs**

Authorizes such sums as may be necessary for the Commissioner to make annual grants to state boards, colleges and universities, and public education agencies to reduce the cost of borrowing funds for the construction of residential schools and dormitories.

8. **Consumer and Homemaking Education (Part F)**

Authorizes appropriations of $25 million for FY 1970, $35 million for FY 1971, and $50 million for FY 1972 for state programs of education which (a) encourage home economics to give greater consideration to social and cultural conditions and needs, especially in economically depressed areas, (b) encourage preparation for professional leadership, (c) are designed for youths and adults through preparation for the role of homemaker, or to contribute to the employability of such youths and adults through preparation for the dual role of homemaker and wage earner, (d) include consumer education programs, (e) are designed for homemakers, and (f) include auxiliary services such as teacher training, curriculum development and experimental programs. Programs are included under the state plan. One-third of the funds must be spent for programs in economically depressed areas and such funds so expended may be matched on a 90-10 basis.

9. **Cooperative Vocational Education Programs (Part G)**

Authorizes appropriations of $20 million for FY 1959, $35 million for FY 1970, $50 million for FY 1971, and $75 million for FY 1972 for grants to the states for programs of vocational education designed to prepare students for employment through cooperative work-study arrangements. Program must be under the state plan.

10. **Work-study Programs for Vocational Education Students (Part H)**

Authorizes appropriations of $35 million each for fiscal years 1969 and 1970 for state programs to provide work-study arrangements for students in vocational education. Program is a continuation of the work-study program authorized under the Vocational Education Act of 1963.

11. **Curriculum Development**

Authorizes appropriations of $7 million for FY 1969 and $10 million for FY 1970 to enable the Commissioner to make grants to or contracts with colleges and universities, state boards, and other organi-

VOCATIONAL EDUCATION AMENDMENTS OF 1968

Program	Authorization	Matching Provision
1. Grants to States for comprehensive programs and training and research:		50-50
Fiscal year 1969	$355,000,000	
Fiscal year 1970	565,000,000	
Fiscal year 1971	675,000,000	
Fiscal year 1972	675,000,000	
Each year thereafter	565,000,000	
2. Programs for disadvantaged:		up to 100%
Fiscal year 1969	40,000,000	
Fiscal year 1970	40,000,000	
3. Administration of all new programs	*	
4. Administration by O.E. and States of comprehensive programs	*	
5. Work Study:		80-20
Fiscal year 1969	35,000,000	
Fiscal year 1970	35,000,000	
6. Exemplary programs:		up to 100%
Fiscal year 1969	15,000,000	
Fiscal year 1970	57,500,000	
Fiscal year 1971	75,000,000	
Fiscal year 1972	75,000,000	
7. Cooperative Vocational Education:		all or part
Fiscal year 1969	20,000,000	
Fiscal year 1970	35,000,000	
Fiscal year 1971	50,000,000	
Fiscal year 1972	75,000,000	
8. Demonstration residential schools:		up to 100%
Fiscal year 1969	25,000,000	
Fiscal year 1970	30,000,000	
Fiscal year 1971	35,000,000	
Fiscal year 1972	35,000,000	

Program	Authorization	Matching Provision
9. Grants to States for residential schools:		90-10
Fiscal year 1969	$15,000,000	
Fiscal year 1970	15,000,000	
10. Dormitories:		cost above 3%
Fiscal year 1969	5,000,000	
Fiscal year 1970	10,000,000	
11. Consumer and homemaking education:		50-50
Fiscal year 1970	25,000,000	1/3 to 90%
Fiscal year 1971	35,000,000	
Fiscal year 1972	50,000,000	
12. Curriculum development:		up to 100%
Fiscal year 1969	7,000,000	
Fiscal year 1970	10,000,000	
13. National Advisory Council:		
Fiscal year 1969	100,000	
Fiscal year 1970	150,000	
Fiscal year 1971	150,000	
Fiscal year 1972	150,000	
Fiscal year 1973		
14. Vocational education professions development:		Sec. 552
Fiscal year 1969	25,000,000	Individual grants
Fiscal year 1970	35,000,000	Sec. 553 up to 100%

*Such sums as may be appropriated

The above are authorization figures which were passed by the last Congress. It remains to be seen what the next Congress will see fit to appropriate to implement vocational and technical education programs. If Congress should see fit to make a full appropriation, next school year could be a banner year in vocational and technical education.

Fig. 12-5.

zations, to promote the development and dissemination of vocational education curriculum materials.

12. **Training and Development Programs for Vocational Education Personnel**

Authorizes appropriations of $25 million for FY 1969 and $35 million for FY 1970 to enable the Commissioner to give Leadership Development Awards (stipends) to vocational education personnel to attend institutions of higher education having approved vocational education leadership development programs. Includes a cost of education allowance payment to the institution of up to $3,500 per year.

Also authorizes the Commissioner to make grants to state boards to pay the cost of carrying out cooperative arrangements for the training or retraining of experienced vocational education personnel, including exchange of teachers with skilled technicians in industry, inservice training programs, institutes, and familiarizing teachers with new curricular materials.

The new and added resources for vocational education indicate some new and special areas of emphasis. These implications seem apparent:

1. The states and local communities must create a universal continuing system of vocational education to serve the occupational training needs of all persons of all ages in all communites. Such programs must utilize all resources available to the community.
2. The primary mission of vocational education is that part of a total program of education that prepares a person for employment or for advancement in a job. However, vocational education must now assume more responsibility for prevocational courses and programs, for guidance and counseling, and for the development of programs and projects designed to reorient the school curriculum to the end that all students have better knowledge and understanding of the world of work.
3. Vocational education must greatly expand its offerings in job preparation through the technique or process of cooperative work-study programs.
4. Emphasis must be given to the preparation of vocational education leadership and to upgrading of personnel and inservice training for new vocational education personnel.
5. More vocational education programs must be designed to serve the special needs of the disadvantaged and the handicapped.[4]

Constant changes in congressional action and funding for vocational and technical education will require that leadership be exercised in being alert to changes in this or succeeding legislation.

Economic Opportunity Act of 1964

The $947.5 million dollar act was signed into law by President Johnson as Public Law 88-452. Commonly referred to as the "Anti-Poverty Bill," the educationally-oriented measure is a combination of about a dozen programs.

Elementary and Secondary Education Act of 1965

The Elementary and Secondary Education Act of 1965 (ESEA) was the first major legislation enacted by the 89th Congress. Keyed to poverty, ESEA virtually doubles the amount of federal aid available to schools. There are five major provisions in this legislation.

TITLE I provides for payment of one-half the average per pupil expenditure for children from families with an income below $2000 per year.

TITLE II authorizes distribution of $100 million to the states for acquisition of library resources, including textbooks and audio-visual materials.

TITLE III authorizes distribution of $100 million for grants to local schools for establishment of supplementary education centers. An extremely wide range of activities may be authorized under this title. Under its terms, school authorities are required to cooperate with other educational and cultural interests in the community. The specially designed activities which might be included in a supplementary education center are specialized instruction, including mobile services.

TITLE IV makes another $100 million available over the next five years for regional educational research and training facilities.

TITLE V appropriates $25 million to strengthen state departments of education. Grants are made available to undertake special projects which will improve services rendered to local school districts.

Funds under the first three titles go to local schools. Funds under Titles IV and V go to other agencies.

National Defense Education Act

When the National Defense Education Act was first enacted in 1959, Senator Majority Leader Lyndon B. Johnson commented, "History may well record that we have saved liberty and saved freedom when we undertook a crash program in the field of education." When Johnson became President, he later signed a bill amending and extending the NDEA; he reminisced that "first things must still come first."

NDEA encompasses many types of aid in various programs, several of which provide direct benefits to local schools; although sometimes such benefits do not take the form of cash payments.

TITLE I furnishes a guide to the general provisions of the act.

TITLE II authorizes $180 million for a loan program to assist college students.

TITLE III authorizes $90 million annually for a federal-state matching grant program from which local schools derive direct benefits. These funds may be used to purchase materials and equipment which will strengthen instruction in science, mathematics, history, civics, geography, modern foreign languages, English, and reading. Industrial Arts was added to this title in 1967 and this should help strengthen this subject area.

TITLE IV provides for graduate fellowships to help colleges meet the need for an increasing number of teachers.

TITLE V appropriates nearly $25 million for matching grants to the states in support of guidance and counseling programs in public schools. Such grants can be used for both testing and guidance programs with special emphasis in junior and senior high schools.

TITLE VI provides support for programs which furnish training for foreign language teachers.

TITLE VII authorizes direct grants-in-aid to local school districts for experimentation and development of new education media. Special attention is directed to new methods of utilizing audio-visual systems.

TITLE VIII was replaced by the Vocational Education Act of 1963.

TITLE IX authorizes the National Science Foundation to provide for a general science information service.

TITLE X provides grants for state education agencies to improve statistical services.

TITLE XI appropriates $32 million annually for grants to support operation of teacher training institutions open to elementary and secondary school teachers.

TITLES III, V, and VII are of direct interest to public schools. In addition, TITLES VI and XI provide training for teachers already in the schools.

Vocational Education Act of 1963

The Vocational Education Act of 1963 opened the door to the establishment of comprehensive vocational education programs at the secondary school level. This act, Part A of Public Law 88-210, provides for allocations to the states, based on proportionate population in various age groups. No state is allotted less than $10,000 annually. The Vocational Education Act reserves an appropriation for research and demonstration grants authorized by the Commissioner of Education. Distribution of vocational education funds is contingent upon a state plan submitted by the agency having jurisdiction over vocational education activities.

Local school officials are urged to maintain a close contact with field offices of the Labor Department's Bureau of Employment Security. This office can advise school officials of the skills which are in greatest demand.

The vocational education program is intended to provide a means to meet the needs of the labor market. Nearly $18 million was available during the fiscal year 1966 for vocational education research and demonstration projects. Several hundred R & D projects have been approved since 1963 with payments ranging from $1500 to well over one million dollars. Most of these grants have gone to institutions of higher education and other nonprofit research organizations. Public schools may, however, participate in this program and are urged to do so.

The Amendments of 1968 essentially rewrote the 1963 Act.

Manpower Development and Training Act of 1961

The manpower Development and Training Act of 1961 (MDTA) can provide substantial assistance in supporting school adult vocational education programs. MDTA activities include testing, counseling, and referral for training or retraining of unemployed or underemployed workers. Arrangements for such training are channeled through the U.S. Office of Education and the appropriate state agency responsible for vocational education.

MDTA offers financial aid in training youths 16 years of age or older, including dropouts. Furthermore, priority for such training is granted to programs which will result in a reasonable expectation of employment, either locally or within the same state. MDTA activities are initiated by Labor Department officials in local offices of the Bureau of Employment Security. Unemployed and underemployed persons are tested and counseled to determine their needs for education and training. Based on the unfilled demand for various skills, such persons are selected for appropriate training. Recommendations of the local employment security office are then forwarded through state and regional offices to Washington. The Manpower Administration refers the matter to the Office of Education which is charged with the responsibility of providing a suitable program. The state vocational education agency is then requested to make necessary arrangements at the local level. (In most cases this means the public schools.)

It is generally up to local school officials to establish the requirements of a proposed MDTA program, including its estimated cost. Assuming that the local school district is capable of undertaking the proposed MDTA program, at reasonable cost, the U.S. Office of Education authorizes the state agency to proceed. Payments are made to the state which, in turn, distributes the funds to local school authorities. MDTA payments do not affect state allotments under the Vocational Education Act of 1963.

Area Vocational-Technical Education

The concept of Area Vocational-Technical Schools embraces training for all who need it. Specifically, the Vocational Education Act of 1963 and the 1968 amendments provide for training of high school students; full-time study for persons who have completed or left high school; persons employed but who need training or retraining to achieve stability or advancement in employment; and for persons who have academic, socio-economic, or other handicaps that prevent them from succeeding in the regular vocational education programs.

Issues in Vocational-Technical Education

Who will be responsible for vocational and technical education in America? Will it be the public schools, including high schools, area vocational schools, and community colleges? Will it be other governmental agencies such as the Job Corps and Labor Department or private industry and private trade schools? Most leaders firmly believe that the best and most efficient method is for free public education to have the responsibility for this important part of the education of young Americans.

How will funds be provided for vocational and technical education? In spite of increased federal appropriations for these programs, there is still a serious shortage of monies to accomplish the job. In comparing federal appropriations for vocational and technical education in the United States to those in Canada, we find that federal appropriations in Canada amount to approximately ten times as much per capita as in the United States. If the per-capita appropriation for vocational education at the federal level were to equal that authorized in Canada in 1967, the United States would have to spend at least ten times as much at the federal level. Vocational education today is truly everybody's business.

New Perspectives for Vocational Teachers

For the first time in history, the availability of federal funds, Congressional initiative, and national approval have provided broadened possibilities for schools on several levels to participate in expanded programs in the field of vocational and technical education. In secondary schools throughout the nation, large numbers of young people are now being served with improved programs of vocational and technical education.

The great numbers in post-secondary institutions who now have a wide choice of vocational opportunities in the fields of industry, manufacturing, technical occupations, health occupations, business, distribution, and agricultural endeavor, indicate the extent to which both financial help and moral support from state and federal sources are producing measurable program results.

In several states, industrial education centers, technical institutes, junior colleges, and community colleges have seen the challenge which the new legislation affords and have seized the opportunity to provide needed vocational education as part of a wide spectrum of choices for individuals—both on the all-day preemployment training level and on the adult and extension level.

Vocational Education Stands Tall

With popular enthusiasm, with public support, and with funds to provide not only "quality" vocational education but also breadth of vocational opportunities, the time has come for the vocational educator to recognize his position on the education team, and while extending and improving his own highly specialized competency, to recognize also the valid contributions made by others.

Vocational education as a dynamic force in the nation has "arrived;" its relationship to the burgeoning economy of the nation and its sociological effects have been acknowledged and demonstrated in the Congress and established throughout the nation. Thus, personnel who are or who will teach in institutions offering vocational education opportunities would be well advised to adopt a truly positive attitude rather than the defensive one characteristic of earlier vocational education enthusiasts. Vocational educators should now stand tall in the councils of educators. They should make their contributions knowing well that stature and respect is now part of the vocational enterprise.

Internships

The internship, not yet fully developed in the nation, has been demonstrated as one of the most effective means of helping prospective faculty members acquire many of the competencies needed to perform effectively as teachers of vocational or related vocational subjects.

Diversified Programs

Programs should be available for girls interested in developing skills in typing, stenography, the use of clerical machines, home economics, or a specialized branch of home economics which, through further work in college, might lead to such professions as dietitian. Distributive education should be available if the retail shops in the community can be persuaded to provide suitable openings. If the community is rural, vocational agriculture should be included. For boys depending on the community, trade and industrial programs should be available. Half a day is required in the 11th and 12th grades for this vocational work. In each specialized trade, there should be an advisory committee composed of representatives of management and labor.

The school administration should constantly assess the employment situation in those trades included in the vocational programs. When opportunities for employment in a given trade no longer exist within the community, the training program in that field should be dropped. The administration should be ready to introduce new vocational programs as opportunities open in the community or area. In some communities, advanced programs of a technical nature should be developed; these programs often involve more mathematics than is usually required for the building trades or auto mechanics programs.

Advisory Committees

Purpose of Advisory Committees

The purpose of advisory committees is to provide a link between the school and the community through which their activities may be coordinated. Their function is to counsel with and advise the school with respect to improving the vocational program, to foster closer cooperation between agriculture, industry, business, the home, and the school and thus to aid in the development of an educational program which will more adequately meet the needs of the community. They have no administrative or legislative authority and are not created to usurp the prerogatives of boards of education and administrative staffs.

Such groups are referred to under various names, but the title is not so significant as the purpose. Whether they are called boards, commissions, councils, or committees, the important thing is that they serve in an advisory capacity. Many schools prefer to use the word "committee" because "council" or "board" denotes a certain degree of legislative authority, while "advisory committee" implies advice, investigation and reporting back, but does not include any legislative or administrative responsibilities.

Kinds of Advisory Committees

Advisory committees are set up to perform many different services in connection with the school's vocational program. Sometimes they serve in a general advisory capacity, sometimes as advisors for a particular field or occupation or for a special phase of the program. Temporary advisory committees may also be appointed, for a single specific task, to be disbanded upon the completion of their work.

General Advisory Committee

A general advisory committee is appointed to assist in the development and maintenance of the entire vocational education program offered by the school or school district. It helps to ascertain the training needs of the service area, to keep the program realistic and practical, to develop community understanding and support of the methods and objectives of vocational education, and to build prestige and respect for vocational education. The chief values of such committees are their importance in producing good public relations and in keeping the program of vocational training in tune with the demands of the community.

Some Imperative Educational Needs

The past emphasis on matching the best man with an existing job must be replaced with emphasis on providing a suitable job for each man or equipping the man to fill a suitable job. Emphasis now placed on manpower as an economic resource must also be placed on employment as a source of income and status for workers and their families.

An opportunity must be provided the individual to improve his employment status and earnings and to adapt to a changing economic environment and an expanding economy.

Career consciousness must be integrated throughout the schools in order to enlarge the number of options and alternatives for individual pupils—both in terms of occupations and higher education.

The study of the world of work is a valid part of education for all children—it documents for youth the necessity of education, both academic and vocational.

Industry is investing billions of dollars in technological devices and equipment required to produce complex products. Unless we can also produce technically trained people to use and operate that equipment, it will be useless.

Our economic survival depends on the knowledge and skills of our employees.

The impact of technological development on the social, economic, and educational sectors of our lives has impelled industry to seek a closer partnership with the educational community.

Both industry and the schools have recognized common problems and a common mission. That mission is to collaborate in establishing a continuing program of vocational and technical courses in order to improve the standards of the educational system, and to qualify students for employment in jobs available in the community.

One problem which we have not yet surmounted is how to educate the less gifted student. An expanding technology demands that we find ways to teach people who have little education or have poorly developed learning skills. Although the answer is complex, the aim is to identify what should be taught, to whom it should be taught, and how to teach it.

Much of the progress that takes place must begin with the teacher training institutions. They really hold the key to the promotion and progress of vocational programs. In vocational education we may receive large amounts of money and lose much of our potential progress because teachers are not available or poorly prepared. In the final analysis, it still falls on the teachers' shoulders. Many of us wait and ask: where is the pattern, the model? In most cases you will not get one. You must move ahead on your belief, experience and dare to innovate.

Achieving the goal of better secondary schools requires a focus on change. School administrators and classroom teachers need constantly to seek new ways to organize classes, new methods of instruction, and new ways of utilizing staff resources so that they will better serve the needs of youth and American life.

Change is the order of the day. All in education must keep alert to new developments and be ready to exercise leadership.

References

1. "A Job for the Schools," *School Shop*, May, 1961.
2. *An Act*, Amendments To The Vocational Education Act of 1963, Public Law 90-576, 90th Congress, HR 18366, October 16, 1968.
3. Arnold, Walter, *Industrial Arts and Vocational Education*, May, 1965.
4. *AVA Like It Is*. Washington, D. C.: American Vocational Association.
5. *Education for a Changing World of Work*. Washington, D. C.: Department of Health, Education, and Welfare. (Report of the Panel of Consultants for Vocational Education)
6. *Industrial Arts In Education*. Washington, D. C.: American Industrial Arts Association, American Council of Industrial Arts Supervisors, April, 1961.
7. *Vocational Education in the Next Decade*. Washington, D. C.: Department of Health, Education, and Welfare, January, 1961.
8. "Vocational Education Today and Tomorrow," Philadelphia: Philadelphia Public Schools, February 25-26, 1966. (Report of a conference on vocational education)

Appendix A

Departmental Bulletins
Express School Policies

Typical List of Bulletins

Opening the School Year

Instructions for Closing Shops, Laboratories and Classrooms

Policies for Vocational Graphics Arts

Enrollment Report

Typical List of Bulletins

Bulletins available from the office in the Education Service Center for the Department of Industrial Arts and Vocational-Technical Education

**Bulletin
Number**

1	Instructions for Writing Requisitions
2	Resale Deposits
3	Instructions for Use of Receipt and Refund Books
4	Methods of Making Deposits of Resale Money to Treasurer
5	Opening of the School Year
6	Steps in Teaching (Preparation or introduction, Presentation, Application and Evaluation)
7	Safety Instruction
8	Responsibilities of Industrial Arts Instructors
9	Methods of Instruction
10	Recommendations of Production, Sales, and Economy
11	Design
12	Industrial Cooperative Training in the Tulsa Public Schools
13	Vocational-Industrial Classes
14	Distributive Education
15	Requirements for Good Tool Racks or Panels
16	Practical Work in Shop Classes
17	Related Study in Junior High School Shop Classes
18	General Safety
19	Shop Painting – Using Color Dynamics
20	Reading Skills and Habits Needed in Industrial Arts
21	Self-Appraisal Questions for Instructors of Industrial Arts and Vocational-Technical Education Classes
22	Personnel Responsibility Chart
23	Suggested Industrial Arts and Vocational-Technical Education Classes
24	Instructions for Closing Shop
25	Instructions for Vocational Teachers
26	Suggestions for Shop Organization and Management
27	Safety Rules
28	Safety Rules – While Using Spray Gun
29	Motivation

30   Vocational Guidance for Industrial Arts and Vocational-
         Technical Education
31   Industrial Arts Education
32   Details Pertinent to Assignments
33   Employment Code for Vocational Students
34   Financial Report

Opening the School Year

Industrial Arts and   Bulletin No. 5
Vocational-Technical Education
Tulsa Public Schools

TOPICS FOR STUDY AND EMPHASIS 1968-1969

Expansion of Vocational-Technical and Industrial Arts Education

Vocational-Technical Education Center — Post-Secondary
         Data Processing
         Chemical Technology
         Mid-Management
         Professional Secretary
         Technical Electronics
         Technical Drafting and Design
Webster High School
         A new drafting room under construction.

Kettering said, "You can't push on anything that is going faster than
you are."

Improvement of Instruction

Implementation of Curriculum Materials
Development of Instructor Guides
         Power Mechanics 9-12
         Drafting 7-12
         Metals and Machines 7-12
         Electricity-Electronics 7-12
Inservice Education (on request to Dr. Alexander)
         Development of instructors guide for Drafting 10-12. First
                semester, Tuesdays, 4:00-6:00, 6 or 12 weeks.
         Development of instructors guide for Power Mechanics 9-12.
                First semester, Tuesdays, 4:00-6:00, 6 or 12 weeks.
         Evaluation, interpretation and practice of School Shop Safety

7-12. First or second semester, Tuesdays, 4:00-6:00, 6 sessions.

Curriculum Evaluation and Development for Vocational Education Courses 11-12. Second Semester, Tuesdays, 4:00-6:00, 6 sessions.

Extension courses in T & I Education to be offered in the Tulsa area.

Vocational Guidance

Industrial arts teachers have a definite responsibility for vocational guidance. A bulletin is available with suggestions as to how we can do a better job of guidance, especially in the family of occupations related to the subject you teach.

Organization

Department chairmen activities and responsibilities.

Organization for efficient operation and control of equipment and supplies using student personnel.

Plans for carrying on class with substitute teacher.

Management

Inventory equalization and supply storage

Teacher-Pupil class area arrangement and operation

Records and Record Keeping

Related study and shop or laboratory practice

Department Organization

Department to be organized by subject areas, grades 7-12, for the school year 1968-1969.

Professional Organizations

Consideration should be given to joining professional organizations. Dues are as follows: AIAA – $15.00; OIAA – $5.00; AVA – $8.00; OVA – $1.00; T & I – $2.00; DE – $2.00; Tech – $5.00.

All dues to be paid to representatives of each division. Do not send direct to OVA. The department office will be glad to handle the dues.

Teacher liability group insurance available for $1.12 if you are a member of AIAA or AVA.

Calendar

Four-State Industrial Arts and Vocational Education Conference, October 2 & 3, 1970, at Pittsburg, Kansas.

OEA Workshop, Tulsa District, October 9, 1970.

OEA State Meeting, October 22 & 23, 1970, Oklahoma City.

American Vocational Association Convention, December 4-9, 1970, New Orleans.

American Industrial Arts National Convention, April 7-11, 1969, Las Vegas.

OPENING OF SCHOOL

Starting the Class

The activities connected with starting a class are of vital importance. They are equally important to both the teacher and the student. They afford the teacher an opportunity to "get off on the right foot," to get the class started in the direction he wishes it to go, and to gain and hold control of the situation. To the student, it is an opportunity to "size-up" the teacher, to gain a "preview" of what is in store, and to become a part of the class organization. Much of the future success of the course depends upon getting a good start. It is imperative, therefore, that every effort be made to prepare for the important first day.

It is extremely doubtful if any two teachers will use exactly the same method or techniques for starting a class. This is as it should be, for every teacher is a unique individual and will necessarily put something of himself into the teaching situation. There are, however, certain principles relating to starting a class which have proven their worth and which may be used to advantage by other teachers. The method used will vary according to the grade level and the type of course offering.

Factors That Promote Learning

1. Favorable Learning Situations
2. Active Rehearsal
3. Distributed Practice (Start to Work)
4. Meaningful Units
   (Break it down)
   History - categories - parts
   Each unit must have completeness
5. Use of Aids
6. Knowledge of Progress (Score)
   Success begets success
   Failure begets failure
   (Let students know at all times where they stand.)

Course Outlines

All shops, laboratories and classrooms should have copies of Instructor Guides, course outlines, and other instructional materials on their inventories. See that such materials are added to your equipment inventory.

Course outlines and Instructor Guides should be left in the room or shop for use by the teacher assigned.

Audio-Visual Materials

Please use a written requisition when requesting films from the Instructional Media Department. The school office should have a supply of the request forms for your use. The forms are available in the Instructional Media office.

"Where the Action Is," a sound and color film on Vocational-Technical Education is available through the Instructional Media Center. (EXCELLENT)

Accident Reporting

It is the responsibility of every shop teacher to make detailed written reports of any accident of any consequence whatever, which happens in his shop. This report should be made out immediately after the accident has happened. An injury is considered an accident when a doctor's attention is needed or when the student is out of school one-half day or more because of the injury. *Forms* for reporting accidents are available in the principal's office.

Safety Devices and Instructions

We want to re-emphasize the importance of making sure all equipment in shops is properly equipped with the necessary safety devices. It is the responsibility of each teacher to see to it that all equipment is properly guarded while the equipment is being used. If repair or installation of safety equipment is needed, a requisition should be written and sent to this office. Industrial concerns require workers to use these safeguards and we should train our students in safe work habits. If you give explicit instructions on the use of equipment, require that proper safety devices be used at all times, and remain in your shop when equipment is being used, you are less liable for injuries which might occur in your shop.

Safety equipment is to be made available to provide protection to students and personnel working with materials and machines dangerous to vision or the respiratory system. Equipment needed for this protection has been provided to all shops and laboratories where safety glasses, goggles, and respirators are needed. A plan of hanging, cleaning, and sanitizing to be instituted.

Eye Safety

Schools in Oklahoma shall provide safety goggles as approved by the National Safety Council for all personnel using materials and machines that may damage the vision of such personnel because of flying particles, intense light, severe heat or other harmful effects.

Vocational classes will be provided with sets of safety glasses or goggles to be assigned to the student for his use. Such equipment to be turned in at the end of the year or replaced if lost or broken.

Industrial arts classess will have a set for the shop and will need to be used by students in each class. This is an added safety effort. The cooperation of all students and teachers will be needed in our safety program during 1970-1971.

Respirators

An act relating to schools requiring use of approved respirators where needed in the opinion of the State Health Department as approved by the National Safety Council. The equipment to be in sufficient number to protect teachers and students in classes using or handling toxic materials or other substances, which may cause damage to the respiratory system. Respirators to be maintained in satisfactory working condition.

Tool Breakage and Loss

The reports which are made at the end of each school year, indicating the loss and breakage of tools and equipment, should be carefully examined by each instructor. The loss of tools and other items of equipment alone is not the most important factor involved in these reports. If students are allowed to develop the habit of taking tools for their own use, or permitted to use tools and equipment carelessly, bad habits and attitudes on the part of the boys are being formed. It is essential that we eliminate the tool losses by changes in shop management and tool handling methods and devices. This is a responsibility for each individual teacher in his own assignment.

Shop Maintenance

The teachers in the shops of this department were employed because of their training and mechanical ability. I need not mention to you the necessity of applying your mechanical ability in the upkeep of your equipment before greater damage is done to it. This is a responsibility of each teacher and indicates good management in the shop. *Set up oiling schedule.*

Inventories

All inventories should be checked at the beginning of the school year, preferably the week before school actually starts, and a report made in writing to this office as to whether or not things are in order. *Do not wait until next* May to bring up discrepancies; take care of this while it is fresh in mind. A number of resale and board inventories are too large. An effort will be made to transfer needed basic supplies to other teachers. *You can help by sending a note to the office listing supplies* that could be transferred. Make an effort to use your supplies that may be of a special nature and not in general use by other teachers.

Delivery of Supplies

Teachers will be in their building starting August 7 to August 28, getting ready for the opening of school when they are not attending meetings. Supplies may be delivered on or before this date, depending upon when and how ordered.

School supplies from the department catalog are delivered by the warehouse. Record prices at time of purchase so you may have costs for your supply inventories. List supplies and prices delivered by vendors on purchase orders.

Use of Supplies for Shop Maintenance and Repair

Do not use resale supplies for repair or maintenance work. Request for certain supplies to be utilized in the conduct of their work, or the making of equipment for their department, should be filled from supplies purchased from respective budgets.

Use of Resale Supplies for Other Departments of the School

Do not utilize supplies from the Industrial Education Department for making building changes or for providing equipment or supplies for other departments. If work is done for the Activity Fund, individuals, etc., the same procedure should be followed as is used with students for resale materials. In doing work for other departments, materials are furnished by that department through requisitions from their department office or the principal.

Supply and Equipment Lists

You will receive your copies of lists of supplies and equipment left at check out time. Check immediately to see if there are discrepancies and return immediately to this office with a note explaining what is wrong and the matter will be checked at once. Do not wait until the end of the school year to report discrepancies.

Band Saw Blades

Band saw blades are handled on an individual basis, either by the roll or blade. Send your request directly to your school office, following outlined procedure for outside vendors. Maintenance and Repairs for sharpening and brazing; Supplies by Board if new blades. Blades to be brazed and sharpened will be handled by a saw service. Circular and hand saws will also be handled by a saw service. Follow procedure as outlined.

Jointer Knives and Squaring Shear Blades

Jointer knives and squaring shear blades are handled in the same manner as band saw blades.

Shop Changes

You are requested to make no major changes in your shop without the approval of the department office and principal.

Aprons

In the senior high school, cost of aprons and having them laundered is to come from supplies by the board or resale, depending on the type of program.

Aprons for junior and senior high school students may be provided by debiting to the *resale account* a charge for apron use. Ten cents (10c) per semester is a suggested amount. It will take approximately two or three years to pay for a set of aprons by this method. (This plan is optional to both student and teacher.) NOT REQUIRED

Exchange of Items

Do not return materials to a merchant unless approved by Purchasing.

Purchases

No supplies are to be purchased directly from the merchant with resale funds.

Requisitions must be written for all supply purchases. Follow instructions in Bulletin No. 1 — Instructions for Writing Requisitions.

The Tulsa Public Schools have a ruling to the effect that all supplies used in the shops are to be purchased through the Purchasing Department. *Do not purchase* items and then request confirmation. Anticipate your needs in advance because it takes several days for a requisition to be approved and processed. Some vocational shops, *with prior approval*, use a monthly open charge account, as recommended by the department office and approved by purchasing.

Transfer of Materials

When transferring materials from one shop to another, the regular transfer sheet, Order for Transfer, must be used and a copy sent to the department office. All supplies on this transfer must be priced. All transfer sheets should be turned in promptly. *Do not hold* them until near the close of the school year. The person making the transfer of materials should initiate the proper forms which are available through the department office. This office will request pick up for warehousing, so credit can be given on your account.

Printing by School

All requests for printing jobs done by our vocational printing classes are to be charged through the department office when supplies by the board or resale accounts are to be used in payment of materials.

Requisitions

All items listed on requisitions should carry *complete* specifications if you are to receive the correct items.

Equipment

All equipment *worn-out* or broken is to be held until final checking at the close of the school year, unless removed during the year by this office. The department chairman will help in evaluating these items.

Junior High Drawing and Printing

Junior high school *"drawing"* supplies are *resale.* Please debit to each student's resale deposit *.30* to cover cost of paper, pencil, eraser, and envelope. These items are to become the property of each student paying for them. Junior high *"printing"* students should be charged *.30* from their resale account to pay for printing booklet.

Junior High Electricity

Student manual at *.48* from resale deposit.

Area Vocational-Technical Education Center

This year marks the sixth year of operation of the Vocational-Technical Center. It is located at 3420 South Memorial. Some twenty-five occupational areas will be offered in 1970-1971. All are invited to visit the Center and become familiar with its program.

Adult Education

It is necessary in many instances for our shops to be used by adult groups in the adult education program. The more service which any school shop can render the people in the community, whether they are adults or people of regular school, the more nearly the expenditure for the equipment can be justified.

Teaching Aids

All teachers should develop teaching aids to be used in improvement of instruction. Any items to be developed should have prior approval if materials required will amount to more than can normally be absorbed in your resale. Teaching aids should become a part of the room inventory.

Projects

Projects are an important part of every shop, laboratory or drafting room. Samples of beginning projects should be available for use by the instructor at the beginning of each unit. Such samples to be handled as a teaching aid and as such to become a part of the room inventory.

Production Group Projects — Research

It is recommended that all junior high school instructors select, plan and produce at least one item on a production basis. This could be a seasonal project or one developed anytime after basic tool skills and processes have been learned. Booklets on "Teaching Industry Through Production," may be checked to teachers in the junior high school for use in planning such an activity. Senior high school instructors should consider such an activity.

Salvage — Metal, Storage Batteries

All salvage engines, scrap steel and worn out storage batteries are to be removed from your shop by requisition only. This will give us a record of worn out batteries and engines for our inventory and as to disposition of same. Explain details of salvage.

Books

Books are to be requisitioned through your principal. All books, state adopted or those purchased outright, are to be listed on your equipment inventory. You should have an up-to-date list of text and reference books. A system of marking, storage, and checking *all* books should be developed.

Approved: Hiram Alexander   M. J. Ruley, Director
             Assistant Superintendent   Homer Towns, Assistant
             for Instruction   August 1970

Instructions for Closing Shops, Laboratories and Classrooms

Bulletin No. 24 – 1970
Industrial Arts and
Vocational-Technical Education
Tulsa Public Schools
1970-1971

1. Easier and More Efficient Checking of Inventories

A typed carbon copy of all supplies received this school year is being sent along with these instructions. This includes items received through Warehouse requisition, direct purchase on purchase orders, and any surplus items from department stock. Current prices have been charged for Warehouse items. Since this is the first year for handling requisitions through different channels, some items have been missed by the department office. It is most important that *all* items received be listed and charged to their respective accounts. A total of the amount we show on our books is enclosed for the Supplies by Board and Supplies for Resale accounts.

The *buddy* system is to be used in checking inventories. Please help one another in checking all inventories in each of our facilities. Every effort to make the best check possible will be needed if we are to obtain the kind of inventory each teacher wants and that the department needs.

You should start checking inventories not later than May 17, 1970. Remember you will have a limited time to do this checking. It is desirable that you check your equipment and supplies at the same time. Make arrangements with your building teachers or the one who will help you check. List all items sent to your shop which we may have failed to include on your inventory. Price all equipment at replacement cost. List *all* books, visual aids, projects, or teaching aids purchased from any source (so designate) on your equipment inventory. This gives everyone a ready source of *all* equipment, tools, and books which may be needed at any time. With the many sources of books as state adopted textbooks, books for the Elementary-Secondary Education Act, principals' allocation, new school initial purchase, we need to know allocations and a complete record. Please list on your yellow inventory such items. When the office pink copy of inventory comes to you, would like such items listed, so our white office copy of inventory may be completed.

With our new Warehouse system it is not necessary to carry large inventories of supplies. Plan your program of instruction, then order accordingly.

Do not stop class work to check inventories.

Have all "Supplies for Resale" listed and in a convenient manner for checking. It is suggested that all long pieces of lumber be labeled with chalk or by tag, and all short pieces be placed together. Have your lumber sorted according to specie. This is also true of iron and steel. Have your long pieces of iron and steel listed according to length and/or weight (see supply catalog for conversion of length and weight).

Sheets for listing "Supplies for Resale" and "Supplies by the Board" inventories are being sent to you with this bulletin. MAKE THEM OUT IN DUPLICATE. These SHEETS MUST ALL BE PRICED. You can get prices from the pink typed inventory sheets included with this bulletin, and from last year's teachers' pencil yellow copy of inventory list. Please re-check your totals – on units and totals. *Send* in the original copy of these inventories not *later* than *Wednesday, May 22, 1970. ORIGINAL* copies of *INVENTORIES MUST* be *sent* to this office, before you come in to check out. You will bring the carbon copies of all inventories and other reports at your final check out in the office *ON* or *BEFORE Friday, May 29, 1970.*   (Vocational teachers see Item No. 8, this bulletin.)

The pink equipment inventory is being sent out early so your yellow equipment inventory, and our pink copy may be brought up-to-date. The pink copy to be returned to this office with other inventories. Please *add items not on your* inventory. *List serial numbers* of *all* equipment. Check ID numbers assigned to VEA '63 equipment to be sure they are listed.

Arrangement of tools in tool cabinets, rooms, or storage areas with corresponding grouping on inventory lists make for easier and more effective checking.

Any equipment loaned to other instructors, or which is not in your shop at the time of inventory, will be checked as "lost" or "stolen".

Tools which are surplus, worn-out and broken, are to be removed from your equipment inventory and boxed for storage. If the broken tools can be repaired this will be done, and they will be returned to you and placed on your inventory again. Mimeographed sheets for listing above will be supplied, and should be made out in duplicate. One copy is for the office and will be turned in with your reports, and the other is for the instructor. If these items are to be picked up by school truck, so designate on check sheet. These items should be priced. (Use available catalogs for replacement price.)

The department office wishes to thank each of you for your help in taking inventories as suggested.

2.   Storage of Equipment and Tools During the Summer

Be sure your tools are properly stored in a secure location at the close of the school year and if need be, have them oiled.

If your room is to be remodelled during the summer, arrangements should be made for storage.

Remove saws, blades, and stones from your power machines. Also dismantle those which can easily be damaged if used by an untrained person. Be sure windows in shops that are away from the main building are bolted.

Some of you will need to box your tools and store them in the main building if painting or remodelling is to be done.

All personal equipment and supplies should be removed from your shop. Add any items of equipment or supplies which may have been overlooked on your inventory.

3.   Delivery of Supplies and Equipment for the School Year 1970-1971

With our new warehouse system, it is not necessary to carry large inventories. Plan your program of instruction, then order accordingly.

Refer to instructions for writing requisitions. Teacher initiates request, Form No. 76, for supplies (board and resale) (Maintenance and Repair of Equipment) (Equipment — New or Replacement).

A.   Supplies from Industrial Education Warehouse Catalog on a request (indicate intended use). Channel through department chairman to your principal's office so requisition can be issued.

B.   Supplies not in catalog. On individual request channeled through your chairman to your principal's office so requisitions can be issued.

C.   Maintenance and repair requests for parts to be purchased on RQ-1 Requisition. Repair of equipment by Maintenance on RQ-2 Requisition. Request written by teacher, channeled through department chairman to your school office.

D.   Equipment, new or replacement, request issued through department chairman and channeled to Department Office, Room 308, Education Service Center, for requisition to be written.

E.   Warehouse delivery or pick-up on RQ-1 Requisition. Material transfer made by memorandum on approved form through Department Office, Room 308, ESC.

There will be *no* spring requisition as in the past (once a year ordering). The Warehouse will stock catalog items which are to be ordered as noted in previous bulletins. Order your needs during the year as required, but in quantity and in advance of need. Deliveries from the Warehouse are made to each school once a week. Please allow time for requisition to flow through ESC to Warehouse.

This means a large inventory will not be necessary in catalog items. Other supplies not in catalog should be for school year needs and with only a small carry over as needed for starting a school year. A smaller inventory at the close of the year will expedite end-of-year closing.

All other procedures of inventories, deposit of resale funds, and other supervisory and administrative details as followed by this department will be in use until notified (see bulletins and Instructors Handbook as here applicable).

Remember!!! All material received: resale, board and equipment is to be placed on respective inventories before check out time.

4. Summer Repair Jobs

Send in a list of any repair jobs which need to be done during the summer months. Make this request on the regular Form No. 76, and mark it "Summer Work." Send in this request by May 10, or before. This means repair on equipment listed on your inventory. *Building repair requests should go to your principal.*

5. General Instructions

At the close of the school year, when you are checking out in the office, we are asking that you turn in all copies of your inventories: *"Supplies for Resale," "Supplies by the Board,"* and *"Equipment."* Also leave any plans pertaining to your shop, or notations which might be helpful to any new teacher taking over in a new shop. These will be placed in a large envelope with the name of the shop and present teacher's name written on it. Sometimes we have a teacher leave us for a new job during the summer, and it is very difficult to locate inventories unless they have been left in the office. If you are not to be back in your present assignment, there will be a number of added items to be checked.

6. Course Outline

A copy of your course outline to be checked in at the end of the year if bound department copies are not available.

7. Equipment Inventories — Pink Copies

Please make an attempt to list replacement prices on all tools and equipment. It would be helpful if more specifications could be listed for all machines. Belt sizes, serial numbers of motors, model numbers. Such information would help many times in requisitioning repair or parts for machines in your shop or laboratory.

8. Vocational-Technical Teachers

Vocational-Technical teachers will have assigned numbers for all VEA '63 items purchased that cost over $50.00. Please be sure such numbers are recorded on your inventory, with serial numbers, etc. Install markers or labels on all VEA '63 equipment with assigned numbers. We must be ready at all times for an audit.

All end of semester class reports should be in by May 29, 1970, so they may be processed. Teachers who will be on duty fulfilling their contract until June 5, 1970, may have until *June 2* to check in other local reports.

9. Teaching Aids and Shop Projects or Problems

Teaching aids and display projects or problems are to be listed on your inventories the same as other equipment.

10. Books

All Books should be listed on your equipment inventory. Note State adopted, and all books furnished from your building allocation.

Special Instructions

Each teacher should come by the office at the close of the school year and check out. Some of you do not have as much to check as others. We need to know your summer address, disposition of keys, and your enrollment by semesters. A clearance slip is received when items listed have been checked.

The earlier you are able to check out, the better for all concerned. All instructors should be checked out by the close of the school year, Wednesday, May 29, 1970, except as noted.

Vocational-Technical Teachers see Bulletins No. 25 and No. 32 for details pertinent to your assignments.

Note: Call the office before you come in to check out. We will try to work by a schedule if at all possible.

Approved: Hiram Alexander   M. J. Ruley, Director
           Assistant Superintendent   Homer Towns, Assistant Director
           for Instruction   Industrial Arts and
                                 Vocational-Technical Education

Check List

1. Copy of "Supplies for Resale" inventory with prices and totals, Bring tape if you have added the figures on the adding machine.
2. Copy of "Supplies by the Board" inventory with prices and totals.
3. Copy of "Equipment" inventory. All items prices at replacement cost.
4. Copy of financial report. (Those who do not have resale will need to fill in part of this report: enrollment for the first and second semester.)
5. BE SURE to bring *all receipt* and *refund* books to the office. The auditor will check before final clearance.
6. Disposition of keys to shop. All shop keys, including door key, storage cabinet keys, supply room keys, etc., should be turned in to your school office at the close of the school year. (See your principal.)
7. Summer address.
8. All library books borrowed from this office are to be returned.
9. Copy of course outline — if not a bound department copy.
10. *Vocational personnel* — application for certification.

11. *Vocational Follow-Up* — Per instructions as specified by the division from the State Department.
12. All *vocational* records and reports.
NOTE: *Call* the *Office* before you come in to check out. We will try to work by a schedule if possible.

Policies for Vocational Graphic Arts

To: Vocational Graphic Arts Instructors — Printing and Lithography
                                                     Photography
                                                     Commercial Art

From: M. J. Ruley, Director Vocational-Technical Education

Date: August 22, 1956; Revised May 8, 1961; Revised November 16, 1962; Revised October, 1970

Subject: Procedures and Policies for Operation of Vocational
          Graphic Arts

Participating Departments Approval: Division of Instruction, Division of
          Secondary Education, Division of Business Management

1.   The purpose of this program to be for training those junior and senior students who have selected a specific area of graphic arts as a trade. Classes to meet for a period of fifteen (15) hours each week, which includes related technical instruction and actual shop practice.

2.   Training to be of a type that will give students approximately the same experiences as they will find in a commercial shop. Jobs to be obtained within the Tulsa Public Schools, such as forms of different types of the operation of the various departments of the school, and for various organizations and activities within the schools, or other non-profit organizations.

3.   That no job be done that will normally compete with commercial establishments in this community.

4.   That printing services be available *only* to school or school affiliated groups.

5.   With these general policies the final selection of jobs to be done in the shop to be left to the discretion of the instructor.

6.   All supplies used for a job to be furnished by those requesting the work done, or furnished by the school from stock. Retail prices of all supplies at the quantity price of the supplies for the job plus 20% will be charged. This 20% to be used in payment for cleaner, wiping cloths, material wasted in the process of instruction, and other miscellaneous costs not covered in the basic charge. Receipts to be written for total cost of job when money received. One department of the school cannot pay another for materials used. Follow correct procedure in doing

work for other departments of the school – that of having supplies needed furnished for the job.

7.   That special projects submitted must: (a) be approved by the building principal; (b) be paid for by the group requesting the service; (c) fit into the instructional program as determined by the instructor.

8.   That no school stationery, letterheads, envelopes, etc., bearing any identification with the Tulsa Public Schools be imprinted in these classes. (See 1960-1961 Administrative Rules and Procedures, page 83.)

9.   Printing of forms used in this department, other than minor jobs, to be cleared through the director's office in order that some uniformity be established where there is more than one program of a kind in the system.

10.   A certificate will be issued to students who complete the course and have shown excellent employable qualities, such as skill, technical knowledge, good work habits and character.

Approved: Hiram Alexander
              Assistant Superintendent
              for Instruction

Enrollment Report

INDUSTRIAL ARTS AND VOCATIONAL-TECHNICAL EDUCATION
TULSA PUBLIC SCHOOLS
First Semester – 1969-1970

Industrial Arts

Senior High	Enrollment		Industrial Arts Enrollment			% of Boys in Industrial Arts				
	Total	Boys	Boys	Girls	Total	69-70	68-69	67-68	66-67	65-66
Central	2302	1151	648	30	678	53.6	68.6	63.9	59.5	59.4
East Central	1410	705	428	4	532	60.7	56.3	66.7	68.5	74.7
Edison	1866	933	458	12	470	49.0	57.2	51.4	53.3	52.6
Hale	2366	1183	593	18	611	50.1	53.4	56.7	48.1	53.5
McLain	1638	809	522	.4	526	64.5	76.4	86.3	91.8	100.9
Memorial	2352	1176	569	12	581	48.3	48.0	56.7	47.6	43.6
Rogers	2625	1313	819	10	829	62.3	66.4	71.0	70.0	52.2
Washington	1111	556	286	23	309	51.4	43.6	47.3	40.6	51.9
Webster	916	458	263	6	269	57.4	64.1	67.8	58.4	75.2
TOTAL SR. HIGH 69-70	16,586	8,284	4,586	119	4,705	55.3	60.2	63.1	59.8	63.5

SENIOR HIGH SCHOOL – Total Enrollment   16,586
                    Industrial Arts Enrollment   4,705
                              % Enrolled   28.3 of Total Enrollment
                              % Enrolled   55.3 of Boys Enrolled

Junior High	Enrollment		Industrial Arts Enrollment			% of Boys in Industrial Arts				
	Total	Boys	Boys	Girls	Total	69-70	68-69	67-68	66-67	65-66
Anderson	496	248	116	0	116	46.7	40.0	40.3	44.3	49.1
Bell	983	492	266	0	266	54.0	55.6	48.8	51.7	55.3
Byrd	1219	610	138	0	138	22.6	29.0	34.4	31.6	--
Carver	686	343	299	46	345	87.1	86.2	85.8	86.7	82.7
Cleveland	1031	516	314	31	345	60.8	62.9	61.2	65.1	63.2
Clinton	1056	528	357	63	420	67.8	69.5	68.0	72.0	73.9
Edison	1380	690	307	0	307	44.5	44.2	38.5	43.7	43.7
Foster	671	336	185	0	185	55.0	58.2	53.0	--	--
Gilcrease	1130	565	405	25	430	71.6	71.6	73.8	63.2	66.4
Hamilton	1064	532	330	65	395	62.0	59.3	68.2	59.8	60.8
Horace Mann	584	292	187	0	187	64.0	53.8	59.4	47.7	45.1
Lewis & Clark	636	318	160	0	160	50.3	51.8	51.8	64.3	63.6
Lowell	203	102	97	0	97	95.0	85.0	80.5	85.0	99.0
Madison	625	313	230	11	241	73.4	71.7	73.4	70.3	72.3
Monroe	1114	557	359	50	409	64.4	66.0	68.8	61.7	61.9
Nimitz	989	495	271	0	271	54.7	54.7	44.3	50.2	53.7
Roosevelt	675	338	204	0	204	60.3	73.0	58.3	61.9	42.7
Skelly	906	453	235	0	235	51.8	49.9	55.3	49.2	--
Whitney	1405	703	339	0	339	48.2	45.2	51.9	53.1	47.6
Wilson	895	448	230	0	230	51.3	45.5	54.3	33.7	45.3
Wright	771	386	166	0	166	43.0	47.9	45.4	38.2	36.2
TOTAL JR. HIGH 69-70	18,519	9,265	5,195	291	5,486	56.0	56.1	56.7	55.5	54.0

JUNIOR HIGH SCHOOL — Total Enrollment   18,519
Industrial Arts Enrollment   5,486
% Enrolled   29.6 of Total Enrollment
% Enrolled   50.0 of Boys Enrolled

Approved: Hiram Alexander   M. J. Ruley, Director
Assistant Superintendent   Industrial Arts and
for Instruction   Vocational-Technical Education

SUBJECT	7	8	9	Total	10, 11 & 12	68-69	67-68	66-67	Total
Drawing & Planning General Woodwork	2273	122	246	2641		2903	2818	2815	
General Metals General Electricity	833	657	584	2074		1779	1788	1749	
Elementary Printing Industrial Crafts	71	521	179	771		830	899	668	
Drafting					1594	1624	1636	1502	
Electronics					637	617	583	455	
Machine Shop					439	685	664	618	
Photography					145	147	144	173	
Power Mechanics					913	944	1017	906	
Printing					112	131	114	128	
Tailoring					86	68	67	67	
Woodworking					779	783	758	646	
Total 1st Sem. 69-70	3177	1300	1009	5486	4705				10191
Total 1st Sem. 68-69	3267	1343	902	5512	4999				10485
Total 1st Sem. 67-68	3141	1415	949	5505	5053				10558
Total 1st Sem. 66-67	3060	1310	862	5232	4580				9812
Total 1st Sem. 65-66	3051	1355	756	5156	4612				9768

Subject	Number of Classes
Junior High	
Woodwork and Drawing	99
Metals and Electricity	79
Industrial Crafts and Printing	30
	TOTAL 208

Senior High	
Drafting	65
Electronics	25
Machine Shop	22
Photography	5
Power Mechanics	36
Printing	5
Tailoring	3
Woodwork	35
	TOTAL 196

Vocational Education

School	V-T Center Enrollment	Self-Contained Enrollment	Total	% Enrolled — 11 & 12 Grades				
				69-70	68-69	67-68	66-67	65-66
Central	53	214	267	17.6	17.4	19.4	16.3	8.5
East Central	87	66	153	17.5	15.3	17.5	14.0	3.5
Edison	38	0	38	3.1	2.5	2.9	2.9	.04
Hale	85	57	142	9.2	9.5	9.2	8.1	5.7
McLain	76	125	201	20.4	16.3	17.3	7.0	4.5
Memorial	36	0	36	2.4	2.2	1.8	3.3	2.1
Rogers	135	188	323	18.8	17.1	17.6	16.3	8.2
Washington	45	153	198	32.3	33.3	35.0	17.3	13.2
Webster	36	81	117	20.3	23.6	27.3	25.6	12.8
TOTAL	591	884	1475	14.0	13.5	14.9	12.9	6.7
Berryhill	3		3					
Bixby	19		19					
Broken Arrow	28		28					
Collinsville	26		26					
Glenpool	5		5					
Jenks	7		7					
Bishop Kelly	11		11					
Liberty	13		13					
Owasso	28		28					
Skiatook	4		4					
Sperry	10		10					
Union	17		17					
TOTAL	171		1646					

	69-70	68-69	67-68	66-67
Total 11 & 12 Grade Enrollment (9 high schools)	10,480	10,201	9,951	9,462
Vocational Enrollment (9 high schools)	1,475	1,379	1,477	1,223
% 11 and 12 Grade Enrolled	14.0	13.5	14.9	12.9
TOTAL VOCATIONAL ENROLLED (County Included)	1,646	1,498	1,595	1,295

	Enrollment	Number of Classes
TRADE AND INDUSTRIAL EDUCATION		
Aeromechanics	76	4
Auto Body Repair	40	2
Auto Mechanics	103	6
Cabinet Making and Millwork	30	2
Commercial Art	40	2
Cosmetology	133	6
Diesel Mechanics	34	2
Drafting	74	4
Electronics	36	2
Machine Shop	79	5
Photography	33	2
Printing	63	4
Refrigeration and Air Conditioning	35	2
Small Engine Repair	30	2
Tailoring	14	1
Welding	105	5
Total Day Trade	925	51

	Enrollment	Number of Classes
TRADE AND INDUSTRIAL EDUCATION (continued)		
Industrial Cooperative Training		
Central	29	1
Rogers	29	1
Washington	29	1
Total ICT	87	3
Total	1012	54
TECHNICAL EDUCATION (V–T Center)		
Electronics	20	2
Chemistry	5	1
Drafting and Design	30	2
Total	55	5
DISTRIBUTIVE EDUCATION		
Central	33	3
East Central	66	3
Hale	43	2
McLain	44	3
Rogers	59	3
Webster	30	2
Total	275	16
BUSINESS EDUCATION		
Data Processing (Unit Record)	40	2
Stenography	20	2
Stenography	20	2
Cooperative Office Education		
Central	18	1
Hale	14	1
Rogers	39	2
Washington	22	1
Webster	21	1
Total	174	10
HEALTH OCCUPATIONS		
Dental Office Assistant	19	1
Medical Office Assistant	20	1
Total	39	2
HOME ECONOMICS EDUCATION		
Child Care	32	2
Sewing Services	23	2
Food Services	21	2
Total	76	6
AGRICULTURE		
Horticulture	15	2
Total	15	2
POST HIGH SCHOOL ENROLLMENT		
Chemistry Technology	5	
Computer Programming	63	
Drafting and Design	32	
Mid-Management	24	
Professional Secretary	28	
Electronics Technology	17	
Special	1	
Total	170	

Appendix B

Sample Forms

Requisition

Equipment Inventory

Equipment for Survey or Disposal

Supplies for Resale Inventory

Supplies Furnished by Board Inventory

Resale Report

Excerpt from Local Catalog of Supplies and Small Equipment

Application for Vocational Education

Application Blank for Cooperative Vocational Training

Application Blank for Area Vocational-Technical Program

Permanent Record and Follow-Up Card

Employer's Rating Sheet on Trainees

Instructor's Guide Sheet

Project Card

Project Plan Sheet

Vocational Education Completion Certificate

Certificate of Appreciation

Standard Student Accident Report Form

National Standard School Shop Safety Inspection Check List

Job Description—Local Director

248

Requisition

TULSA PUBLIC SCHOOLS
INDUSTRIAL ARTS AND VOCATIONAL EDUCATION DEPARTMENT

Date_____196____

Please furnish the following and charge to—

SUPPLIES FOR SALE	[ ]
SUPPLIES FURNISHED BY BOARD	[ ]
MAINTENANCE AND REPAIRS	[ ]
REPLACEMENT OF EQUIPMENT	[ ]
NEW EQUIPMENT	[ ]

N° 2010

Teacher_____Shop_____School_____

QUANTITY	UNIT	DESCRIPTION SIZE, COLOR, WEIGHT, CATALOGUE NUMBER, ETC.

Order from_____ Address_____

App._____   Signed_____
                                                    Teacher

INSTRUCTIONS—Send one copy to the department office.   Check-mark in the correct square purpose for which items will be charged.
List items by categories.

Form 76

Teacher .... (Year) ....
Teacher .... (Year) ....
Teacher .... (Year) ....

EQUIPMENT INVENTORY
Industrial Arts and Vocational Education
TULSA PUBLIC SCHOOLS

Page ....
School ....
Shop ....

LINE	YEAR	YEAR	YEAR	YEAR	UNIT	NAME AND DESCRIPTION	Unit Price	YEAR	YEAR	YEAR
	ADD	ADD	ADD	ADD						
1										
2										
3										
4										
5										
6										
7										
8										
9										
10										
11										
12										
13										
14										
15										
16										
17										
18										

Checked by .... (YEAR) ....
Checked by .... (YEAR) ....
Checked by .... (YEAR) ....

(MAKE THIS OUT IN TRIPLICATE)

Voc. Prin. Form 26

SYMBOLS
W—Worn out (Incapable of Repair)
B—Broken (Can Be Repaired)
S—Stolen
L—Lost
T—Transferred (To Whom Transferres)

Equipment for Survey or Disposal

Worn Out, Broken, Lost or Stolen Equipment
Industrial Arts and Vocational Education
Tulsa Public Schools

Name of Instructor _____

Name of School _____

Date _____

(Record on this sheet all equipment which is worn out, broken, lost or stolen.)

Quan-tity	Name of Item	W	B	L	S	Unit Price	Total Price

Make two copies: 1 for office
1 for instructor

PUT QUANTITY IN PROPER COLUMN

Supplies for Resale Inventory

Industrial Arts and Vocational Education
Tulsa Public Schools

Instructor_____Shop_____ School_____

Quan- tity	Unit	Name of Item	Unit Price	Total Price

Make this inventory in *duplicate.*

Date_____

Send: 1 copy to office immediately
after inventory check.
1 copy to office when checking out

Supplies Furnished by the Board Inventory

Industrial Arts and Vocational Education
Tulsa Public Schools

Instructor_____ Shop_____ School _____

Quan-tity	Unit	Name of Item	Unit Price	Total Price

Make this inventory in *duplicate.*   Send: 1 copy to office *immediately*
                                                    after inventory check.
Date_____   1 copy to office when checking out

Resale Report

Industrial Arts and
Vocational-Technical Education
Tulsa Public Schools

FORM No. 53

Report for period of _____
(Period as Indicated)

Instructor _____ School _____ Shop_____

1. Total cash carried over from last report. (Item No. 7 previous report.) $_____
2. Total receipts from resale during the period. Send in receipts for this period only, regardless of whether page is full or not. This amount corresponds with the total *pink* receipts from your Receipt Book No. 1A-4, sent in at this time. $_____
3. Total amount of refunds during the period. This amount corresponds with the total *blue* receipts from your refund book sent in at this time. $_____
4. Amount overpaid last report. (Item No. 8 previous report) $_____
5. Total amount owed for the period. (No. 1 plus No. 2 minus No. 3 and No. 4, the amount to be recorded here.) $_____
6. Total amount of resale money turned to school treasurer for the period indicated. (If you have not actually deposited this money, do not list.) $_____

Treasurer's Receipt No.	*Date*	*Amount*
_____	_____	_____
_____	_____	_____
_____	_____	_____
_____	_____	_____
_____	_____	_____
_____	_____	_____
_____	_____	_____

7. Total cash on hand at end of period. (Item No. 5 minus No. 6.) $_____
8. Amount overpaid for period. $_____

   Note: Mail this report each period to the department office, 323 Education Service Center. REPORTS ARE DUE ON THE FOLLOWING DATES: *October 1, February 1, April 1, and Final Check Out Date*

   Send the report on the above dates whether you made any transactions or not. *Deposits* with the *school treasurer* should be *made* as often as *necessary* to *keep* the *amount* of *cash* on hand to a *minimum.* The treasurer's office *close* their books at 2:00 on the last day of each month.

RESALE MONIES SHOULD BE DEPOSITED WHEN THE AMOUNT EXCEEDS $100.00. YOU ARE NOT TO HOLD RESALE MONEY UNTIL THE END OF THE SCHOOL YEAR !

DO NOT KEEP MORE MONEY ON HAND THAN YOU CAN AFFORD TO REPLACE IF IT IS LOST!

Excerpt from Local Catalog of Supplies and Small Equipment

INDEPENDENT SCHOOL DISTRICT NO. 1
OF TULSA COUNTY, OKLAHOMA
1969-1970

Instructions

Items in this catalog are to be requisitioned on Form RQ1. Please do not include catalog items for warehouse issue and items for purchase on the same requisition. The original, first and second copies of the requisition are to be forwarded to the education service center for approval. Retain the third or last copy of the requisition for comparison with delivery.

List items on your requisition in the same order as they appear in the catalog. The stock number must be shown followed by the quantity, unit of measure and description. Please use the unit of measure as shown in the catalog when, for example, the unit of measure is dozen and you require twelve, please requisition one dozen, not twelve each, etc.

Please do not order brand name or substitute items when similar specified items are available in the warehouse.

Refer to your departmental bulletin for information in detail on requisitioning. Complete the intended use section in accordance with those instructions.

The clerk at your school will have a general instruction sheet on the proper preparation of a requisition.

Use Form RQ-2 for service repair.

All requisitions are to be signed by the building principal or the departmental supervisor.

Table of Contents

Dept. Code	Stock Number	Unit of Measure	Item Description	Cost Per Unit
Printed Forms				
58	211-005	Each	Charts, Isometric for Drawing, Junior High	$ .04
58	211-008	Each	Books, Junior High Printing, Unit 1 Thru 9	.31
58	211-009	Each	Books, Junior High Printing, Unit 10 Thru 18	.31
58	211-012	Pkg.	Cards, Project, 4 in x 6 in, Pkg/100	.53
58	211-018	Each	Plan Sheets, Woodwork Project, Senior High	.03
58	211-020	Each	Auto Mechanics Service Order — VE-28	.02
58	211-021	Each	Manual, Student, Experiences with Electrons, by Rex Miller and Fred Culpepper Jr., McKnight & McKnight	.50
Chemicals				
58	211-050	Qt.	Acetone	.79
58	211-053	Qt.	Acid, Muriatic	.63
58	211-054	Qt.	Acid, Sulphuric	.79
58	211-055	Qt.	Ruby Fluid	.85
58	211-057	Cake	Sal Amoniac, ½ Lb. Cake	.32
58	211-060	Lb.	Soldering Salts, 1-Lb. Can	.66
58	211-061	Can	Soldering Paste, 2-Oz. Can	.13
58	211-062	Can	Soldering Paste, 1-Lb. Can	.98
58	211-065	Lb.	Zinc Chloride	1.05
Drawing and Drafting				
58	211-080	Each	Compass, Pencil, Post No. 889E or Equal, 5¾ in Bow, Center Adjustment, 3/16 In. to 9 In. Range	1.50
58	211-082	Each	Points Compass, Eagle	.03
58	211-084	Each	Compass, Pencil No. 576 Eagle	.18
58	211-085	Each	Layout Dye or Fluid, Dy Kem — 8 Oz., Half Pint	1.30
58	211-086	Tube	Leads Compass, 2H, 12 to Tube	.13
58	211-087	Tube	Leads, Compass, H, 12 to Tube	.13
58	211-090	Roll	Tape, Drafting, ¾ In. Wide by 10 Yds., Scotch	.36
58	211-093	Each	Board, Drawing, Basswood, Wood End Cleats, 16 In. x 21 In., Equal to Post No. 7253	1.88
58	211-096	Doz.	Erasers, Ruby, Firm Red Small, Junior High, No. 312	.39
58	211-099	Pair	Klip Tacks with Screws	.26
58	211-102	Doz.	Pencils, Drawing, Aviator 2H or Equal Junior High	.53
58	211-105	Each	Ruler, Wescott No. 150 or Equal, 1¼ In. Wide Scaled by 1/16th, Flat No Metal Edge, 12 In., Junior High	.05
58	211-108	Each	Scales, Drafting, Architect, 12 in. Triangular, Post No. 7301DH or Equal, Hardwood, Imitation Boxwood Finish, Die Engraved, Junior High	.54

Application For Vocational Education

TULSA PUBLIC SCHOOLS
Tulsa, Oklahoma

Name ....Date ....

Address ....---

Telephone ....---

I desire to become a member of the Vocational Class in.. next year.

I will then be a
Senior

Junior

MY PRESENT CLASS SCHEDULE IS: PLANNED FOR NEXT YEAR:

1. ....   0. ....
2. ....   1. ....
3. ....   2. ....
4. ....   3. ....
5. ....   4. ....
6. ....   5. ....

6. ....

---

a. Number of times absent so far this year ....

b. Number of times tardy so far this year ....

c. To what school organizations, if any, do you belong?..

d. What are your hobbies, if any? ....

e. Give two reasons why you wish to join this class..

OK. of present instructor in this subject ....

Indicate your FIRST and SECOND choice of the subjects listed below:

Auto Mechanics	Machine Shop ....
Auto Body Repair............	Welding ....
Drafting	Business Ed. (Machines)............
Drafting and Design............	Printing (Offset)............
Electronics	Commercial Art ....

Radio-TV Servicing............	
Medical-Dental Office Assistant............	
Commercial Sewing	
Cosmetology	
Others	

Signature of Applicant ....

A list of completed subjects and grades earned:

9th Grade	Sem. Grades 1	2	10th Grade	Sem. Grades 1	2	11th Grade	Sem. Grades 1	2
1.								
2.								
3.								
4.								
5.								
6.								

PARENT'S APPROVAL

I understand the plan of The Area Vocational-Technical Education Program, and it is with my consent and approval that my (son-

daughter) ....be assigned to the educational schedule as checked above.

Parent or Guardian _____ Date _____

Address _____ Telephone _____

THE SPACES BELOW ARE RESERVED FOR COUNSELORS' USE ONLY.

(Information relevant to counseling and guidance as recorded on cumulative record)

Signature _____ Counselor

_____ HIGH SCHOOL

_____ Local School

Signature _____ Vocational Counselor

AREA VOCATIONAL-TECHNICAL CENTER

Application Blank for Cooperative Vocational Training (reverse side)

Check below any special skills, or interests which you have:

_____ Art, Drawing	_____ Lettering	_____ Woodwork
_____ Auto Mechanics	_____ Modeling	_____ Printing
_____ Drive a car	_____ Make change	_____ Laboratory Technician
_____ Electricity	_____ Machine shop	_____ Selling
_____ Filing	_____ Mathematically minded	_____ Drafting
_____ Gift wrapping	_____ Mechanically inclined	_____
_____ Hand writing	_____ Meet the public	_____
_____ Have bicycle	_____ Scientific interest	
_____ Have driver's license	_____ Welding	

What type of work do you prefer? Mark XX

What type of work would you do? Mark X

DISTRIBUTIVE	OTHERS	TRADE AND INDUSTRIAL	OTHERS
_____ Advertising	_____	_____ Drafting	_____
_____ Display	_____	_____ Electrical	_____
_____ Stock work	_____	_____ Metal	_____
_____ Sales work	_____	_____ Wood	

List subjects you have had in high school.

Sophomore	Junior	Senior
1. _____	_____	_____
2. _____	_____	_____
3. _____	_____	_____
4. _____	_____	_____
5. _____	_____	_____
6. _____	_____	_____

PARENT'S APPROVAL

I understand the plans of the Cooperative Vocational Education Program, and it is with my consent and approval that my (son or daughter)

_____ may be assigned to a work schedule with an employer, and to related study classes as a part of

his regular course of study.

Parents or Guardian _____ Date _____

Address _____ Telephone _____

Please fill out in ink or type   TULSA PUBLIC SCHOOLS   Date _____

AREA VOCATIONAL-TECHNICAL EDUCATION PROGRAM

APPLICATION BLANK

_____ *Local High School*

1. Applicant _____ _____ _____   Sex _____ Classification _____
              Last   First   Middle

2. Home Address _____   Telephone _____

3. Date of Birth _____ _____ _____   Age _____
                 Month   Day   Year

4. Parent or Guardian _____ Occupation _____

5. Where Father Works _____

6. Where Mother Works _____

7. No. of Brothers _____ Ages _____ Working? _____

8. No. of sisters _____ Ages _____ Working? _____

9. State Condition of Your Health _____

10. Explain Any Physical Weakness _____

11. Social Security No., if any _____

12. What Classes do you enjoy most? _____

_____

THIS SPACE

FOR

PHOTOGRAPH

IF

AVAILABLE

Present High School Schedule			
Pr.	SUBJECT	TEACHER	ROOM
1.			
2.			

13. What are your hobbies? _____

14. To what school organizations do you belong? _____

15. What is your vocational objective? _____

16. Are you employed? Employer's name _____

17. Hours of work _____

Schedule For Next Year

Pr.	SUBJECT	TEACHER	ROOM
1.			
2.			
3.			
4.			
5,			
6.			

3.		
4.		
5.		
6.		

WORK EXPERIENCE

KIND OF WORK	EMPLOYER	ADDRESS	TELEPHONE

Application for Area Vocational-Technical Program (reverse side)

Please fill out in ink or type

TULSA PUBLIC SCHOOLS

COOPERATIVE VOCATIONAL EDUCATION PROGRAM

APPLICATION BLANK

First Occupational Choice _____

Other Choices _____

1. Applicant _____ Sex _____ Year You Graduate _____

2. Home Address _____ Telephone No. _____ Date _____

3. Date of Birth _____ Age _____ Height _____ Weight _____

4. Parent or Guardian _____ Occupation _____

5. Where Father Works _____

6. Where Mother Works _____

7. No of Brothers _____ Ages _____ Working? _____

8. No. of Sisters _____ Ages _____ Working? _____

9. Church Preference _____ Nationality _____

10. State condition of Your Health _____

11. Explain Any Physical Weakness _____

12. How many times were you absent last year? _____ tardy? _____

13. Social Security No. _____

14. What classes do you enjoy most? _____

15. What are your hobbies _____

+---+
| |
| APPLICATION |
| _NOT_ |
| COMPLETE |
| UNTIL YOUR |
| PICTURE FILLS |
| THIS SPACE |
| |
+---+

PRESENT HIGH SCHOOL SCHEDULE			
PD.	SUBJECT	TEACHER	ROOM
1.			
2.			

16. To what school organizations do you belong?

17. Do you plan to go to college?

18. What are your plans after graduating?

19. How did you learn about this program?

Attach a letter of application stating why you wish to enter this program.

| 4. |
| 5. |
| 6. |

NOT TO BE FILLED IN BY APPLICANT

	GOOD	AVE	POOR		GOOD	AVE	POOR
Attendance				Personality			
Scholarship				Appearance			
Character				Intelligence			
Initiative				Dependability			

Present Number of Credits?

Required Subject to graduate.

WORK EXPERIENCE

KIND OF WORK	EMPLOYER	ADDRESS	PHONE

GIVE REFERENCES—ONLY ONE OF WHICH MAY BE A TEACHER

NAME	ADDRESS	PHONE	BUSINESS OR OCCUPATION
1.			
2.			
3.			

Student   _Coordinator_

Form VE - 6

PERMANENT RECORD AND FOLLOW UP CARD

VOCATIONAL EDUCATION—TULSA PUBLIC SCHOOLS

STUDENT .... Date of Birth .... 19 .... -19

Date Enrolled .... Age When Enrolled .... Grade When Enrolled .... 19 .... -19

19 .... -19

Employer .... Employer ....

Address .... Address ....

Tel. No. .... Tel. No. ....

Kind of Business .... Kind of Business ....

Occupation .... Occupation ....

Date Began .... Date Began ....

Date Left .... Date Left ....

No. Months .... No. Months ....

Hours Work .... Hours Work ....

Wages—Week .... Wages—Week ....

Reason for Leaving .... Reason for Leaving ....

....

Graduate .... If "No" State Reason ....

(Yes or No)

Date Left Program ....

Home Address .... Tel. No. ....

Name of Person for Reference .... Address .... Tel. No. ....

FOLLOW-UP RECORD

DATE	EMPLOYER	OCCUPATION	WAGES WEEK	NEW ADDRESS

Employer's Rating Sheet on Trainees

Name..

Occupation...

Training Agency...

Grade Symbols

A . . Superior quality of work   D . . Below quality of work expected

B . . Good quality of work   F . . Unsatisfactory work

C . . Satisfactory quality of work

(Encircle Letter Designating Grade)

Attendance	A	B	C	D	F
Dependability	A	B	C	D	F
Cooperation	A	B	C	D	F
Quality of Work	A	B	C	D	F
Production	A	B	C	D	F
Initiative	A	B	C	D	F
Safety	A	B	C	D	F

....
Coordinator

Remarks..

....

....

Date ....Signed ....

NOTE: Please place in envelope, seal, and return by trainee. Please be frank in making out this rating sheet. One-half unit of high school credit, each semester, is given on this rating. Each trainee spends four hours in school each day, one hour of which is spent in study of subjects related to his particular job. Suggestions for this study from employers, or any printed trade material loaned student by employer will be appreciated.

INSTRUCTOR'S GUIDE SHEET

Job or Subject _____

Educational Outcomes:

I. Introduction or Preparation

II. Presentation

Teaching Outline	Teaching Techniques, Aids and Devices

Instructor's Guide Sheet (reverse side)

III. Application:

IV. Test or Check-up:

Tools and Materials:

References:

Assignment:

Project Card

Information may be entered on both sides of the project card.

M T W T F	M T W T F	M T W T F	M T W T F	M T W T F	M T W T F
1	4	7	10	13	16
2	5	8	11	14	17
3	6	9	12	15	18

PROJECT	GR.	S	F	COST	DEPOSIT

Form IA-4—10M-954

TULSA SECONDARY SCHOOLS

INDUSTRIAL ARTS WOODWORKING SHOP

PROJECT PLAN SHEET

STUDENT   PERIOD   NAME OF PROJECT   DATE

NOTE.: A shop sketch need not be scaled to size. Use straight edge to secure reasonably satisfactory sketch. Keep this plan sheet in assigned place to prevent loss.

(Top Side View)

(Front Side View)

(Right Side View)

Project Plan Sheet (reverse side)

STOCK BILL (finished size)

No. Pieces	Name of Part	Thickness	Width	Length	Kind of Wood

LUMBER BILL (rough size)

How Many	Name of Part	Thickness	Width	Length	Kind of Wood	Cu. In.	Bd. Ft.	Price Per Ft	Cost
				TOTAL					

PROCEDURE STEPS:

1. ....
2. ....
3. ....
4. ....
5. ....
6. ....
7. ....
8. ....
9. ....
10. ....

Vocational Education Completion Certificate

SENIOR HIGH SCHOOL

VOCATIONAL EDUCATION

TULSA PUBLIC SCHOOLS

This Certifies That _____

has attended _____ hours and has satisfactorily completed the requirements

of this course in

Date Issued _____

_____
Instructor

_____
Director of Vocational Education

_____
Principal

Vocational Education Completion Certificate (reverse side)

_____

Signature of student

_____

Occupation for which training was given

VOCATIONAL EDUCATION RECORD

School years	Units of instruction	Clock hours

To assist the bearer in finding the position, either in private employment or in the military service, for which he is best fitted, the Tulsa Public School issues this Certificate as a Record of Instruction and Training.

CERTIFICATE OF APPRECIATION

TULSA PUBLIC SCHOOLS

VOCATIONAL EDUCATION

AWARDED TO

In grateful appreciation for the cooperation given The Tulsa Public Schools in serving in an educational capacity for the purpose of assisting Tulsa youths in achieving their educational objectives.

PRESENTED THIS_____ DAY OF_____ 19_____

_____
DIRECTOR

_____
PRINCIPAL

_____
SUPERINTENDENT OF SCHOOLS

STANDARD STUDENT ACCIDENT REPORT FORM
Part A. Information on ALL Accidents

1. Name: _____ Home Address: _____
2. School: _____ Sex: M □; F □. Age: _____ Grade or classification: _____
3. Time accident occurred: Hour _____ A.M.; _____ P.M. Date: _____
4. Place of Accident: School Building □   School Grounds □   To or from School □   Home □   Elsewhere □

5. **NATURE OF INJURY**

Abrasion	_____	Fracture _____
Amputation	_____	Laceration _____
Asphyxiation	_____	Poisoning _____
Bite	_____	Puncture _____
Bruise	_____	Scalds _____
Burn	_____	Scratches _____
Concussion	_____	Shock (el.) _____
Cut	_____	Sprain _____
Dislocation	_____	
Other (specify) _____		

DESCRIPTION OF THE ACCIDENT

How did accident happen? What was student doing? Where was student? List specifically unsafe acts and unsafe conditions existing. Specify any tool, machine or equipment involved. _____
_____
_____
_____
_____
_____
_____
_____
_____
_____
_____

PART OF BODY INJURED

Abdomen	_____	Foot _____
Ankle	_____	Hand _____
Arm	_____	Head _____
Back	_____	Knee _____
Chest	_____	Leg _____
Ear	_____	Mouth _____
Elbow	_____	Nose _____
Eye	_____	Scalp _____
Face	_____	Tooth _____
Finger	_____	Wrist _____
Other (specify) _____		

6. Degree of Injury: Death □   Permanent Impairment □   Temporary Disability □   Nondisabling □
7. Total number of days lost from school: _____   (To be filled in when student returns to school)

Part B. Additional Information on School Jurisdiction Accidents

8. Teacher in charge when accident occurred (Enter name): _____
    Present at scene of accident: No: _____ Yes: _____

9. **IMMEDIATE ACTION TAKEN**

First-aid treatment _____ By (Name): _____
Sent to school nurse _____ By (Name): _____
Sent home _____ By (Name): _____
Sent to physician _____ By (Name): _____
Physician's Name: _____
Sent to hospital _____ By (Name): _____
Name of hospital: _____

10. Was a parent or other individual notified? No:___ Yes:___ When:_____ How: _____
     Name of individual notified: _____
     By whom? (Enter name): _____
11. Witnesses: 1. Name: _____ Address: _____
     2. Name: _____ Address: _____

12. **LOCATION**

Specify Activity		Specify Activity		Remarks
Athletic field	_____	Locker	_____	What recommendations do you have for preventing other accidents of this type? _____
Auditorium	_____	Pool	_____	
Cafeteria	_____	Sch. grounds	_____	
Classroom	_____	_____ shop	_____	
Corridor	_____	Showers	_____	
Dressing room	_____	Stairs	_____	
Gymnasium	_____	Toilets and		
Home Econ.	_____	washrooms	_____	
Laboratories	_____	Other (specify)	_____	

Signed: Principal: _____ Teacher: _____

Make in Duplicate

Tulsa Schools-Safety-1-5000-58

NATIONAL STANDARD SCHOOL SHOP SAFETY INSPECTION CHECK LIST

Prepared by the Joint Safety Committee of the
AMERICAN VOCATIONAL ASSOCIATION — NATIONAL SAFETY COUNCIL

Date _____

INTRODUCTION

A safe environment is an essential part of the school shop safety education program. The safe environment will exist only if hazards are discovered and corrected through *regular* and *frequent* inspections by school personnel—administrators, teachers and students. Safety inspections are to determine if everything is satisfactory. Inspections may be made at the request of the board of education, the school administration or upon the initiative of the teacher. Some communities have drawn upon the cooperative service of professional safety engineers, inspectors of state labor departments, insurance companies and local safety councils to supplement and confirm inspections by school personnel.

The National Standard School Shop Safety Inspection Check List, recommended by the President's Conference on Industrial Safety is an objective inspection procedure for the school shop.

DIRECTIONS

WHO INSPECTS?

This will depend upon local policies. It is recommended, however, that shop teachers, and students—the student safety engineer and/or student safety committee—participate in making regular inspections. This not only tends to share responsibility but stimulates a broader interest in the maintenance of a safe school shop.

WHEN TO INSPECT?

As a minimum, a safety inspection should be made at the beginning of every school term or semester. More frequent inspections may be advisable.

HOW TO INSPECT?

Inspections should be well planned in advance. Inspections should be systematic and thorough. No location that may contain a hazard should be overlooked. Inspection reports should be clear and concise, but with sufficient explanation to make each recommendation for improvement understandable.

FOLLOW-UP

The current report should be compared with previous records to determine progress. The report should be studied in terms of the accident situation so that special attention can be given to those conditions and locations which are accident producers. Each unsafe condition should be corrected as soon as possible in accordance with accepted local procedures. A definite policy should be established in regard to taking materials and equipment out of service because of unsafe conditions. The inspection report can be used to advantage as the subject for staff and class discussion.

CHECKING PROCEDURE

Draw a circle around the appropriate letter, using the following letter scheme:

S — Satisfactory (needs no attention)
A — Acceptable (needs some attention)
U — Unsatisfactory (needs immediate attention)

Recommendations should be made in all cases where a "U" is circled. Space is provided at the end of the form for such comments. Designate the items covered by the recommendations, using the code number applicable (as B-2). In most categories, space is provided for listing of standards, requirements or regulations which will have local application only.

A. GENERAL PHYSICAL CONDITION

1. Machines, benches, and other equipment are arranged so as to conform to good safety practices. . . . . S A U

2. Condition of stairways. . . . . S A U

3. Condition of aisles. . . . . S A U

4. Condition of floors. . . . . S A U

5. Condition of walls, windows, and ceiling. . . . . S A U

6. Illumination is safe, sufficient, and well placed. . . . . S A U

7. Ventilation is adequate and proper for conditions. . . . . S A U

8. Temperature control. . . . . S A U

9. Fire extinguishers are of proper type, adequately supplied, properly located and maintained. . . . . S A U

10. Teacher and pupils know location of and how to use proper type for various fires. . . . . S A U

11. Number and location of exits is adequate and properly identified . . . . S A U

12. Proper procedures have been formulated for emptying the room of pupils and taking adequate precautions in case of emergencies S A U

13. Lockers are inspected regularly for cleanliness and fire hazards. S A U

14. Locker doors are kept closed. . . . . S A U

15. Walls are clear of objects that might fall. . . . . S A U

16. Utility lines are properly identified. . . . . S A U

17. Teachers know the procedure in the event of fire including notification of the fire department and the evacuation of the building. S A U

18. Air in shop is free from excessive dust, smoke, etc. . . . . S A U

19. _____ S A U

20. _____ S A U

21. _____ S A U

22. _____ S A U

23. Evaluation for the total rating of A. GENERAL PHYSICAL CONDITION . . . . S A U

Shop Safety Inspection Check List (cont)

B. HOUSEKEEPING

1. General appearance as to orderliness.............. S A U

2. Adequate and proper storage space for tools and materials.
   S A U

3. Benches are kept orderly.................... S A U

4. Corners are clean and clear.................. S A U

5. Special tool racks, in orderly condition, and provided at benches and machines .... S A U

6. Tool, supply, and/or material room is orderly......... S A U

7. Sufficient scrap boxes are provided............... S A U

8. Scrap stock is put in scrap boxes promptly........... S A U

9. Materials are stored in an orderly and safe condition.... S A U

10. A spring lid metal container is provided for waste and oily rags.
    S A U

11. All waste materials and oily rags are promptly placed in the containers .... S A U

12. Containers for oily rags and waste materials are frequently and regularly emptied .... S A U

13. Dangerous materials are stored in metal cabinets..... S A U

14. Machines have been color conditioned.............. S A U

15. Safety cans are provided for flammable liquids....... S A U

16. Bulk storage of dangerous materials is provided outside of the main building .... S A U

C. EQUIPMENT (continued)

5. All equipment control switches are easily available to operator.
   S A U

6. All machines are "locked off" when instructor is out of the room.
   S A U

7. Brushes are used for cleaning equipment............ S A U

8. Nonskid areas are provided around machines......... S A U

9. Machines are in safe working condition............. S A U

10. Machines are guarded to comply with American Standards Association and local state code................... S A U

11. Adequate supervision is maintained when students are using machines and dangerous tools...................... S A U

12. Tools are kept sharp, clean and in safe working order S A U

13. All hoisting devices are in safe operating condition... S A U

14. Machines are shut off while unattended............. S A U

15. Adequate storage facilities for tools, equipment, etc., not in immediate use .... S A U

16. _____ S A U

17. _____ S A U

18. _____ S A U

19. _____ S A U

20. Evaluation for the total rating for C. EQUIPMENT.. S A U

17. A toe-board or railing around a mezzanine used for storage or washing facilities .... S A U
18. Materials are stored in an orderly and safe condition on this mezzanine .... S A U
19. Flammable liquids are not used for cleaning purposes ..... S A U
20. Floors are free of oil, water and foreign material...... S A U
21. Floors, walls, windows, and ceilings are cleaned periodically. S A U
22. _____ S A U
23. _____ S A U
24. _____ S A U
25. _____ S A U
26. Evaluation for the total rating for B. HOUSEKEEPING S A U

C. EQUIPMENT

1. Machines are arranged so that workers are protected from hazards of other machines, passing students, etc.............. S A U
2. Danger zones are properly indicated and guarded...... S A U
3. All gears, moving belts, etc., are protected by permanent enclosure guards .... S A U
4. All guards are used as much as possible............. S A U

D. ELECTRICAL INSTALLATION

1. All switches are enclosed............................ S A U
2. There is a master control switch for all of the electrical installations .... S A U
3. Electrical outlets and circuits are properly identified . S A U
4. All electrical extension cords are in safe condition and are not carrying excessive loads............................. S A U
5. All machine switches are within easy reach of the operators. S A U
6. Electrical motors and equipment are wired to comply with the National Electric Code............................... S A U
7. Individual cut-off switches are provided for each machine. S A U
8. Machines are provided with overload and underload controls by magnetic pushbutton controls......................... S A U
9. No temporary wiring in evidence..................... S A U
10. _____ S A U
11. _____ S A U
12. _____ S A U
13. _____ S A U
14. Evaluation for the total rating for D. ELECTRICAL IN-STALLATION .... S A U

Shop Safety Inspection Check List (cont)

E. GAS

1. Gas flow to appliances is regulated, so that when appliance valve is turned on full, the flames are not too high........... S A U

2. Gas appliances are properly insulated with asbestos or other insulating material from tables, benches, adjacent walls, or other flammable materials .... S A U

3. No gas hose is used where pipe connections could be made. S A U

4. Gas appliances have been adjusted so that they may be lighted without undue hazard.............. S A U

5. Students have been instructed when lighting gas appliances to light the match first before turning on the gas.......... S A U

6. There are no gas leaks, nor is any odor of gas detectable in any part of the shop.......... S A U

7. Shop instruction has been given concerning the lighting of gas furnaces operating with both air and gas under pressure.. S A U

8. When lighting the gas forge, goggles are worn....... S A U

9. When lighting the gas furnace, the following procedure is used: (a) light the match; (b) turn on the gas; (c) drop the match in the hole in top of the furnace.......... S A U

10. In shutting down the gas furnace, the gas valve is closed before the air valve.......... S A U

11. _____ S A U

12. _____ S A U

13. _____ S A U

14. _____ S A U

15. Evaluation for the total rating for E. GAS.......... S A U

F. PERSONAL PROTECTION (continued)

13. _____ S A U

14. _____ S A U

15. _____ S A U

16. Evaluation for the total rating for F. PERSONAL PROTECTION. S A U

G. INSTRUCTION

1. Shop Safety is taught as an integral part of each teaching unit. S A U

2. Safety rules are posted particularly at each danger station. S A U

3. Printed safety rules are given each student.......... S A U

4. Pupils take a safety pledge.......... S A U

5. Use of a safety inspector.......... S A U

6. Use of a student shop safety committee.......... S A U

7. Use of safety contests.......... S A U

8. Motion and/or slide films on safety are used in the instruction. S A U

9. Use of suggestion box.......... S A U

10. Use of safety tests.......... S A U

11. Use of safety posters.......... S A U

12. Talks on safety are given to the classes by industrial men. S A U

F. PERSONAL PROTECTION

1. Goggles or protective shields are provided and required for all work where eye hazards exist.................. S A U

2. If individual goggles are not provided, hoods and goggles are properly disinfected before use................ S A U

3. Shields and goggles are provided for electric welding.. S A U

4. Rings and other jewelry are removed by pupils when working in the shop.. S A U

5. Proper kind of wearing apparel is worn and worn properly for the job being done................................ S A U

6. Leggings, safety shoes, etc., are worn in special classes such as foundry, etc., when needed.......................... S A U

7. Respirators are provided for dusty or toxic atmospheric conditions such as when spraying in the finishing room........ S A U

8. Provisions are made for cleaning and sterilizing respirators. S A U

9. Students are examined for safety knowledge ability.. S A U

10. Sleeves are rolled above elbows when operating machines. S · A U

11. Clothing of students is free from loose sleeves, flopping ties, loose coats, etc. .... S A U

12. _____ S A U

13. Tours are taken of industrial plants as a means of studying safety practices .... S A U

14. Periodic safety inspections of the shop are made by a student committee .... S A U

15. Men from industry make safety inspections of the shop S A U

16. Student shop safety committee investigates all accidents S A U

17. A proper record is kept of safety instructions which are given, preferably showing the signature of student on tests given in this area .... S A U

18. Rotate students on the Shop Safety Committee so that as many students as possible have an opportunity to participate... S A U

19. _____ S A U

20. _____ S A U

21. _____ S A U

22. _____ S A U

23. Evaluation for the total rating of G. INSTRUCTION S A U

H. ACCIDENT RECORDS

1. There is a written statement outlining the proper procedure when and if a student is seriously hurt...................... S A U

2. Adequate accident statistics are kept.............. S A U

3. Accidents are reported to the proper administrative authority by the instructor .... S A U

Shop Safety Inspection Check List (cont)

H. ACCIDENT RECORD (continued)

4. A copy of each accident report is filed with the State Department of Education .... S A U

5. Accident reports are analyzed for instructional purposes and to furnish the basis for elimination of hazards............. S A U

6. _____ S A U

7. _____ S A U

8. _____ S A U

9. _____ S A U

10. Evaluation for the total rating of H. ACCIDENT RECORDS. S A U

I. FIRST AID

1. An adequately stocked first aid cabinet is provided... S A U

2. The first aid is administered by a qualified individual S A U

3. The school has individuals qualified to administer first aid. S A U

4. _____ S A U

5. _____ S A U

6. _____ S A U

7. _____

8. Evaluation for the total rating of I. FIRST AID..... S A U

RECOMMENDATIONS

Code No.

Job Description

Position: Director of Industrial Arts and Vocational-Technical Education

Responsible to: Assistant Superintendent for Instruction, and others in staff relationships

Qualifications: The qualifications set forth in the State Plan for the local director and/or assistant directors of Vocational Education are as follows:

The minimum qualifications for Local Directors shall be a degree from a standard four-year college approved for teacher training with *a major in a vocational education field* and two or more years of teaching experience in an approved vocational education program. They shall hold a valid teaching certificate or credential in a specific vocational field, and preferably should have competency sufficient to direct and assist in the area of vocational guidance and counseling.

The State Board for Vocational Education approved a policy on June 11, 1965, to allow reimbursement on a 12-month basis to school districts employing a qualified, full-time, local director and/or assistant directors of Vocational Education under the following conditions:

A school district employing 13 or more qualified, full time, reimbursed vocational education teachers may qualify for a local director of Vocational Education and the salary may be reimbursed up to 50%.

A school district employing 24 or more qualified, full-time, reimbursed vocational education teachers may also qualify for an assistant director of Vocational Education, whose salary may be reimbursed up to 50%.

Such reimbursement must be requested by the local Board of Education and must have the approval of the State Director of Vocational and Technical Education.

Industrial Arts: MS in Industrial Education, Major in Industrial Arts

Duties and Responsibilities:

SEE ATTACHED LIST

DUTIES OF THE DIRECTOR AND ASSISTANT DIRECTOR OF INDUSTRIAL ARTS AND VOCATIONAL-TECHNICAL EDUCATION

M. J. Ruley, Director
Homer B. Towns, Assistant Director
Tulsa Public Schools
1969

Administrative and Executive Duties

Provide assistance to administrators in the interpretation and initiation of industrial arts and vocational-technical programs.

Assist in coordination of industrial arts and vocational programs on the elementary, junior high, senior high, and post-secondary school levels.

Assist in the development of a consistent philosophy of elementary, secondary, and post-secondary education.

Make appropriate professional and community contacts.

Attend staff meetings.

Attend and participate in school, community, and professional meetings and conferences.

Recommend advisory committees on vocational education. Hold meetings with the committees.

Work with Oklahoma Employment Service. (Job Outlook.)

Cooperate with other agencies aiding in the further development of vocational education.

Coordinate and administer vocational programs. Cooperate closely with adult education in and with program of vocational-technical education.

Work with community committees on specific instructional materials.

Prepare budgets, including department and vocational.

Promote summer programs for high school students and adults.

Arrange special programs (open house, etc.) for parents to acquaint them with vocational training.

Observe instruction of vocational programs and solicit aid of state specialists where needed.

Attend area and state conferences and workshops for vocational education, industry, business, etc.

Conduct follow-up of all vocational students including adults and out-of-school youth.

Establish standards and guidelines for new programs.

Recommend to State Director for approval all applications for vocational education programs.

Recommend to State Director for approval all claims covering expenditures for the operation of the vocational education programs.

Recommend any new policies, or changes in policies, affecting the various divisions.

Cooperate with teacher training staffs in the development of the pre-service and inservice teacher education programs.

Assist in the recruitment of industrial arts and vocational-technical teachers. Assist in the certification of teachers in their respective field.

Promote state and national youth programs.

Promote by discussion, conferences, and the use of printed materials, the establishment of vocational courses wherever needed, and explain to school authorities the operation of federal and state laws for vocational education.

Supervise and assist in the conducting of surveys, studies, and investigations affecting the vocational education programs.

Provide for adequate records and reports to be submitted to federal, state and local boards on vocational education programs.

Correlate industrial arts and vocational-technical supervisory activities with those of other supervisors in order to promote an integrated, coordinated educational program.

Interview prospective teachers as requested.

Assist in the assignment of industrial arts and vocational-technical instructors.

Conduct orientation program for new teachers.

Work with state vocational departments.

Keep teacher education institutions and available industrial arts and vocational-technical teachers informed of position openings.

Write articles for local and national professional publications.

Prepare and edit bulletin or newsletter to keep instructors, administrators, and community informed on practices, policies, and happenings in the field of industrial arts and vocational-technical education.

Receive visitors.

Conduct inspection tours.

Receive and interview sales representatives.

Professional Improvement

Conduct individual teacher conferences.

Hold group meetings.

Interchange ideas and information between teachers.

Encourage and assist teachers to conduct needed research.

Encourage teachers to attend summer session and other professional improvement activities.

Help evaluate the services of industrial arts and vocational-technical education departments and individual teachers.

Arrange for displays and exhibits.

Promote participation in local and national awards programs.

Encourage teachers to to write articles for professional publications.

Conduct research to improve overall program.

Introduce experimental procedures in selected schools.

Visit each instructor as needed and at least each quarter.

Consult with administration on teacher transfers and advancement.

Plan and provide place and facilities for inservice training classes.

Plan demonstrations and sample lessons for teacher groups.

Report in writing or orally, when requested by principal, the evaluation of a visit:
Evidence of good student-teacher relationship
Appearance of teacher
Size of class
Teaching procedures used
General appearance of facilities

Ventilation and lighting
Condition of tools and equipment
Safety devices and safety rules employed

Mannerisms of teacher
Instructor's use of English
Instructional aids used
Extent to which outcomes are met
First aid equipment and supplies
Instructor's lesson plan
Records of student progress
Records of inventory, purchase, and requests

Instructional Program

Hold individual and group conference for consideration of instructional problems.
Direct (assist in) the development and publication of instruction guides (including course of instruction outlines) for all areas (revision and supplemental material).
Implement (help in implementing) the courses of instruction.
Establish and maintain a safety program.
Review instructional material from other school systems.
Keep teachers informed of effective teaching procedures.
Direct (assist in) textbook evaluation.
Keep instructors informed of current literature.
Encourage instructors to use new industrial products and procedures.
Work with and through department chairmen for implementing total program.
Develop teaching aids.
Assist teachers in planning field trips.
Distribute material concerning occupational information.
Sponsor workshops for developing teaching aids and instructor guides.
Compile and distribute lists of audio-visual aids available.

Facilities, Equipment and Supplies

Set up (assist in setting up) standards for equipment and supplies.
Analyze needs and recommend purchase of supplies both for warehouse and vendor purchase.
Recommend acceptable types and makes.
Prepare (assist in preparing) specifications.
Recommend changes, repairs, and replacements.
Supervise (assist in) installation of equipment.
Prepare standard lists for equipment and supplies.
Process requisitions per established policies and procedures.

Responsible for inventories of equipment supplies for resale and supplies by
board, including keeping records on all **NDEA VIII, ESEA, VEA '63,**
surplus, and gift equipment.

Advise and assist in planning of construction and remodeling shops with
department of building and planning, principal, department chairman,
and teacher.

Plan shop layouts.

Prepare (assist in preparing) preliminary plans and estimates for constructing,
remodeling.

Make recommendations on lighting, heating, and ventilation.

Typical Course Descriptions

Industrial Cooperative Training Program

Refrigeration and Air Conditioning

Junior High School Industrial Arts

INDUSTRIAL COOPERATIVE TRAINING

IN TULSA

The Public Schools and Employers Prepare Youth for Employment

---

Fold on dotted line

The
Industrial Cooperative Training Program

in Tulsa

is administered by the

Vocational Education Department

of the

Tulsa Public Schools

in co-operation with the

State Board for Vocational Education

Division of

Trade and Industrial Education

Stillwater, Oklahoma

For further information call:

Coordinator ....

School ....

Telephone ....

Coordinators may be reached by telephoning their respective senior high schools.

Printed by Vocational Printing Class, Central High School

Fold on dotted line

Training for Leadership in

INDUSTRY

SCHOOL

HOME

CHARLES C. MASON
Superintendent of Schools

HIRAM ALEXANDER
Assistant Superintendent For Instruction

M. J. RULEY
Director of Vocational - Technical Education

Advantages to the School

The I.C.T. program provides a channel for projecting the school into the community. It adds an average of 20 additional courses to the school curriculum, with students receiving instruction through production which meets present day standards.

1. Provides shop facilities in industry.
2. Furnishes actual working conditions.
3. Provides training opportunities on actual jobs.
4. Keeps the school informed of employment possibilities and the need for training.

Purpose

The I.C.T. program is designed primarily for high school students to get both education, and experience while still in school.

Bridging the gap between school and employment has always been a problem. High School graduates are forced to take whatever jobs they can get, in many instances without regard to individual aptitudes and preferences.

Job applicants are asked, "Have you had any training or experience?" The I.C.T. student has had specific training and experience - and his employment is simply increased to a full time basis after graduation.

Who Can Enroll

Any Junior or Senior, 16 years of age, who has an earnest desire to learn a trade, and whose school record is satisfactory, may apply for enrollment in Industrial Cooperative Training.

Application for this training should be made to the Coordinator of the I.C.T. program.

— Fold on dotted line —

Advantages to the Student

The I. C. T. program is designed primarily for students who do not plan to go to college. However, should the student decide to go to college, he will find no difficulty in entering.

The I. C. T. Program provides many advantages to the student.

1. Gives vocational training and actual experience.
2. Provides financial assistance while in school.
3. Stimulates an interest to complete high school.
4. Gives an opportunity to develop the student's individual aptitudes and interests.
5. Provides opportunity for vocational counseling and guidance.
6. Provides an opportunity to explore a chosen vocation.
7. Provides an opportunity to become established in his chosen field.

Advantages to Employers

1. Through the I. C. T. program, the employers have an opportunity to secure the most promising young people in the community for their personnel.

2. Coordinators have counseled with prospective trainees, and have a complete record of each individual, available for the employer's benefit.

3. The school makes the trainee's job a part of his school studies.

4. Employers are encouraged to suggest items of technical information and to supply special material for study in school.

5. Employers become a part of the public school, thereby promoting good school-community relations.

6. An economical education and training program.

— Fold on dotted line —

How The ICT Program Works

The I.C.T. student completes all his required subjects such as English, History, etc., and graduates from high school along with the rest of his classmates. In addition he has an opportunity to study about his occupational objective since a period is scheduled before the regular school day begins.

On the job, the student spends a minimum of 20 hours per week learning a trade or occupation gaining experience, which will enable him to continue working full time in his chosen field upon graduation from high school.

The student receives school credit and wages for time spent on the job. This money has, in a number of instances, made it possible for the student to complete his high school education.

Occupations

Training can be given in practically any industrial occupation which requires a training period of 2000 clock hours.

The occupation must be suited to the apprenticeship type of training, and one in which there is sufficient related and technical information available for study.

Some of the occupations, furnishing such a training period are:

Auto Mechanics
Baking
Beauty Operator
Business Machine Repair
Cabinet Making
Carpentry
Cook
Cleaning and Pressing
Drafting
Dental Technician
Foundry work
Laboratory Technician
Machine Shop

Meat Cutting
Nurse Aid
Pattern Making
Photography
Plating
Printing
Radio and T. V. Repair
Sheet Metal Work
Shoe Repair
Watch Repair
Welding
Plumbing

EDUCATIONAL OPPORTUNITIES

In The

Tulsa Area Vocational Technical Center

INSPIRATION — TOMORROWS

CHALLENGES — TODAYS

REFRIGERATION AND AIR CONDITIONING

PROGRAM

TULSA AREA

VOCATIONAL-TECHNICAL CENTER

Vocational-Technical Education
TULSA PUBLIC SCHOOLS
in cooperation with the
STATE BOARD
FOR VOCATIONAL EDUCATION

— Fold on dotted line —

TULSA AREA
Vocational-Technical Center
INFORMATION

OPERATION

The Vocational-Technical Center is a department of each participating high school. Students enrolled spend one-half day at the Center and one-half day at the home high school.

REQUIREMENTS FOR ENTRANCE

Enrollment in a high school in Tulsa County and recommendation by a high school counselor. Some courses have specific requirements, or prerequisites that are described in separate course descriptions.

SELECTION OF STUDENTS

Careful attention is given to selection of students for admission. Only those students who can reasonably be expected to profit by the instruction are selected for enrollment. General school records and exploratory experiences and activities are carefully reviewed in determining whether or not a prospective student has the ability, aptitude, and interest needed to master the skills and knowledge required in the occupation. General education is important in the program for all students enrolled in vocational and technical courses.

CREDITS

Credits earned at the Center are sent to the home high school of each student to become a part of the student's permanent record. The credits will count toward graduation, and the student will graduate from his home high school. However, Certificates of Achievement are issued from the Center.

VOCATIONAL COURSES

The objective of vocational courses is to teach occupational skills and related information which will benefit a person entering employment.

TECHNICAL COURSES

These courses provide basic scientific and mathematical knowledge and specialized training required of the specific industry. The curriculum is preparatory for a post high school Associate Degree program. Technical mathematics and science is included in the curriculum of the technical programs, and one of the credits earned in a technical program will be technical mathematics or technical physics.

THE INSTRUCTIONAL PROGRAM

The instructional program is conducted by teachers who are occupationally competent through bona fide salary-earning experiences in the occupation, and who have received instruction in the techniques of teaching. The skills and related technical information taught the students are those which are needed by the typical worker in an occupational area. Theory is taught which is related to the skills of the occupation. Advisory committees are used to aid in establishing, maintaining and evaluating the programs.

CHARLES C. MASON
Superintendent of Schools

— Fold on dotted line —

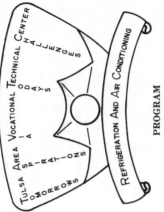

REFRIGERATION AND AIR CONDITIONING

Course Description:

In this course, students receive instruction in the principles of refrigeration and air conditioning equipment and will get practical experience in repairing and servicing small and large equipment of this type. The mathematics and physics related to this field will be stressed as well as the general theory of refrigeration and its application to refrigeration and air conditioning equipment. Household refrigeration units, refrigerator drinking fountains, commercial refrigerators and standard air conditioning refrigeration units are used as study materials and projects.

Some Course Points:

Fundamentals of electricity—fundamentals of refrigerant circuits—electric and pressure—operated controls, overhaul and repair of refrigeration units—adjustment and repair of relays, timers, and thermostats—fundamentals of commercial refrigeration units—fundamentals of heating units—installation and maintenance of equipment — related physics and mathematics.

Entrance Requirements:

The course is open to juniors who are mechanically inclined and indicate a sincere interest in the field. Approval of the home high school and technical center counselors is required.

Length of Course:

This is a two-year course starting in grade eleven. Three units of credit may be earned each year.

Job Description:

The refrigeration and air conditioning mechanic installs and repairs industrial, commercial and domestic air conditioning units. Installing new air conditioning or refrigeration equipment, the mechanic puts the motors, condensers, and dehumidifiers in proper position following design specifications. He connects duct work, refrigerant lines and other piping, and then connects the equipment to an electrical power source. He installs electrical controls and checks the electric power entering the motor. After completing the installation and connecting the recording and gauging devices, the mechanic starts the unit and tests it for proper performance and for leaks. He also adjusts the pumps, dehumidifiers, filters and other components. The mechanic may install air conditioning equipment ranging from small self-contained units to large central-plant-type systems. When air conditioning and refrigeration equipment becomes inoperable, the mechanic must diagnose the cause and make necessary repairs.

Job Opportunities in the Field:

A considerable number of air conditioning and refrigeration mechanics are employed in shops that specialize in the repair and maintenance of commercial, industrial and home air conditioning and refrigeration equipment. There is work for construction companies, air conditioning or refrigeration equipment manufacturers, heating and air conditioning contractors and dealers. Some are employed by department stores, hotels, restaurant and food store chains, factories, warehouses and other establishments large enough to require fulltime maintenance men. The use of air conditioning in offices and stores is expected to increase greatly. The use of refrigeration as a means of preserving food and other perishable items has grown greatly in recent years. Refrigeration is also becoming increasingly important in some kinds of manufacturing and in research laboratories.

Courses Offered at the

VOCATIONAL-TECHNICAL CENTER

AEROMECHANICS

AUTO BODY REPAIR

AUTO MECHANICS

BUSINESS EDUCATION
(Bookkeeping and Office Procedures)

BUSINESS EDUCATION
(Stenographic)

BUSINESS MACHINES
(Data Processing)

COMMERCIAL ART

COSMETOLOGY

DENTAL OFFICE ASSISTANT

DIESEL MECHANICS

FOOD SERVICES

HORTICULTURE

MACHINE SHOP

MATERIAL FABRICATION

MEDICAL OFFICE ASSISTANT

OFFICE MACHINES REPAIR

OFFSET PRINTING

REFRIGERATION and
AIR CONDITIONING

SEWING SERVICES

SMALL ENGINES REPAIR

TECHNICAL DRAFTING AND DESIGN

TECHNICAL ELECTRONICS

VOCATIONAL DRAFTING

VOCATIONAL ELECTRONICS
(Radio-TV Service)

WELDING

POST-HIGH SCHOOL COURSES:

DATA PROCESSING
(Computer Programming)

CHEMICAL TECHNOLOGY
(Industrial Chemistry)

— Fold on dotted line —

Course Descriptions
for
Offerings in the
Industrial Arts Education Department

Junior High School (Grades 7 through 9)

LEVEL I, Exploratory; LEVEL II, Basic; LEVEL III, Advanced

The junior high school industrial arts program offers rich experiences to all seventh grade boys and girls in a series of exploratory industrial arts activities. This program consists of a sequence of four exploratory courses including drafting, woods, metals, and electricity/electronics. Each of these courses is offered for a 9 week period.

After completing this cycle, eighth grade students may pursue the drafting, metals, and woods areas in basic courses or they may choose to take exploratory courses in plastics — industrial crafts or printing. Many combinations of offerings may be chosen in the 9 to 18 weeks courses in the basic subjects or the 9 weeks courses in the two exploratory subjects.

Ninth grade students may enter advanced classes in metals and machines, which include a unit in power mechanics, or woods. Drafting 1 may be offered to ninth grade students. All of these industrial arts classes are electives and apply as credits toward high school graduation in the "doing" subject requirements.

The junior high school industrial arts courses are conducted in limited general shops, each representing a broad industrial field. For example, general metal includes exploratory experiences in bench metal, sheet metal, ornamental iron, metal casting, welding and elementary machine shop practice.

Industrial arts activities are housed in especially designed shops or laboratories. The classes meet one hour each day, five days per week.

Seventh Grade Industrial Arts

Seventh Grade Industrial Arts includes work in exploratory drafting, electricity/electronics, metals, and woods. These courses are designed to acquaint the students with the language and to provide experiences in each area that will help him to determine whether his abilities and interests lie in that particular field.

Exploratory Drafting — 7-D

Exploratory Drafting provides the student with the opportunity to investigate some of the problems in and relative to the language of drafting. It provides a means by which a student may learn to visualize and express graphically his own ideas and interpret the ideas of others; it provides for self-expression through planning and doing. It is offered in the seventh grade for a period of 9 weeks.

Exploratory Electricity/Electronics — 7-E

Exploratory Electricity/Electronics for the junior high school deals with very simple principles and their direct application to some concrete experiments, problems, or projects. At this level a student should become interested in electricity for what it does for us. This course is offered for 9 weeks in the seventh grade depending on the schedule.

Exploratory Metals — 7-M

Exploratory Metals is designed to provide the student with a knowledge of the tools, materials, and finishes in the different areas of metal work. It provides varied experiences that correlate closely with other areas of learning in the curriculum in the junior high school. Areas include bench metal, sheet metal, ornamental iron, foundry. This course is offered for 9 weeks in the seventh grade.

Exploratory Woods — 7-W

Exploratory Woods provides the student with the opportunity to investigate the problems in, and relative to, the fundamentals of woods. It provides for self-expression through tool manipulation and handling of lumber and other materials in constructing simple projects. It provides varied experiences that correlate closely with other areas of learning in the curriculum of the junior high school. This course is offered for 9 weeks in the seventh grade.

References

Books

Adams, Harold P. and Frank G. Dickey, *Basic Principles of Supervision.* New York: American Book Company, 1953.

Association for Supervision and Curriculum Development, *Individualizing Instruction.* Washington, D.C.: The Association, 1964.

____, *Leadership for Improving Instruction,* 1960.

____, *Perceiving, Behaving, Becoming: A New Focus on Education,* 1962.

____, *Role of Supervisor and Curriculum Director in a Climate of Change,* 1965.

____, *Supervision: Emerging Profession,* 1969.

Barr, A. S., William H. Barton, and Leo J. Brueckner, *Supervision, A Social Process.* New York: Appleton-Century, 1955.

Bartley, John A., *Supervision as Human Relations.* Boston: D. C. Heath Company, 1953.

Bakamis, William, *Improving Instruction in Industrial Arts.* Milwaukee: The Bruce Publishing Company, 1966.

Baughman, Dale M., Wendell G. Anderson, Marle Smith and Earl W. Wiltse, *Administration and Supervision of the Modern Secondary School.* West Nyack, N.Y.: Parker Publishing Company, Inc., 1969.

Beal, G. M., et al, *Leadership and Dynamic Group Action.* Ames, Iowa: The Iowa State University Press, 1962.

Briggs, Thomas H. and Joseph Justman, *Improving Instruction Through Supervision.* New York: The Macmillan Company, 1952.

Ericson, Emanuel E., *Teaching the Industrial Arts,* Peoria, Ill.: Chas. A. Bennett Co., Inc., 1956.

Eye, Glen G., and Lanore A. Netzer, *School Administrators and Instruction.* Boston: Allyn and Bacon, Inc., 1969.

____, *Supervision of Instruction, A Phase of Administration.* New York: Harper and Row, Publishers, 1965.

Gibson, Oliver R., and Herold C. Hunt, *The School Personnel Administrator.* Boston: Houghton Mifflin Company, 1965.

Hamilton, Robert R., *Legal Rights and Liabilities of Teachers.* Laramie, Wyoming: School Law Publications, 1956.

Harman, Calvin and W. E. Rodenstengal, *Public School Administration.* New York: Ronald Press, 1954.

Lane, Willard R., Ronald G. Corwin and William G. Monahan, *Foundations of Educational Administration – A Behavioral Analysis.* New York: The Macmillan Company, 1968.

Likert, Rensis, *The Human Organization.* New York: McGraw-Hill Book Company, 1968.

Linder, Ivan H., and Henry M. Gunn, *Secondary School Administration: Problems and Practices.* Columbus, Ohio: Charles E. Merrill Books, Inc., 1963.

Mays, Arthur B., and Carl H. Casberg, *School Shop Administration.* Milwaukee: The Bruce Publishing Company, 1950.

McGregor, Douglas, *The Human Side of Enterprise.* New York: McGraw-Hill Book Company, 1960.

McKean, Robert C., and H. H. Mills, *The Supervisor.* Washington, D.C.: The Center for Applied Research in Education, Inc., 1964.

Melchoir, William T., *Instructional Supervision.* Boston: D. C. Heath Company, 1950.

Morphet, Edgar L., Roe E. Johns, and Theodore L. Reller, *Educational Organization and Administration.* Englewood Cliffs, N. J.: Prentice-Hall, Inc., 1967.

Ostrauder, Raymond H., and Ray C. Dethy, *A Values Approach to Educational Administration.* New York: American Book Company, 1968.

Sachs, Benjamin M., *Educational Administration, A Behavioral Approach.* Boston: Houghton Mifflin Company, 1966.

Wiles, Kimball, *Supervision for Better Schools.* Englewood Cliffs, N.J.: Prentice-Hall, Inc., 1967.

Bulletins and Booklets

A Guide for Developing Administrative Policy in Industrial Arts Education. Los Angeles: Los Angeles County Schools.

A Guide to Improvement of Industrial Arts in Oklahoma Schools. Oklahoma City: State Department of Education, 1965.

A Guide to Improving Instruction in Industrial Arts. Washington, D.C.: American Vocational Association, 1968.

A Guide to Teaching Industrial Arts. Minneapolis: Minneapolis Public Schools.

A Plan for Industrial Arts. Hartford: Connecticut State Department of Education, 1967.

An Act – Amendments to the Vocational Education Act of 1963, Public Law 90-576. Washington, D.C.: 90th Congress, HR 18366, October 16, 1968.

Area Vocational Education Programs. Washington, D.C.: American Vocational Association, 1966.

AVA Like It Is. Washington, D.C.: American Vocational Association.

Bulletin on Industrial Arts and Vocational Education. Tulsa, Okla.: Tulsa Public Schools.

Bulletin to Members of the American Council of Industrial Arts Supervisors. Washington, D.C.: American Industrial Arts Association, 1959.

Burnham, Reba and Martha King, *Supervision in Action.* Washington, D.C.: Association for Supervision and Curriculum Development, 1961.

Educational Values in Club Programs. Washington, D.C.: Department of Health, Education and Welfare.

Education for a Changing World of Work. Washington, D.C.: Department of Health, Education and Welfare (Report of Panel of Consultants for Vocational Education).

Facts You Should Know – Occupational Distribution a Factor in Educational Planning. Washington, D.C.: American Vocational Association.

Guide for Industrial Arts Education in California. Sacramento: State Department of Education.

Guide for Planning and Equipping Industrial Arts Shops in California Schools. Sacramento: State Department of Education, 1956.

Handbook for Instructors of Industrial Arts and Vocational Education. Tulsa, Okla.: Tulsa Public Schools, Bulletin No. 6.

Hamburg, Merrill C., *Problems of the Industrial Arts Supervisor.* Washington, D.C.: American Council of Industrial Arts Supervisors, American Industrial Arts Association.

Harris, Ben M., and Kenneth E. McIntyre, *A Manual for Observing and Analyzing Classroom Instruction.* Austin, Texas: Extension Teaching and Field Service Bureau, 1964.

Hoyt, Kenneth, *The Challenge of Guidance to Vocational Education.* Washington, D.C.: American Vocational Association, 1965.

Implementation – New Designs for the Challenge of the 1970's. Washington, D.C.: American Vocational Association, 1968.

Improving Industrial Arts Teaching. Washington, D.C.: Department of Health, Education and Welfare, Conference Report, June, 1960.

Industrial Arts Education. Washington, D.C.: Department of Health, Education and Welfare, Conference Report, 1960.

Industrial Arts Education – Organization and Administration. Albany: The University of the State of New York, State Education Department, 1960.

Industrial Arts in Education. Washington, D.C.: American Industrial Arts Association, American Council of Industrial Arts Supervisors, 1961.

Industrial Arts Handbook. Jefferson City: Missouri State Department of Education, Bulletin 7B.

Organization and Administration for Industrial Arts Education. Columbus: Ohio State Board of Education, 1959.

Policies and Procedures. Oklahoma City: Oklahoma State Department of Vocational and Technical Education.

Suggested Responsibilities of a State Supervisor of Industrial Arts. Washington, D.C.: American Vocational Association.

Summary of a Principal-Supervisor Inservice Conference. Tulsa, Okla.: Tulsa Public Schools, 1954.

The Bridge Between Man and His Work – Vocational Education. Washington, D.C.: Department of Health, Education and Welfare, 1968.

The Industrial Arts Teacher. Washington, D.C.: American Industrial Arts Association, 1959.

The Role of the Supervisor in Educational Leadership. Tulsa, Okla.: Tulsa Public Schools, 1960.

Vocational Education Today and Tomorrow. Philadelphia: Philadelphia Public Schools, 1966 (Conference on Vocational Education).

Vocational Education, Bulletin No. 1. Washington, D.C.: Department of Health, Education and Welfare, 1958.

Vocational Advisory Committees. Washington, D.C.: American Vocational Association, 1950.

Vocational Education in the Next Decade. Washington, D.C.: Department of Health, Education and Welfare, 1961.

Vocational Education for American Youth. Washington, D.C.: American Vocational Association.

What Do You Know About Your Tulsa Schools? Tulsa, Okla.: Tulsa Public Schools, 1960.

What Makes Education Vocational? Washington, D.C.: American Vocational Association, 1965.

Will Your Child Get a Quality Education? Washington, D.C.: National Education Association.

Your Professional Organization. Washington, D. C.: American Vocational Association.

Your Public Relations. Washington, D. C.: American Vocational Association, 1954.

Periodicals

"Administering Industrial Education," *Industrial Arts and Vocational Education,* May, 1961.

Arnold, Walter, *Industrial Arts and Vocational Education,* May, 1965.

"A Job for the Schools," (Editorial), *School Shop,* May, 1961.

Diamond, Thomas, "Teacher's Letters," *School Shop,* February, 1957.

Editorial, "Opinion," *Industrial Arts and Vocational Education,* October, 1960.

Goldstein, Harry, "Vocational Education in the Next Decade," *Industrial Arts and Vocational Education,* April, 1961.

Greer, Edith S., "Human Relations in Supervision," *Education,* December, 1961.

James, H. M., "Responsibility of the State Department in Improving Industrial Education," *Industrial Arts and Vocational Education,* September 1961.

Kyte, G. C., "This Is the Kind of Supervision that Teachers Welcome and Appreciate," *Nation's Schools,* July, 1961.

Mathews, Chester O., "Self-Improvement of Supervisors," *Educational Leadership,* Educational Leadership, *May, 1959.*

Newell, Clarence A., "Selection for Leadership," *Educational Leadership,* December, 1962.

Ramsey, Curtis P., "Leadership in Instructional Improvement," *Education,* December, 1961.

Schindler, Rainman E., "Leadership Training in Underdeveloped Neighborhoods," *Adult Leadership,* June, 1963.

Index